Praise for Archetypes at Work

"As we confront the challenge and opportunity of change in the world around us, this powerful and engaging book will help all of us to craft an exciting journey that will help to draw out much more of our potential and increase our impact. You can't afford to miss this one!"

John Hagel, management guru, Chairman, Center for the Edge

"It is rare that one finds a book that breaks new ground with such brilliance and relevance. Hillman and Olivier show us how, as major organs of the psyche of both self and world, archetypes give us our essential connections, and without them we would lose the gossamer bridge that joins spirit with nature, mind with body, and self with the metabody of the universe. Archetypes are organs of Essence, the cosmic blueprints of How It All Works. The dialectic inherent in the blueprint gives us the opportunity of finding our own path through the highs and lows of the 10 principal archetypes and their astrological equivalents. The authors themselves are sons of fathers who became archetypal through their celebrated lives in theatre and psychology. Thus, so wisely informed, and ingenious in their own studies and experience, they offer reflections and activating processes to manage the dilemmas of we who have grown up ignorant of the Timeless Beings who inform our lives and actions. With the help of this deeply original work, we discover that we are characters in the drama of the Anima Mundi, the Soul of the World. In this discovery we push the boundaries of our own human story and gain the courage to live mythically ourselves with the character and passion to help heal our world."

Jean Houston, scholar, philosopher and researcher in Human Capacities

"Understanding archetypes and how they manifest in our collaborations is a window into the powerful unconscious dynamics of our organizations. Richard and Laurence have lighted a path to greater clarity on how people work together, and why we fail."

Eliot Frick, CEO, Bigwidesky

"We are involved as part of this Earth in an evolution that is very likely unprecedented, certainly unknown in our conscious memory. To survive, simply to stay afloat with love and joy for each other, we must anchor ourselves to, or discover the flowing currents of, realities deep beneath most conscious attachments of the body and mind and heart. The ancient archetypal currents described here so playfully and usefully by Richard and Laurence are like life-saving charts to help us navigate these flooding times. We have a lot of creative positive imagining to do. We have to change ourselves, like actors in a new play. This book, this work of acting in an eternal frame, is invaluable for us all."

Mark Rylance, actor

"Richard's work on archetypes has played a powerful role on the Oxford Strategic Leadership Programme. Leaders come from all over the world for a week to explore the opportunity of their leadership. With Richard, they are able to reflect on their habitual strengths as well as the shadows these can cast; the archetypal approach also enables them to examine those 'characters' within themselves that they avoid or turn away from. The programme gives them room to rehearse a fresh archetypal repertoire to the benefit of their leadership and the future of their organizations."

Tracey Camilleri, Director, Oxford Strategic Leadership Programme,
Associate Fellow, Saïd Business School

"As an executive working on a global scale, I constantly look for ways to exercise leadership with deeper awareness and greater skill. Laurence Hillman's work has proven invaluable to me. By focusing my attention on the myriad of archetypal energies that form my internal landscape, I have become much more successful in aligning my internal resources to external reality; making me a much more mindful leader and skilful manager."

José M. Román, Assistant Vice President for Research,
New York University

"This is an extraordinary new way of looking at leadership – practical and powerful. For me personally and for my entire leadership team, this work has been transformational in growing a complex organization. This is the best new leadership book to come out in a very long time. If you are a leader, read it!"

Heather Shea, CEO, United Palace of Spiritual Arts

"I've never come across a clearer, calmer, wiser or more powerful model than this for guiding us through the complexities of life and work: Olivier and Hillman's approach is simply a revelation. After reading it, I took a big box of leadership, management and personal development books to the charity shop: thanks to Archetypes at Work, I just don't need them anymore. This is my one guide for the next 10 years."

Simon Anholt, Founder of the Good Country Index

"We spend the lion's share of our productive lives at work, but so often life goes out of our work. This soul-stirring book reveals the secret of re-enlivening our thinking, leading and working by sourcing the deepest channels and patterns of intelligent life made visible as leadership capability."

Aftab Omer, President, Meridian University

"In our company, understanding archetypes and their implications has become an integral part of our thinking regarding all team-based work and a fundamental component of our leadership development. By giving us a common language to discuss our business needs, and a framework to implement strategies to enhance our strengths and address our deficiencies, we have seen improvement in both team performance outcomes as well as team dynamics."

John B. Zachry, Chairman and CEO, Zachry Group

Archetypes at Work

Evolving your story,
one character at a time

Laurence Hillman
Richard Olivier

Matador
9 Priory Business Park,
Wistow Road, Kibworth Beauchamp,
Leicestershire. LE8 0RX
Tel: 0116 279 2299
Email: books@troubador.co.uk
Web: www.troubador.co.uk/matador
Twitter: @matadorbooks

ISBN 978 1838593 483

British Library Cataloguing in Publication Data.
A catalogue record for this book is available from the British Library.

Printed and bound by CPI Group (UK) Ltd, Croydon, CR0 4YY

Matador is an imprint of Troubador Publishing Ltd

FSC
www.fsc.org

MIX
Paper from
responsible sources
FSC® C016486

To our families,

and to our fathers,

without whom we may never have met

ABOUT THE AUTHORS

Laurence Hillman, PhD

Born and raised in Zürich, Switzerland, Laurence began to study astrology at the age of 16 and this has remained his passion for over 40 years. As a professional archetypal coach, he specializes in helping his clients understand their deeper purpose and their life's calling – especially in these challenging times. In his role as a consultant he helps leaders and organizations understand their archetypal patterns and advises on high-level decision-making.

Laurence has lectured internationally and conducted workshops at the Globe Theatre in London, taught at Findhorn, at Jean Houston's Mystery School and at Pacifica Graduate Institute, and he has been a repeated guest lecturer at Washington University in St. Louis.

He is the author of *Planets in Play: How to reimagine your life through the language of astrology*, and the co-author of *Alignments: How to live in harmony with the universe*. Laurence holds a PhD in psychology with a focus on Transformative Leadership, an MBA, an MCM (Masters in Construction Management) as well as a degree in Architecture. He has travelled extensively in more than 40 countries and is fluent in five languages.

Richard Olivier

Awarded Thought Leader 2013 by the Best Practice Institute, Richard Olivier is Artistic Director and founder of Olivier Mythodrama. He works internationally as a leadership development consultant, keynote conference speaker and workshop leader. He was a guest speaker at the

World Economic Forum in Davos in 2003 and 2009 and collaborates with many other global organizations.

Richard is the founding voice within Mythodrama – a new form of experiential learning which combines great stories with psychological insights, creative exercises and organizational development techniques to explore issues faced by modern leaders. He has worked extensively in the fields of Organizational and Personal Development, and his work today is at the leading edge of bringing the world of theatre into the development of authentic leaders.

From 1998–2003 he was the Master of Mythodrama at Shakespeare's Globe Theatre and is an Associate Fellow of Saïd Business School, University of Oxford.

He is the author of *Inspirational Leadership: Henry V and the Muse of Fire* and Artistic Director of Leadership Lab, resourcing the transition to life-affirming culture.

Laurence Hillman and Richard Olivier

TABLE OF CONTENTS

ACKNOWLEDGEMENTS

We are extraordinarily grateful for the generous support we have received from many corners. How can we ever thank all the people who helped shape us along the path to finalize this book? To the teachers who guided us, the clients who listened to us, the supporters who experimented with us, and the friends who encouraged us to keep on – without you this book would never have been completed. A special thank-you is due to all at Olivier Mythodrama who embraced our early crazy ideas and helped us ground them in reality and business practice, particularly Michael Boyle, Lesley Quilty, Nick Ross, Greg Kirwan and Scott Young. Many thanks too to Phyllida Hancock, Bee Davison, Phil Atkinson, Ben Walden and Daren Jacobs for all efforts to support the company as we embarked on our Labs. We thank Susannah Lear for her editorial wisdom and support as well as her endless patience. We feel very blessed to have a world-class poet contributing to this work, so a huge thank-you to our good friend and colleague William Ayot for his poems included in these pages. We also thank the many consulting and coaching clients over the years who have taught us how to apply our theory in action, particularly those whose stories are included here.

Laurence adds: A humble thank-you to my family for showing endless patience as I became absorbed in this work which meant time away from my remarkable wife of 30 years, Cindy, and our outstanding daughter, Gabrielle. I am thankful to a large number of friends who, with their own creative efforts, have inspired me to keep going, including Ray Grasse, Jim Ibur, Rob Way, Heather Shea, Elizabeth Nelson and Laura Page. This work would never have been possible without the considerable trust instilled in me by my clients for over 40 years, especially those who dared explore their depths beyond conventional wisdom. Deep gratitude also goes to Meridian University and my cohort there, and particularly to Aftab Omer, Melissa Schwartz and Jean Houston for opening up the world of leadership to me in ways I had never imagined. And finally, a special thank-you to my co-conspirator in this archetypal adventure, to Richard: it is a rare and beautiful experience in life to find a productive relationship like we have. Thank you for believing in this work, for your trust, and for being a true friend.

Richard adds: We may never have had the courage to write this if it were not for the early adopters who allowed us to experiment with our emerging methodology. Participants on Mythodrama Project workshops at the Findhorn Foundation, Schumacher College, Hawkwood College and the United Palace of Spiritual Arts in New York. Courageous Programme Directors at the Oxford Saïd Business School, especially Tracey Camilleri and Marc Thompson, and the Bill and Melinda Gates Foundation, especially Katherine Kahn. John Zachry and Jenny Trefzer at the Zachry Group, Sara Niese and Wolfgang Loess from the Daimler Vice President Promotion Seminar; we would not know how effective this work would be for senior leaders without your support and encouragement. My wise supervisor Alan Mulhern for helping enable dreams and mitigate nightmares. My wonderful wife of 33 years, Shelley, who has now endured the rather tortuous writing process of her husband four times. And my friend and writing partner Laurence, who has been the guardian of this wisdom for over 40 years and who has generously shared all he knows and continues to learn as we truly begin to see Archetypes at Work™!

PREFACE

We, the authors, Laurence Hillman and Richard Olivier, first met in April 1996 in New York, at the 70th birthday celebrations of James Hillman, world-renowned archetypal psychologist, and Laurence's father. Richard was there because James was the American publisher of Richard's book about the relationship with his father, the famous actor, Laurence Olivier. Though our fathers never met, the fact that James was an admirer of Laurence's film of *Henry V* may have played a part in the French spelling of his son's name.

Our shared experience of growing up in the shadow of high-performing, brilliant (and often absent) fathers drew us immediately into deep conversation and is still a topic of mutual interest to this day. By the time we left New York two days later we both had a sense that there was some deeper reason for our connection, and we committed to stay in touch across the Atlantic. We also started a somewhat tongue-in-cheek private club which we named "The Son Also Rises..."

We first worked together in 1998 at Shakespeare's Globe Theatre in London, where Richard was Master of Mythodrama and a guest director. Alongside James Hillman and the Globe's Artistic Director and leading actor, Mark Rylance, we were exploring how the wisdom of the archetypes infused the works of Shakespeare – and how both could be used to help individuals gain more self-awareness and insight into their own lives, whether at work or home. As Shakespeare has Hamlet say to a group of actors: "The purpose of playing... is to hold a mirror up to nature". This combination of archetypal wisdom and rehearsal techniques proved itself to be remarkably effective in activating meaningful personal development for those who experienced it at the Globe (the workshop we developed is described in more detail in Appendix 1). We both took great inspiration from this first experiment into our different working practices – Laurence in personal coaching and Richard in leadership development and consulting. We continued to run workshops together once or twice a year for the next 17 years.

In 2015 we co-founded an Archetypal Research Lab to explore how the 10 Archetypes that had been the basis of Laurence's coaching practice for 40 years could be applied to leadership as well as team and organizational development. Over the past four years we have been working intensively together to research, experiment and test our theories in practice. It was out of this Lab that the Archetypes at Work™ method was born. Richard brought the 10 archetypes into the leadership development programmes run by his company, Olivier Mythodrama. Laurence developed a bespoke practice, working with CEOs across the USA to apply the method, and used this research to create the thesis for his PhD that explored and confirmed the usefulness of an archetypal approach to leadership consulting.

The method has now been thoroughly "road-tested". It has been successfully applied to a wide range of individuals and organizations across many sectors, including charitable foundations, NGOs, government departments and Fortune 500 companies. Along the way over 5,000 managers and leaders have assessed themselves using the archetypal framework described here, and they have found it easy to understand, meaningful to engage with, and practical to apply. As they have recognized their own behaviours in the Archetypes, they continue to improve their work and lives. Being able to describe both their gifts and difficulties in an imaginative, yet systematic, way offers them tools to develop into more insightful and reflective people who understand themselves and the world better. Many have given feedback to us about how this has profoundly changed their perspective on themselves and on their relationships. The insights they gained by understanding their archetypal patterns, both at work and in their private lives, has set many on a path to deep personal development. We hope our readers, whatever their background, will echo their experiences, using the knowledge gained in this book to become "future-fit" for an increasingly complex and fragile world.

Apologia

We offer several big ideas and assumptions in this book – all the way through, from the Introduction to the last Appendix. Any attempt to fully explain or justify these would take another book of equal length, so for the sake of easy understanding and practical application we have avoided this here. We hope you will take our premises in the provocative spirit in which they are intended. Take them on as working assumptions if you can, or put them aside as the authors' personal opinions, if you wish.

We are also both aware of the privileged position we hold in the current world: being white, male and birthed into successful, well-resourced families. Our feminist friends are only too willing to remind us that, on a bad day, this can lead to us exhibiting MPS syndrome – Male, Pale and Stale. We hope that this book represents a good day. Our shared belief is that the hope for the future will come primarily from the non-male and non-pale members of our global village. We also trust that there can be an appropriate place for everyone's contribution. This is ours.

Laurence Hillman and Richard Olivier,
September 2019

INTRODUCTION

"We do not live most of the time in exalted states. The content of our stream of consciousness is usually not so lofty. Our psychic life is more like a squabbling theatrical company trying to rehearse a play we don't even know the name of."

CHARLES SIMIC

The pitch

We, the authors, believe that humanity has reached a crucial moment in history – a turning point – and in order to survive and thrive in the future we will need all the help we can get. We further believe that a deep understanding of the 10 Archetypes outlined in this book can be an invaluable tool to help people engage with personal, professional and cultural development in this increasingly complex and fragile world.

Overview

This book is aimed at those who want to develop or increase their insight, agency and effectiveness at work and in life. These Archetypes are "at work" all the time, whether we are aware of them or not. Becoming aware of them will increase your ability to respond to any situation effectively. We use the word "leader" in its broadest sense; we believe that everyone has the capacity for leadership and that leadership operates at all levels in life, not just in more formal organizational settings, including "taking the lead" in your own life.

The frame of the 10 Archetypes provides a template for you to understand the dynamics that underpin individuals, situations and collective cultures. You will first learn how to identify these dynamics and then how to change them, as and when necessary. You will have the opportunity to diagnose your own archetypal pattern, either in the workbook pages within this book as you go along, on a separate notebook, or on a free downloadable attachment (www.archetypesatwork.com/freedownloads). You will be introduced to practical tools to develop access to new desired Archetypes.

We use a selection of approaches to give you the insights you need, including mini case studies of those we have previously coached, creative writing and poetry commissioned especially for this book.

The big picture

As we write this, we are aware that many old certainties have fallen by the wayside, and many trusted institutions have betrayed our trust or suffered a breakdown of some kind in the recent past. Whether in politics, religion, finance or law, none of the old certainties seem unshakable now. This seems to be a symptom of a larger malaise: that as a species we are currently "between stories".

Every age in human history has a narrative thread that runs through it, a world view that gives the ruling class their strength and the prevailing cultures of that time their credibility – and everyone else a context for sense-making. As history has shown, every so often a world view runs out of steam, eventually to be replaced by another. We seem to be in such a time.

Many of us see that the old story that we have been living with since the beginnings of the Industrial Revolution (what Joanna Macy calls "the Industrial Growth Society") is not working anymore, but we do not yet see a tangible new story taking shape or taking its place. Given the multiple current and likely future crises that we are already being warned about – including the climate crisis in all its known and as-yet unknown manifestations, refugees, water shortages, pollution, wars and global debt, to name a few – it seems that we are at a crossroads. Can we create a great turning towards a new, more sustainable and socially just story for the many? Or will we stubbornly refuse to read the writing on the wall and suffer a great collapse, with only the few surviving and thriving on the other side of it? Many future thinkers and thought leaders alive today believe that our very existence as a species on the planet is now hanging in the balance. Most predict that things will get a lot worse before they get any better (apart from politicians seeking election it seems – but then few votes are won by saying, "This is going to hurt, but our descendants will thank us"). So, rather than sitting around and waiting it out, what can we do?

Activating archetypal wisdom

The core of our work is based on activating archetypal wisdom. This draws on profound cultural images and transformational teachings from past societies and combines these with effective modern techniques to create the desired future.

Many past cultures have survived and thrived through huge transitions. Those we are most familiar with seem to have two things in common: 1) they found or developed ways to access archetypal wisdom; and 2) they created exercises, rituals and rites of passage that allowed that wisdom to be imagined, embodied and then expressed. This was certainly true of the Ancient Greek world, the full flowering of the Roman Empire and the transformative period that became known as the Renaissance. Accessing archetypal wisdom and then activating it are the key principles of Archetypes at Work™.

The big picture context for this work is the urgent need for a change in our collective human culture, but the completion of this shift is unlikely to occur within our lifetimes. Cultural change is slow and unpredictable and, for many, feels so far away from their day-to-day reality that it can also lead to a sense of disempowerment: "It's so big, what can I as an individual possibly do?"

Changing your story – one character at a time

Within this bigger picture, a large majority of those reading this book will have some agency; and one of the most tangible ways to utilize that agency is to keep developing ourselves.

The world is getting increasingly complex, and to understand it, and interact with it, we need ready access to as many faculties as we can develop. To become "future-fit" means having a felt understanding of a multiplicity of approaches to life itself. The ability to extend your perspective to embrace a range of approaches therefore becomes critical.

While reading this book we will be prompting you to come up with your own answers to some pretty big questions: Who am I now? Who do I want or need to be in the future? How am I going to get there? Increasing your knowledge of the Archetypes will give you access to a fuller range of these faculties. As the world changes, we too must change and adapt ourselves to new circumstances. Understanding your current archetypal patterns and developing lesser accessed parts of yourself is a practical, proven and powerful way to repattern yourself for the future. This, we believe, will benefit you both professionally and personally.

Having spent the majority of our professional lives in the development field, we can reliably inform you that very few people let go of an old story and step into a new one easily or, indeed, willingly. There are usually two very different circumstances that enable the personal shift, which we could loosely refer to as the stick and the carrot. The stick operates in a situation that feels like "do or die" – where there is no option but to change. The carrot works via a compelling picture or dream of a desired future that is inspiring enough to enable the individual to abandon the comfort of an old identity and the story that reinforced it. The latter can be engendered in some people by a passionate belief in a better future, or by an inner commitment to continuous development. For many, it is prompted by a nagging discomfort with the present, an intuition that we could be more, and an interest in figuring out what that could be. For any and all of these motivations to change, we offer a metaphor and a tool to help. The metaphor is:

> *If you want to evolve your story, first change the characters on your inner stage.*

As touched upon in the Preface, our tool is the unique combination of archetypal wisdom combined with theatre practice. In essence, the 10 Archetypes we work with (and which we will introduce you to very shortly) operate like characters – and we will invite you to think of them as 10 key actors on your inner stage. And as all good dramatists know, the easiest way to change a story that is getting stuck is to introduce a new character. This will shift the action in a new direction, often one the existing characters could not have imagined. This is as true in your life as it is in drama and fiction. You can change your story by changing a Leading Actor on your inner stage. So, while the notion of changing your story may be understandably daunting, the notion of simply bringing a new character onstage is, we hope, considerably more encouraging!

Part One of this book will take you on a journey that teaches you how to recognize the 10 characters in your life and in the world, and to realize the impact they have on you. Much of what we do every day is automatic and remains out of our conscious awareness. When you use the methods outlined in this book to make your behaviour patterns conscious, you learn to recognize archetypal patterns in yourself and also in the world around you. This enables you to increase the benefits of what is most helpful (what we call the "Gifts") and tone down what is overplayed (thereby mitigating the impact of what we call the "Shadows of Too Much"). You can also choose, if you wish, to cultivate what is missing or underplayed (to reduce the impact of what we call the "Shadows of Too Little").

Part Two then offers a series of techniques to help you nudge your story into a new direction whenever you need to (what we call "expanding your repertoire"). These techniques draw on the primary interdisciplinary fields of archetypal psychology, leadership development, experiential learning and techniques from theatre. We synthesize these into practical methods to help you imagine and then rehearse new possibilities for who you choose to be, what you choose to do, and how you choose to do it. We call this "Acting-In" the desired future. Part Two closes with a template for a personal Archetypal Development Plan to help you integrate the learning and decide on final development goals.

What are Archetypes?

Archetypes are the underlying patterns of human nature and experience that recur throughout history and across all cultures. They are the organizing factors and primordial principles that lie behind appearances but give things and people their distinct energetic footprint. As such they are – often invisibly – "running the show". They deeply inform the character we present to the world as an individual, and the culture we present to the world as a collective. They inform our values and motivations, and often dictate our mindset and behaviour. The better we understand these patterns, and the more consciously we use them, the more effective we will be.

Archetypes seem to be subtly coded into human consciousness and have been expressed by every culture known to anthropologists. In the earliest surviving human art, including the 20,000-year-old cave paintings at Lascaux, there are distinguishable images of chiefs, mothers, warriors, hunters, gatherers and shaman–priests – all archetypal images. In Ancient Greece they projected these Archetypes onto multiple gods with names such as Zeus, Athena and Aphrodite. The Romans borrowed from the Greeks deities, often projecting their gods onto the visible planets of our solar system. Mars became simultaneously the god of war and a planet in the sky. The Renaissance, up through the time of Shakespeare, revisited these old ideas and re-visioned many of them for their modern time. And throughout the 20th century, with the emergence of Swiss psychiatrist Carl Jung and depth psychology, followed by James Hillman and archetypal psychology, Archetypes became an established, modern way of looking at patterns of action and behaviour. We can recognize Archetypes in ourselves and also in patterns in the world. We never see an Archetype in its pure form (as they are primordial images) but will see countless representations and manifestations of them throughout our lives.

Over the last many decades of exploration and practice, we have found that the palette of the 10 Archetypes presented in this book can provide an invaluable frame. Through it we can see all of life's circumstances, problems and delights in a meaningful and imaginative way. Together, the 10 Archetypes combine to create a practical, creative and inclusive whole. This book shows the reader a journey of self-exploration through 10 lenses that can accurately describe personality, leadership styles and situations. They apply equally to individuals, teams and whole organizations. They are especially effective when there is a recognized need for a shift to become "future-fit".

As authors, we have followed the Ancient Greco-Roman tradition of drawing on the planets in our solar system as inspiration for archetypal images. The 10 we work with are inspired by cultural images that have been associated with these planets by many philosophers, scientists, astrologers and artists throughout human history. For those interested in the philosophical and theoretical roots of this, there is a full explanation in Appendix 1 – though no prior knowledge of these roots is required to apply the learnings presented here and benefit from this book.

Five Realms and 10 Archetypes

Remembering with ease 10 archetypal characters may be a challenge for some, so we created a simple way to divide them into five pairs, each pair presiding over a particular *essential theme or responsibility* in leadership and life, what we call the *Five Realms*...

The Five Realms

Going counter-clockwise (and in brief), the Realm of **Order** illuminates how we organize our life and work, the realm of **Relationship** is about how we engage with others, **Creativity** about how we initiate the new, **Change** about how we manage transitions and **Action** about how we get things done. Each Realm contains two Archetypes, which operate in importantly different ways. We will go into much greater detail about each Archetype and the differences from their "Realm partner" in following chapters, but here are the headlines for now, including the key Gifts each Archetype brings.

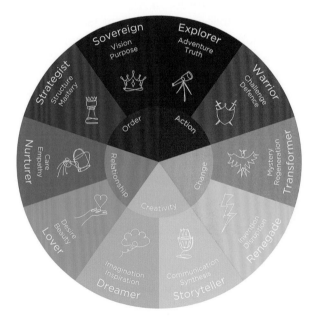

Archetypal Gifts Wheel

Counter-clockwise from the top

The **Sovereign** brings Order through Vision and Purpose, setting the direction for a life or organization while being comfortable at the centre of things, whereas the **Strategist** brings Order through Structure and Mastery, often working backstage to analyse the details, plan precisely and then build the road ahead.

The **Nurturer** creates Relationship through Care and Empathy, giving what is needed to grow and develop others, whereas the **Lover** values a relationship of equals, appreciating Beauty and focusing on what they and others Desire.

The **Dreamer** accesses Creativity through Imagination and Inspiration and is comfortable with the unknown and the irrational, whereas the **Storyteller** enables effective Communication and Synthesis by weaving different ideas into threads, creating coherent, compellingly narratives, and sharing them with relish.

The **Renegade** enables Change through Invention and Disruption, becoming a lightning rod for the future to emerge at pace, whereas the **Transformer** brings the slower more shamanic approach of Mystery and Regeneration, enabling the necessary deaths and rebirths along the path from the old to the new.

The **Warrior** moves into Action assertively, in pursuit of a clear goal, bravely Challenging others and passionately Defending their own territory, whereas the **Explorer** is an expansive optimist, endlessly questing Adventure and Truth, climbing a distant mountain because it is there and seeking profound philosophical wisdom.

Combined, they make an impressive full set of potentials – and the good news is that they are available to all of us, as we each contain their latent potential within. Whereas we are able to draw from all 10, our unique life and work situations will call on them in different ways at different times. Some may always be prevalent, and some may almost always be distant, but they will all be there, one way or another.

One person, many roles

If this is your first introduction to thinking about parts of you as inner characters or figures, it may feel odd to think of the 10 Archetypes as being within you. On one level, it is a useful metaphor for different aspects of the self. On another level, these are powerful energies that you can see and feel as they appear in the world. You can also learn to notice how they show up in you as impulses, habits or attitudes that influence behaviour and subsequent action. This is an extraordinary human ability, and we will be drawing on it extensively throughout the book.

When we accept our innate psychological complexity, we begin to understand some of our habitual inner struggles and can learn to trust that occasional inner confusion can be useful. For instance, we can express some sides of our personality at work and quite different ones at home. Given a particular situation, we will withhold some natural traits from those around us to act appropriately. Sometimes we even have conversations with ourselves, internal arguments: "A part of me wants to take this job, but another part says 'no'". In the language of this book we would say that two Archetypes are having an internal conversation. They both have reasons, instincts and feelings to back up their arguments and advice, as each of us have different inner voices that offer us a variety of agendas and emotions. Together, these inner characters form a loosely integrated whole that we recognize when we look in the mirror. The ability to think of ourselves as having a multitude of inner characters is an extraordinary human capacity, and we will be drawing on it throughout the book.

And so, we invite you to think of the Archetypes as a troupe of actors on your inner stage. Like any group, some will get on and others may be in conflict. Some will be preferred, giving you more satisfaction and sense of identity: "This is me". Others may be ignored or judged as not offering much value or may even surprise you when they show up: "I don't know where that came from – that is not like me".

They all show up - somehow

All 10 Archetypes within us are always present. Even if you do not have easy access to a particular one, it is still in your life. For instance, if you don't like to travel, if new ideas don't particularly interest you and you are not known for your enjoyment of humour, then you probably have difficulty accessing the Explorer. This is because the Explorer is the Archetype that embodies all those things. You could think of the Explorer as a character that you are uncomfortable playing. When you find yourself in a situation that is gregarious and funny to most people, you may want to withdraw. However, just because you are not engaged with your Explorer does not mean that this Archetype is not in your life. It will show up in other people and circumstances you meet in your life. We often find, for example, that people end up with a business or life partner who just happens to play the Archetypes that they don't like. When you go out, your partner may be the life of the party while you stand quietly in the corner. Your partner has taken on one of your inner characters, a very common phenomenon. It is as though you are saying, "I don't know how to play this part, why don't you play it for me?"

We call this tendency to relinquish an Archetype an *externalization*, which we define as a propensity to find others to play the Archetypes within us that we don't. Carl Jung once wrote that, "When a situation is not made conscious, it happens outside as fate." Sometimes externalizations can have more serious consequences. An example is a very creative executive we coached who had a lifelong aversion to the Warrior, having been bullied in school. She tried not to engage in any competitive activities or attitudes but found herself constantly being managed by bullying bosses. Finally, she learned to activate her inner Warrior so that it did not continue to show up outside as "fate". Referring back to the Ancient Greeks, who saw the gods in all things, we sum this up as, "Either you do the gods, or the gods do you". With this we mean that there are energies in life that at times feel compelling. If we are aware of them, we have more choice over how much we "let them in"; if we do not recognize them, they can unconsciously "make us do things".

But why do we find certain Archetypes difficult, troublesome or even distressing? The answer lies both in "nature" (we were born that way) and in "nurture" (we were raised that way). Both led to the current make-up of your archetypal stage.

Archetypal patterns

Your archetypal pattern is the way your inner stage is currently set. You will have the opportunity to fully explore and analyse this in Part One of this book. There are no right or wrong archetypal patterns, only what is true for you at a given point in life. Some of us have a natural flexibility and enjoy shifting from one pattern to another, others are more fixed and prefer to stick with one or two key patterns that work. When new challenges arise, a new archetypal pattern may be required. How to develop this is the subject of Part Two.

What is ahead in Part One: Archetypal Repertoire

Part One enables you to accurately identify your current patterns, Gifts and Shadows.

In **Chapter 1**, **How to use Part One**, we explain how we enter the world of the 10 Archetypes and how the reader can best use the material presented. In **Chapters 2 to 6**, the **Gifts** available from all 10 Archetypes are explored in detail within their appropriate **Realm Chapters of Order**, **Relationship**, **Creativity**, **Change** and **Action**. This will enable you to understand the typical manifestations and energy of each Archetype, both in yourself and in the world around you. At the end of each archetypal immersion you will be invited to make an intuitive assessment of your current relationship with it. How much is the presented Archetype a part of your life and work? Once you have completed this immersion into all 10 Archetypes there will be an optional longer assessment to rank them and assess your current archetypal Gift patterns for life and current working context.

Each Archetype has two Shadows which are also important to understand. **Chapter 7, Archetypal Shadows of Too Much**, explores how all the Archetypes can be overplayed. Any overplayed strength can become a weakness, especially if it is in our blind spot: visible to others but not to ourselves. On a bad day, we can all slip from accessing the gifts of our favourite Archetypes ("you doing the gods") to being possessed by their respective Shadows of Too Much (another way of "the gods doing you").

Chapter 8, Archetypal Shadows of Too Little, explores the opposite pole. There is also a cost when we underplay our least favourite Archetypes. Any Archetype that is firmly pushed off our inner stage will have a limiting effect on our potential. Both these final chapters in Part One are followed by further self-assessment pages ("intermissions"), so you can record and remember the impact of the Shadows of Too Much and Too Little as well.

What is ahead in Part Two: Archetypal Development

Part Two enables you to effectively develop more "future-fit" archetypal patterns.

Chapter 9, How to use Part Two, introduces you to different developmental paths you can take to activate archetypal potentials. You will be able to choose whether to focus on developing a less familiar Archetype or evolving your access to a currently well-developed one.

Chapters 10 to 14, Developing the Five Realms, provide an in-depth selection of proven techniques to activate archetypal wisdom in your less favoured Archetypes. This is particularly helpful to mitigate the effect of any of the Shadows of Too Little you have identified.

Chapter 15, Hybrid Roles: Combining Archetypes for Development, can then help mitigate the impact of any previously identified Shadows of Too Much. This involves creating a new archetypal pattern by bringing a lesser used Archetype onto your inner stage whose Gifts provide an antidote to the Shadow of Too Much of a favourite.

Chapter 16, **Meeting the Archetypes in Others**, provides ideas to help build rapport with other people. This is especially useful when their favourite Archetype corresponds with your least favourite. Meeting the other where they are can significantly increase mutual understanding and alignment.

Chapters 17 and 18, **Evolving Your Core Strengths – Horizontal Integration and Vertical Development**, show how you can further improve what you are already good at. We offer two approaches to enhance the performance of your favourite Archetype. We complete our development journey with early intimations of what the emerging and evolving aspects of each Archetype may offer us and our collective future.

The **Coda** offers a few reflections on what we have presented and how you can further apply it in your life. We call this practice "Developing an archetypal eye". Finally, we include three Appendices. The first one gives a philosophical background on why we use 10 archetypes and explains their cosmological origin. The second is a practical list of all the key words that are spread throughout the rest of the book. The third is a handy list of page numbers if you want to follow a particular Archetype through the whole book.

We are all leaders now

This book is designed to help all readers improve their performance at work and release more potential in their lives. We, the authors, have bridged the humanistic fields of personal and leadership development for many years. From our perspective, the two are intimately linked. If someone is developing as a leader, they will inevitably develop as a person too. The reverse is more rarely stated but we hold this to be true as well: the more you develop yourself as a person the more qualified you are for leadership.

We have had far too many ineffective or tragically misguided leaders in too many places for far too long – and our societies and eco-systems are suffering as a result. We urgently need more emotionally intelligent, self-aware and psychologically mature leaders to step up and help guide the collective into a more sustainable future.

One of the trends already clear in our emerging new age is an enhanced spirt of collaboration and co-operation. The old top-down, command and control, heroic and autocratic styles of leadership were de rigueur in the old story of competitive growth. They are – gradually – losing traction as more democratic, collaborative and collective styles emerge. The old is by no means dead yet and rumours of its demise are often, sadly, exaggerated. But the general trend is clear: as the New Age continues to unfold, the likelihood is that leadership will become more and more shared among more and more people. Increasingly, larger numbers of us will embody leadership in order to take our share of responsibility for the whole. In a time of great transition there will be something for every one of us to co-ordinate or enable. We are all leaders now...

We intend that this work can serve as an inspiration to continuous development, an ongoing reference book and practical guide to help you through the ever-changing seas of life.

We hope you enjoy the journey.

Laurence Hillman and Richard Olivier,
September 2019

Part One

ARCHETYPAL REPERTOIRE

GIFTS, SHADOWS AND ASSESSMENTS

CHAPTER 1
HOW TO USE
Part One

Throughout this work we have at various times strived to inhabit and write not just about the Archetypes but also, to the extent that we are able, from within them. We aim to inhabit their point of view and speak to you, the reader, from their perspective. Our intention is to create a meaningful and three-dimensional character for each, as if each were inhabiting a single persona. However, there may be occasions in which you sense a more two-dimensional character presented – perhaps in one of your favourite characters, for which we apologize in advance; the line between Archetype and stereotype can be a thin one. The attempt to condense an eternal underlying pattern in human nature into an easily comprehensible character can result in occasional over-simplification.

As you read on please remember that you will never meet these 10 particular characters on the street, as it were, "by themselves". Each of us has all of them within ourselves. When they show up in us, they are subtly blended with other Archetypes in our current favoured pattern. So, as you read about one you are more likely to recognize: "I am like that some of the time" or "I know people who operate like this most of the time".

Identifying your archetypal patterns – Gifts

In the next five chapters each Archetype will be introduced in full, using a combination of creative and rational input to give you a comprehensive picture of their unique gifts, including specifics about their appearance, motivation and operation. The invitation is that you use the immersion into each to "try the Archetype on for size" – as if you were visiting an elaborate character costume store and trying 10 different and complex outfits on for size. As you visit each Archetype, we ask you to notice whether this one feels like it fits you mostly, generally, partially or not much. And which of the different character traits and qualities, attitudes and likely priorities for each do fit you at this point in your life and career – and which do not. All of this will be useful information for you to gather, both for your own self-awareness in Part One and to benefit from the more practical applications in Part Two, which will explore what you can do with this new awareness.

After each Archetype you will be invited to make an intuitive judgement as to their likely place on your inner stage. This will be both for what we call your "Core Life Pattern" (who you feel you are at your core) and for your "Current Work Pattern" (what your current working role requires you to be). We lay out four categories to help with this, continuing the theatrical metaphor: *Leading Actors, Major Supporting Actors, Minor Supporting Actors* and *More Offstage Actors*.

A = Leading Actor
This Archetype embodies your favourite natural gifts. It gives you a joyful sense of purpose on your best days. It feels like a trusted and go-to inner advisor.

B = Major Supporting Actor
This Archetype is a favoured back-up. An easy competency you can draw on at will, even if you don't enjoy it as much as your Leading Actors.

C = Minor Supporting Actor
This Archetype has qualities and behaviours you can access when you

have to. An earned competency that you can step into, but you generally choose not to until you need it.

D = More Offstage Actor
This Archetype is less favoured and less used. You may feel uncomfortable with it or about it (for numerous reasons). You may judge it as being of little or no value.

When you have completed your immersion into all 10 Archetypes, we offer a simple self-assessment tool that can help you sort them into your current preferred order (for both Life and Work separately). You will be invited to divide the 10 between the four categories with a minimum of two Archetypes and a maximum of three in each category. We have found that this is the easiest way to create appropriate distinctions and get a sense of the current Life and Work patterns on your inner stage.

Identifying your archetypal patterns – Shadows

As pointed out briefly in the Introduction, each of the Archetypes also has two Shadows which we believe are crucial to understand and assess before you decide on any developmental next steps. We use the notion of Shadows in this work to point out the dangers of Too Much and Too Little access to an Archetype. They will be defined in more detail at the beginning of their respective Chapters, 7 and 8.

We will also explain our understanding of how these Shadows develop. Both share similarities with ways that the Gifts develop (nature and nurture). In addition, Too Much can originate in the human tendency to keep doing more of what we get rewarded for. For example, a natural Warrior will be driven and assertive on a good day, but if these gifts get rewarded and are then used relentlessly, that same person can become an intimidating bully.

Too Little can be a reaction to a previous experience of suffering the consequences of Too Much (usually at the hands of another). For example, some people who have been bullied by aggressive Warriors earlier in life will judge the whole Archetype negatively. They refuse to step into positive Warrior Gifts and can exhibit aspects of the Shadow of Too Little. Here they may be perceived by others as a pushover, find it difficult to motivate themselves or perform with the high energy required to be an obvious choice for promotion. Both Shadows will have a negative impact on our general levels of effectiveness and fulfilment.

As you meet the Shadows, we will invite you to try these on, too, for size – as if on a visit to two very different departments in our imaginary costume store. This is likely to feel less comfortable than trying on the Gifts, as by definition the Shadows are behaviours we tend not to wish upon ourselves and often resent when we see them in others. We encourage you to stick with the process, even through temporary discomfort, as awareness of Shadow material is where the majority of the people we work with find their motivation for change.

Since the implications of both Shadows are of ineffective behaviour, we also imagine that the vast majority of people do not enter these behaviour patterns knowingly, but rather unconsciously. A major benefit of realizing what your Shadows are is that once you are aware of them you are less likely to slip into them quite so often. Most of us, however, will still get triggered into these less than optimal patterns from time to time, especially when we are under pressure. The longer-term antidote to this is understanding their roots (where they came from and how they served you at that time) and then finding an antidote to the behaviour. This antidote usually resides in a Gift inherent in a different Archetype. We explore this and other remedies in Part Two.

Both Shadow chapters are followed by further Self-Assessment pages, so you can record and remember the impact of your personal Shadows of Too Much and Too Little for future reference. And if in doubt about what fits you, particularly with the Shadow of Too Much, feel free to ask a friend!

The journey into the 10 Archetypes

In Chapters 2 through 6 we offer four ways into each Archetype for you to engage with and tune into. We start with a selection of key words that give an overview of the Gifts associated with each. We then move into a more detailed Archetype-appropriate introduction, a piece of creative writing in the manner of its respective character. This is written in the style of each and about a subject naturally associated with each. Your response to each of these will be a clue as to your likely relationship with the Archetype in question. Next is a subjective stream of consciousness section, in which the Archetype speaks in the first person, claiming their gifts, interests, passions and natural offerings for an individual and in the world. You are asked to notice if these feel like you "on a good day" or if they fall outside of your current sense of identity and reach. Each archetypal immersion concludes with an evocative archetypal poem written for this book by our good friend and award-winning poet, William Ayot.

Please turn to the following chapter, Chapter 2, when you are ready to start your immersion into the deeper work presented in this book.

CHAPTER 2

THE REALM OF

Order

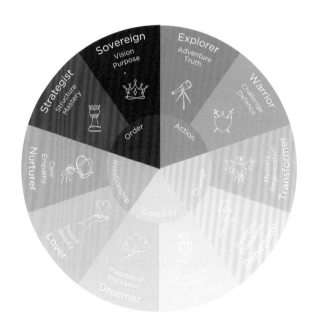

"A mindset that understands order, is a mindset that can understand leadership."

WAYNE CHIRISA

"For nothing matters except life; and, of course, order."

VIRGINIA WOOLF

"The universal order and the personal order are nothing but different expressions and manifestations of a common underlying principle."

MARCUS AURELIUS

"Each move is dictated by the previous one – that is the meaning of order."

TOM STOPPARD

"Order and simplification are the first steps towards mastery of a subject."

THOMAS MANN

"Order is the first law of heaven, and you have to have order to survive on Earth. Figure out what has to be done each day, each week, each year and develop a system to achieve it."

IYANLA VANZANT

"In times of widespread chaos and confusion, it has been the duty of more advanced human beings – artists, scientists, clowns and philosophers – to create order."

TOM ROBBINS

Overview

We begin our deep-dive into the Archetypes with the Realm of Order, where we explore the gifts of the Sovereign and the Strategist. Both help us organize our lives, our work and how we operate in the world. Each has a gift for alignment and selects what is helpful and necessary, but they offer vitally different ways of doing it.

The Sovereign organizes around purpose and vision and radiates a heartfelt passion for a brighter future with a magnetic ability to draw others to them. They are at ease being visible and seen by others as a central point around which everything gathers. They use their energy as an attractor, lighting the way forward with hope and positive pictures of the way ahead.

The Strategist, on the other hand, organizes around form, function and structure. This is the master who creates a logical game plan that others can clearly understand and confidently follow. The Strategist may be more comfortable in the background, away from the spotlight, getting the details right and the numbers to work. They will build the solid foundation that others can rely upon. What they construct others can trust as solid and secure.

The combination of the Sovereign's purpose and the Strategist's structure enables a resilient foundation, an inspiring "North Star" to navigate by and to follow.

Gifts of the Sovereign
Vision and Purpose

"The most courageous act is still to think for yourself. Aloud."

COCO CHANEL

Welcome to the Sovereign!

As we move through the different ways of seeing the gifts of the Sovereign you are invited to notice which of these feels like you on a good day. If a majority of the descriptions that follow feel true for you, it is likely that the Sovereign is either a Leading Actor or a Major Supporting Actor on your stage. If a minority, then the Sovereign is probably a Minor Supporting Actor. If very little or none of this rings true, then the Sovereign is likely a More Offstage Actor. There is no right or wrong in any of this, only what feels true for you at this point in your life. If you recognize elements of the Sovereign that you would like more access to, this is addressed in the later chapters on developing the Archetypes.

We will start with some key words, traditionally associated with Sovereign energy. Please notice how you respond as you read them, holding the question: Does this sound like me on a good day?

KEY WORDS

Royal, Ruler, Visible, Heroic, Luminary, Generative, Playful, Heartful, Magnanimous, Loyal, Present, Spacious, at the Centre of Things

THE SOVEREIGN RADIATES

Purpose, Generosity, Courage, Will, Self-Confidence, Vigour, Strength, Vision, Vitality, Charisma, Ambition

Which of these can you own? Which might feel a bit too much to really claim? Which don't feel like you? You may already have a felt sense of your initial response but please let it "cook" as we explore different expressions of Sovereign energy.

The next piece is an Archetype-appropriate introduction, using a form that suits the naturally theatrical Sovereign: a play. The characters each exhibit Sovereign qualities and gifts. Particularly when you are speaking in a group, running a meeting or "holding court" in some other way, do you feel that you are in the right place or the wrong place? Does it feel comfortable to be holding centre stage and being visible to everyone who is around?

TAKING THE STAGE

A Play in One Act

Cast of Characters

QUEEN ELIZABETH 1: English Monarch in her late 20s
DJIMON KAYLAN: South African Actor in his 40s
KARABO PILLAY: South African Director in her 30s
SUNITA MUDIRA: A Cambodian Community Activist in her 20s
FRANK BRADLEY: An American CEO in his 60s

Setting: Four areas of the stage represent: The Royal Court in London, England, 1558 – A rehearsal room in Cape Town, South Africa, Present – An ecovillage hut in Ashoko, Cambodia, Present – A corporate boardroom in New York, USA, January 2018

Scene 1: Royal Court – the lights come up on a throne – Upstage centre

ELIZABETH (sitting on the throne)

I will be as good unto ye as ever a Queen was unto her people. And persuade yourselves that for the safety and quietness of you all I will not spare if need be to spend my blood. I shall desire you all, my lords (chiefly you of the nobility, everyone in his degree and power), to be assistant to me that I, with my ruling, and you with your service, may make a good account to Almighty God and leave some comfort to our posterity on Earth.

Scene 2: Rehearsal room Nairobi – rehearsing the life story of Nelson Mandela. A pool of light on a prop courtroom Witness Box – Stage left

KARABO (directing DJIMON as NELSON MANDELA in the
witness box)

Good work, Djimon, you've naturally got a felt sense of the great
man's presence. Now see if you can add an even greater inner
conviction; he knows he was born for a reason, *and* – he is ready to
die for it too – so a potent mix of generosity, deep values and the
willingness to sacrifice himself for the greater cause, without regrets.
When you are ready, take it from the top...

DJIMON as NELSON MANDELA –
(standing in the witness box)

Action without vision is only passing time, vision without action
is merely day-dreaming, but vision with action can change the
world. Real leaders must be ready to sacrifice all for the freedom
of their people. I have cherished the ideal of a democratic and free
society in which all persons live together in harmony and with equal
opportunities. It is an ideal which I hope to live and to achieve. But if
needs be, it is an ideal for which I am prepared to die...

Scene 3:   Ecovillage hut – lights up. Downstage centre: Sunita sitting
on a cushion on the floor

SUNITA

Dear friends, our vision is clear, we want to make our country a
better place for our children to live in – and the main obstacle is
also clear; the way that our current government and business leaders
are exploiting the environment, prioritizing short-term growth over
long-term sustainable practice. So, we have to become the voice that
they will listen to; not one of us, not a few of us, but all of us. We
are the generation who have to take responsibility for our collective
future. No generation has had this kind of responsibility before, and
if we do not act soon it may be too late. Our simple message to
those leaders must be: "Remember, the economy is a wholly owned
subsidiary of Ecology!"

Scene 4: Boardroom – Stage right: lights up on Frank at the head of a boardroom table

FRANK (reading from laptop)

I called this special board meeting because of an email that came into my inbox this morning from our biggest fund manager. I'd like to read a couple of excerts [from Annual Letter to CEOs, Larry Fink, CEO of BlackRock, January 2018]:

> "Dear CEO, society is demanding that companies, both public and private, serve a social purpose. To prosper over time, every company must not only deliver financial performance but also show how it makes a positive contribution to society... Companies must benefit all of their stakeholders, including the communities in which they operate... Without a sense of purpose, no company, either public or private, can achieve its full potential."

So, colleagues, it is time we asked ourselves: What role do we play in the community? And how could we start playing on the bigger stage of purpose?

(Lights fade to black)

Could you imagine yourself in any of these roles – metaphorically or in reality? Do those around you know what you stand for or stand against? Where in your life are you making a difference – and how do you stand and become visible for that difference to be made? Many of those with Sovereign as a Leading Actor have at least one space in their lives where visibility is important, but of course it may not be on such a "big stage" as those above. There are as many ways to live the Sovereign as there are people on the planet and the point is to find our own best way of accessing the gifts.

We move on to a more subjective expression of Sovereign gifts, written in the first person. As you read, we invite you to sense which phrases resonate naturally as you hear them in your head. Some may be aspirational (i.e. "I wish I could do this but at present I don't"), and others you may have a negative reaction to ("That's not me and that is not who I want to be"). Again, no right or wrong, just what feels true... today.

Sovereign Gifts - subjective expression

I RECEIVE - I RADIATE - I AM

I create Order around a compelling Vision and exude a soulful sense of Purpose. I am a centre of life force, a shining sun around which others gravitate. I give of myself, freely and generously.

I lead from the heart and have an exuberant, dramatic sensibility. I perform with ease and confidence and enjoy being centre stage in much of what I do. I am strong, vital and fully alive. I have presence and charisma. I shine and enjoy illuminating the way for others.

I claim my right to the throne and hold power easily. I am naturally courageous and willing to stand out in a heroic way. I am playful and enjoy life. I have strong will and determined ambition. I am generative and seek to better any situation I engage in. I am loyal to those who gather around me and seek to reward them appropriately.

Family, friends and colleagues appreciate my willingness to rise above obstacles and remain confident. I enjoy autonomy and take the initiative. I have natural authority and take personal responsibility for my life and work.

I generate compelling visions and serve them with a joyful sense of duty. Those visions often attract others to gather around me. It is easy for me to delegate the details to others. I recognize and have the capacity to bless, often operating as a mentor for others' learning journeys.

Although I enjoy leading from the centre, I am not compulsively drawn to the spotlight. I am aware of the downside of the cult of the hero and look to genuinely empower others to live into their potential.

I live on purpose. I commit to a full and meaningful life. I recognize this is a never-ending journey.

I thrive when my realm is thriving.

Few readers are likely to feel that all of the above is currently active in them. Those who did might not feel the need to read a book about it! A mixture of feeling that some statements are partly true, and others are regularly aspired to, is a good clue that the Sovereign is a key part of your current gift and character. For those thinking that these gifts are too good to be true, you may be right. Nobody has consistent access to all of this throughout a lifetime, but if you relate it more to a specific project or important goal, it may become more realistic. And if you do not recognize yourself in the above, can you think of others in your life that you see accessing these gifts? Most of us will have people we can point to who exhibit a decent amount of the qualities above – although they too may not maintain it consistently (which is where the chapters of the Shadows of Too Much and Too Little will provide more insight).

Last but not least, we offer a poetic invocation to the Sovereign, a piece that looks from the outside at an individual human life and legacy. Have you known people like this? If so, they almost certainly had a strong Sovereign. And like many who naturally shine, sometimes we do not recognize how much they radiate, until they are gone.

Poetic invocation

EULOGY

"How do you want to be remembered..."

J.K. ROWLING

The old church was packed, as if for a wedding –
best business suits and formal dresses;
an air of respect, of gathering the clan.
Looking around, you could see past leaders,
still and thoughtful in pools of remembrance
that drew brave smiles and encouraging looks.
Old friends in the crowd were already weeping
as young Tom Burgess stepped up to speak for her.

"She was our leader, but more than that,
she was our compass, our lodestar and our guide.
She gave this business its raison d'être –
rekindled our hope and lit the way forward.
And me? She taught me to wear the royal face,
to act the part until I grew into it.
'Be who you are' she used to say to me,
smiling – especially on the darker days,
when the markets were scared and the money tight,
when people needed to see that she was there –
calm and confident, enjoying the moment,
bringing us with her to some new beginning.
And yet she didn't want to hog the limelight.
She wanted us all to step into our power.
Her light has gone out, and we will miss her –
but she changed us all and taught us how to shine.
Whatever comes it will be because of her.
She was a giant. She made us who we are."

I swear, if the vicar hadn't started praying,
we'd all have leapt to our feet and cheered.
Outside in the churchyard's autumn sunshine,
as the old guard watched and the hearse drove away,
Wilson, the cynic, who'd spend years fighting her,
turned to me bleakly, with tears in his eyes.
"She lit up our lives. She was like the sun.
We'll never see her like again..."

WILLIAM AYOT

Having read and absorbed this Archetype, we invite you to do an intuitive self-assessment below. You can circle the appropriate letters in the appropriate boxes below or take notes separately as you prefer. This is preparation for the fuller assessment you will be invited to take after the Five Realms chapters.

My Core Archetypal Life Pattern

Now, consider the Sovereign in your personal life and circle A–D accordingly.

A = Leading Actor
Does this Archetype embody your favourite natural gifts? Does it give you a joyful sense of purpose on your best days? Does it feel like a trusted and go-to inner advisor? If so, circle A below.

B = Major Supporting Actor
Is this Archetype a favoured back-up? An easy competency you can draw on at will, even if you don't enjoy it as much as your Leading Actors? If so, circle B below.

C = Minor Supporting Actor
Does this Archetype have qualities and behaviours you can access when you have to? An earned competency that you can step into but you generally choose not to until you need it? If so, circle C below.

D = More Offstage Actor
Is this Archetype less favoured and less used? Do you perhaps feel uncomfortable with it or about it (for any reason)? Do you judge it as being of little or no value? If this is true for you, circle D below.

Sovereign

MY CORE ARCHETYPAL LIFE PATTERN			
A	B	C	D

My Core Archetypal Work Pattern

Now, consider the Sovereign in your work life and circle A–D accordingly.

A = Leading Actor
Does this Archetype represent a key and non-negotiable part of your current work? Do you need to access the gifts of this on most days? If so, circle A.

B = Major Supporting Actor
Does this Archetype represent a needed part of your current work? Do you need to use it regularly, even if not as much as a Leading Actor? If so, circle B.

C = Minor Supporting Actor
Does this Archetype have qualities and behaviours you need to draw on occasionally? A useful support but not currently key? If so, circle C.

D = More Offstage Actor
Is this Archetype rarely if ever used by you at work? Does it feel redundant to your current role or responsibilities? If so, circle D.

Sovereign

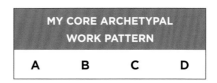

MY CORE ARCHETYPAL WORK PATTERN			
A	B	C	D

This is the first time you are asked to respond intuitively to the Archetypes. We will continue to ask you to respond at the end of each in-depth Archetype immersion.

As you move into the Strategist, notice if this Archetype feels more or less like you than the Sovereign. Do you have a natural or learned preference for one or the other archetypal way of order and ordering?

Gifts of the Strategist

Structure and Mastery

"No wonder so many adults long to return to university, to all those deadlines – ahhh, that structure! Scaffolding to which we may cling!"

MARISHA PESSL

We now progress logically and in an orderly manner into the Strategist. Notice how the energy and the language changes as this new Archetype becomes the focus of our attention and thinking. Consider how the gifts of the Strategist differ from the Sovereign. Please pay careful attention to the different way that this Archetype's gifts are framed and expressed.

We start, as before, with key words that Strategists value and align themselves with. How many of these words do you think of as core parts of your current character? How many would you use to describe yourself?

KEY WORDS

Structured, Rational, Principled, Ethical, Pragmatic, Organized, Controlled, Mature, Contained, Precise, Deliberate, Measured

THE STRATEGIST RESPECTS

Time, Focus, Rules, Mastery, Limits, Discipline, Duty, Hierarchy, Boundaries, Tradition, Wisdom, Objectivity, Goals, Capital, The Establishment, Law and Order, The Truth in Numbers

Notice the different priorities that guide this Archetype. They create different areas of practical importance and focus. How aligned are you with this way of thinking about the world? Very much so, sufficiently, partially or minimally? Each level of access will have a different and ultimately clear impact on how you organize yourself, your life and your work.

The next step in assessment is an Archetype-appropriate introduction for the Strategist: a building manual. Strategists work logically and in a carefully thought through and pre-planned way to achieve measurable results. Lists and numbers are important and preparation vital. *Failing to prepare is preparing to fail!*

Archetype-appropriate introduction

BUILDING MANUAL FOR NEW CONSTRUCTION: FOUNDATION

1. Pre-Construction Assessment
a) Carefully assess the risks and rewards of the project.
b) Spend time to accurately prepare before construction.

c) Start with the bigger eco-system; research the potential dangers of being in a flood plain and/or earthquake zone.

d) Then assess surrounding properties for their architectural features; your new structure is an intrusion into what is already present and will change the landscape. Know what you are entering and what you are building on and adding to.

e) Progress to a detailed site survey, including soil sampling and assessing water drainage.

f) Next walk the site landscape at different hours of the day, mapping the path of the sun to register the hours of light and shade on all sides of the proposed building.

g) Then map a realistic timeline for the construction that takes into account the local climate and likely weather patterns during construction months.

h) Review your budget, add 10% for contingencies – and commit to holding a tight rein on any potential overspend.

2. Construction Preparation and Instructions for Contractors

a) Follow all the building codes in your area.

b) Fence in the building site to prevent theft and/or accidents by unauthorized entry into your jobsite.

c) Ensure you have the right equipment on the site.

d) Keep your work spaces organized, clean from debris and safe, with temporary railings to prevent falling.

e) Anyone entering the jobsite is to wear safety equipment, including a hard hat, eye protection and steel-tipped boots at all times.

3. Commencing Construction

a) Rigorously mark any existing water, electrical, cable, phone or gas lines.

b) Dig a solid foundation beneath the frost line. Avoid the markings in 3a) above.

c) Prepare to keep water from penetrating and weakening your structure.

> **WARNING!**
> *Unless you take the requisite time to follow these steps carefully, whatever you build on top of this foundation will be on shaky ground.*

So, how did you respond to the above? Did you read it slowly while endeavouring to understand each step of the process? Did you check to see if there were any steps missing? Or did you skim it for the main points? Maybe you read it metaphorically as a plan for a sensible life? Or did you find it a bit dull or over-detailed? Each differentiated reaction is a sign of your aptitude for or resonance with the Strategist Archetype itself.

Our next step is into the personal, subjective expression of the Strategist. How they think about themselves from the inside out. Although not many of the following statements may be heard in everyday conversations, they represent the mindset and values that give interior structure to personality and drive behaviours. So please pay attention to which of these you think of as being true for you.

Strategist Gifts – subjective expression

I FRAME – I STRUCTURE – I FOCUS

I am a serious person and I take things seriously. I understand the power of limits and the value of focus. I can therefore discern relevant knowledge in a world filled with too much information.

I improve effectiveness and efficiency. I determine what is essential and eliminate waste. I make things tangible and practical. I take careful note of what is there and then assemble the right pieces in a safe and useful way. Architecture, building, assembly, organizing all connect to my ability to manifest structure.

I say "no" to things that will take me off course. I am single-minded in my focus without being driven. I take measured steps to ensure quality delivery. I prefer quality over quantity. I move forwards in a clear, pre-determined direction and am accountable for pre-agreed outcomes. I am reliable and responsible.

I value trust, honour and integrity. My word is my bond. I keep to deadlines and understand their importance. I know that all things have their time and season. I therefore do not fear endings. I know when to lay things to rest and am willing to sever what is no longer necessary because it has outlived its usefulness. I look for what excess can be removed because it is no longer fit for purpose.

Thresholds are important and not to be rushed. The right journey is always better than the wrong destination. My planned and organized approach lends me natural gravitas. I am often seen as mature and wise for my age. I think things through before acting. I follow tried and tested methods. I prefer the proven to the shortcut, things need to be earned. I do not flap easily and resist making decisions in the heat of the moment.

My wit is dry. I understand the strength that comes from necessary suffering. Steel has to go through fire and tolerate the forging. I respect the elders who have gone before, and teachers who have earned their wisdom.

I maintain ethics in life and business. I look for fair exchange for all involved. I am frugal and sometimes austere. I trust funds and use capital to leverage growth. I do not take unnecessary risks. Boundaries are there for a reason and need to be respected.

There is a lot of information in the above description so you may want to read it again to make sure you have absorbed the weight and detail of it.

You should by now be getting a clear sense of how much this Archetype fits you and where it lives on your inner stage. Leading Actor, a Major or Minor Supporting Actor – or More Offstage?

The final piece now addresses how a natural Strategist in an organization or an institution shows up and is seen. If it is an Archetype that feels further away from you, consider who you know and respect that fits this description.

SATURDAY'S CHILD

Slow and measured, each step deliberate,
he's the one they watch, the grown-up in the room,
the solid rock they need to push back against –
his attentive, pale blue eyes a warning
that they need to be organized, to be ready,
if they are to convince him, to win him over.

Steady Eddie, as safe as houses –
clear in his goals and sure of his tradition –
breathes the numbers and understands capital.
He's a cornerstone of the establishment.
The wannabees laugh at him behind his back
but he's the one that they turn to in a fix.

What he loves is the structure and the rules.
Discipline to him is a kind of comfort;
as a boy he saved his pennies and his sweets
and learned that rewards taste better when delayed.
Now he's a major force to be reckoned with
a builder, a framer, lawmaker, judge.

Watch him at work, see how he operates,
he's not as dull as you may like to think.
Quiet, unassuming and full of integrity,
his practice is the practice of common sense.
He knows you love freedom, respects your ideas
but he is in search of a deeper wisdom –
like Mozart he knows the joy of boundaries
His genius knows the sweetness of limits.

WILLIAM AYOT

So, having read and absorbed this Archetype, we invite you to respond intuitively below. Consider the Strategist both in your personal life and in your work life and then either circle a letter for each or take notes as before. A fuller description of this intuitive assessment appears at the end of the Gifts of the Sovereign section, the first Archetype we explored.

My Core Archetypal Life Pattern

A = Leading Actor (natural favourite)
B = Major Supporting Actor (easy competency)
C = Minor Supporting Actor (earned competency)
D = More Offstage Actor (lesser used)

Stategist

MY CORE ARCHETYPAL LIFE PATTERN			
A	B	C	D

My Core Archetypal Work Pattern

A = Leading Actor (required daily and used most)
B = Major Supporting Actor (often required)
C = Minor Supporting Actor (occasionally required)
D = More Offstage Actor (rarely if ever required)

Strategist

MY CURRENT ARCHETYPAL WORK PATTERN			
A	B	C	D

How prominently does the Strategist appear on your inner stage? Compared to the Sovereign, are these gifts easier or more difficult to claim? Or about the same?

Reflections on the Realm of Order

As we bring our exploration of the Realm of Order to a close, we can recognize some key differences. Where the Sovereign is usually led more by the heart and the soul, motivated by what feels right and purposeful, the Strategist is more often guided by the head and hands, motivated by doing the right things and doing them in the right way. The Sovereign is typically drawn towards the future and what could be, while the Strategist builds on the past. "What have we already learnt that still works well?" The Sovereign, when inspired, may move quickly forwards, confident in their own sense of what should be; the Strategist will think carefully first, weighing the risk and all probable outcomes, before moving slowly and deliberately, wanting proof of concept before a big risk is taken.

Reasonable access to both will be a powerful combination of Ordering principles. You are able to hold a compelling Vison and build a practical Structure to deliver it.

CHAPTER 3

THE REALM OF

Relationship

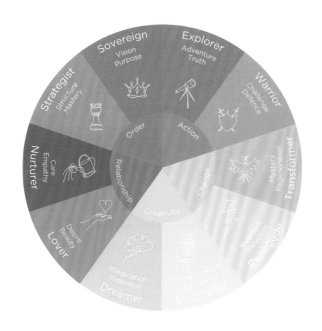

"Let us be grateful to the people who make us happy; they are the charming gardeners who make our souls blossom."

MARCEL PROUST

"The best and most beautiful things in the world cannot be seen or even heard but must be felt with the heart."

HELEN KELLER

"More than half of people who leave their jobs do so because of their relationship with their boss. Smart companies make certain their managers know how to balance being professional with being human. These are the bosses who celebrate an employee's success, empathize with those going through hard times, and challenge people, even when it hurts."

TRAVIS BRADBERRY

"Everyone talks about building a relationship with your customer. I think you build one with your employees first."

ANGELA AHRENDTS

"Every company has two organizational structures: the formal one is written on the charts; the other is the everyday relationship of the men and women in the organization."

HAROLD S. GENEEN

Overview

We continue our exploration with the Relationship Realm and the Archetypes of the Nurturer and the Lover. Both care about how we relate; to ourselves, to each other and to the world around us. Both seek harmony and joy. Both have a natural gift of love and connection but demonstrate this in importantly different ways.

The Nurturer is the classic carer who puts other people and their needs first, always ready to extend a hand and offer support. They sometimes put themselves at the back of the queue when asking for and expecting to receive help themselves. As the Archetype of the "Good Parent", they do not readily expect equal exchange. They value the felt sense that they are here for you. The Nurturer exhibits the kind of loving care we might call "Agape" quite naturally, giving to others and thriving in their growth and development.

The Lover, in relationship with others, shifts between giving themselves, giving *of* themselves and seeking an attractive exchange of give and take. They can appear more self-absorbed, often spending time, energy and money on pleasing themselves. They tend towards partnerships in which both or all parties grow and thrive through increasing knowledge of the other, yearning to experience beauty, pleasure and heart fulfilment. The Lover naturally works with attraction, intimacy and Eros, connecting with others in ways that merge the one into the other, whether in a sexual relationship, a peer group bond or a shared creative endeavour.

We invite you to follow the path into the heart of both and, as much as you can, feel your way into assessing your current access to the Relationship Realm Archetypes.

Gifts of the Nurturer

Care and Empathy

"If I am not good to myself, how can I expect anyone else to be good to me?... I've learned that people will forget what you said, people will forget what you did, but people will never forget how you made them feel."

MAYA ANGELOU

A big warm welcome to the Nurturer. We hope you are sitting somewhere cosy and comfortable with easy access to whatever refreshments will nourish you. If you don't have these available and can find them easily enough, please do take a moment to set yourself up for a comfortable read. (And please do notice if there is a voice in your head telling you *not* to do any of this...)

Now, as you begin to assess your relationship with the Nurturer, which of the following words feel like you on a good day, or even on just a typical day?

KEY WORDS

Supportive, Caring, Reassuring, Protective, Responsive, Instinctive, Parental, Trusting, Nourishing, Sensitive, Empathetic, Receptive, Cosy

THE NURTURER VALUES

Relationships, Potential, Growth, Feedback, Togetherness, Time to Reflect, 'Keeping the Hearth', Legacy, Conservation, Emotional Intelligence, Natural Cycles, Tending Gardens, Feeling at Home, Full-Body Listening

Most of us will feel at home with some of these. Far fewer of us with all of them. They can sometimes feel "counterintuitive" in the working world with its usual high levels of stress and competitiveness. Of course, if we choose to activate this Archetype more fully, the Nurturer can help us respond differently to these pressures.

The Nurturer will naturally have a core place in the raising of healthy children, whether by biological parent/s or other primary care-givers. At work this Archetype often gets typecast as being only of use in Human Resource and Coaching roles but it can and does offer value in any and every role we choose in work and life. We believe it will become increasingly important as humanity acknowledges the cost of the ever-increasing separation from family, friends and nature many of us experience in modern life.

The next piece, written about Nurturing, and in the manner of a Nurturer, is cast as a supportive review of a self-help book. As you read it, please notice if you would be drawn to read such a book (if it existed!) or whether you would decide that it was not really "your thing".

POSITIVE MUSE MAGAZINE

Human potential book of the month review:

"Relational Being – The Invisible Power of The Reassuring Heart"
by Rebecca Amity and Paul Deare

Aimed at a wide audience of parents, teachers, community leaders, healthcare professionals and managers, this book contains the authors' framework for incubating positive human development. They treat the reader throughout as a close friend. They encourage us to reflect on how raising an emotionally stable child, creating conditions in which people thrive, and building an emotionally intelligent workplace, can all be seen to follow a few easy-to-remember guiding principles.

Part 1: Incubation, lays the foundation for mutual trust by paying close attention to "The Nest and the Safety Net". What is the most supportive environment that can be created for growth – and what safety nets can prevent early failures from damaging self-confidence?

In Part 2: Experimentation, we are introduced to their core practices, "The Hand to Guide, The Heart to Care". They use examples from family life, award-winning healthcare initiatives and leading HR practices from the 10 Best Companies to Work For. The principle of the Hand can correct and create appropriate boundaries as well as feed and give gentle direction. The Heart, when opened and appropriately shared, will encourage others to do the same. This builds a coherent field of emotional intelligence in which the many can thrive, mutually supporting each other in ways that encourage collaboration and innovation.

In Part 3: Generation, we are shown the most effective ways to reach a state of "Hands Off, Heart On!" – in which power and autonomy are gradually and willingly handed over to those who are ready. This offers a hand and a heartfelt conversation only when requested. For those not ready to "fly the nest" (what many would call "under-performers"), there are remedial practices that allow for slower but steady progress. Patience allows latent skill and promise to find their own way. Individuals in difficulty are supported to try alternative paths, depending on their individual needs.

A wise tale in the Preface that "No one on their death bed has yet raised their head one last time to say, 'I wish I'd got better grades' or 'I wish I'd increased shareholder value more!'" really hit home for me. Highly recommended for those who recognize that a happy life and fulfilling work is all about people – but don't yet know how to make it so.

Did this review make sense? Did you buy into the premise and follow the stages with interest, or did you lose patience, perhaps thinking that this kind of slow, caring approach is all very well for young children but not for a workforce?

We now move into the subjective Nurturer expression where this Archetype's deepest qualities and feelings about people and life are given a first-person voice. So, with a mind and heart as open as possible, just notice as you read on which phrases feel true for you and which are not active in you at this point in life or work.

Gifts of the Nurturer – subjective expression

I AM HERE FOR YOU – YOU MATTER

I am a consummate care-giver. I embody the value and importance of relationship. I release potential empowered by connection. I naturally balance needs across all areas of life. I bring a family and community feeling to everything.

It pleases me to help others. I find joy in seeing others thrive and grow. I am sensitive to others and anticipate when and how to show up. My generous spirit has no strings attached. I know that the more we give without anticipation of return, the more we will receive, often in mysterious ways.

I care about others and stay in touch, even over distance. My interactions are a genuine exchange of positive energy. I express my feelings easily and encourage others to do the same. I respond rather than react. I take time to slow down and reflect. I notice how things feel on a deep level. I am willing to be open and make myself vulnerable.

I protect and nourish the weak and the neglected; in the house, my community and the world. I am a friendly guardian of space and place, hearth and home. I engage in contemplation and meditation practices. I make sure I have the time and energy to help myself thrive, as well as others.

Nurturers are the keepers of the stories and wisdom from the past. We consciously honour our ancestors and the indigenous world. We keep alive the traditions of our families as well as the tribes and cultures in which we live and work. We cherish happy memories, keepsakes and photographs. We reminisce with colleagues and friends and can enjoy nostalgia.

We have a healthy relationship with food. We enjoy finding the right ingredients, cooking slowly and then feeding others at a big table. We tend our gardens, metaphorically and literally.

We understand how to manage loss in a heartfelt way. We can hold sadness and grief without falling apart and remember the good times in the bad. Ours is a mature feeling world and yet we love giggling with young children. We naturally engage in wise and humorous conversations at every stage of growth. We have deep respect for our parents and grandparents, taking time to look after them as they age.

At work, we champion great day care and flexible hours and contracts. We will actively support the development of co-workers and are not jealous if they are promoted above us. We have the ability to tune into the collective emotional field of a family, a community or an organization. When combined with artistic expression, we can also feel and respond to the shifting moods of the larger culture.

We feel into the potential consequences of actions and ask, "Is this good for me, good for us, good for our planet?"

As you finish this, how much would you say you are aware of doing on a good day? A lot, some or not much? Your responses will determine the likelihood of the Nurturer being either a Leading Actor, a Major Supporting Actor, a Minor Supporting Actor or currently More Offstage.

We complete our immersion into the territory with a poem about a Nurturer at work. Notice who this reminds you of in your workplace, current or past. Was a character like this likely to be a best friend, a valued colleague or an occasional collaborator? Or more like a tolerated necessity, useful to keep others' heads up when things were tough, but of little value to you personally?

Poetic invocation

UNCONDITIONAL

*Like a warm and comforting, fleecy blanket
she holds you in the calm of her attention,
head to one side, doe-eyed and sensitive,
responding to your every shift of feeling –
instinctively breathing in perfect synch
while gently mirroring each mood and gesture.*

(Continues)

(Continued)

This is not a ploy – it's her way of being –
her effortless way of meeting the world.
Hers is the heart that beats for everyone,
the caring core of the organization.
Feedback could have been invented for her,
she thrives on the gifts of growth and belonging.

Her people are her tribe, her source of pride;
her family, her garden, her hearth and home.
She speaks for the earth, for care as necessity,
and like a she-bear, she protects her cubs.

WILLIAM AYOT

So, having read and absorbed this Archetype, we invite you to respond intuitively below. Consider the Nurturer both in your personal life and in your work life and then either circle a letter for each or take notes as before. A fuller description of this intuitive assessment appears at the end of the Gifts of the Sovereign section.

My Core Archetypal Life Pattern

A = Leading Actor (natural favourite)
B = Major Supporting Actor (easy competency)
C = Minor Supporting Actor (earned competency)
D = More Offstage Actor (lesser used)

Nurturer

MY CORE ARCHETYPAL LIFE PATTERN			
A	B	C	D

My Core Archetypal Work Pattern

A = Leading Actor (required daily and used most)
B = Major Supporting Actor (often required)
C = Minor Supporting Actor (occasionally required)
D = More Offstage Actor (rarely if ever required)

Nurturer

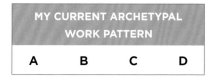

MY CURRENT ARCHETYPAL WORK PATTERN			
A	B	C	D

We hope that you now have a felt sense of the Nurturer and how it plays in you. As we move into the territory of the Lover, notice if this feels more or less like you – or about the same. Do you have a natural or innate preference for one of these two ways of relating?

Gifts of the Lover

Desire and Beauty

"It is an absolute human certainty that no one can know his own beauty or perceive a sense of his own worth until it has been reflected back to him in the mirror of another loving, caring human being."

JOHN JOSEPH POWELL

You are cordially invited to join us as we segue, as elegantly as we can, into the sensual embrace of the Lover. As you start to read this, just raise your eyes from the page and look at your current environment. Is it attractive? Does it appeal to your aesthetic sense of beauty, your sense of style? Are there beautiful things around that can be seen, or even better, touched and felt? Is it a space that you want to spend time in, beyond its practical uses? Or is it purely functional – suited to action but not so much to interaction and attraction? And as you consider this, is this kind of awareness one you often hold as you survey a new scene – or do these questions seem odd or even irrelevant?

Now, see if you can notice what happens inside you as you read the initial lists of words below. Do you respond with a strong "Yes"? Or more of a "Sometimes", "Not really" or "No"?

KEY WORDS

Alluring, Sensual, Sociable, Desirable, Charming, Passionate, Seductive, Creates Longing, Acts as a Muse, Accumulates Self-Worth and Net-Worth

THE LOVER ADORES

Design, Style, Luxury, Money, Pleasure, Relationships, Beauty, Fine Art, Fashion, Decorations, Harmony, Song, Fantasy, Enchantment

Many people in Western cultures value the Lover for playing but not for working. In the world of work the Lover is often underplayed and even repressed – until it spills out at drunken office parties, often in inappropriate ways that cause trouble or regret. But when we banish the Lover because we associate this Archetype principally with sexuality, we also banish design and beauty, style and elegance, harmony and pleasure from our working lives. We then substantially diminish our capacity to do what we love and love what we do: the essential foundation for a purposeful working life.

The Lover awakens longing in us, a deep desire for what brings us satisfaction and pleasure. This includes the yearning to make others feel good as we adjust our relational capacities to suit the moment for maximum harmony. The Lover brings us exquisite intercommunication, what is sometimes called "social intercourse".

Collectively, at this point in human history, much of the Western world struggles to appreciate the deeper gifts of the Lover. This Archetype has

43

in countless ways been hijacked by a consumer culture that surrounds us incessantly. The advertising industry knows how effectively "sex sells" and how attractive, dressed-up images compel our attention more than ordinary ones. As a result, most of us in the developed world have grown up with a Lover used and abused as a constant sales tool, insisting that the right clothes, make-up, hair or car will magically make us happy and deliver a perfect soulmate. Many people fall for this easy but limited definition of the Lover – and can end up "borrowing money we don't have, to buy things we don't need, to impress neighbours we don't even like".

So, we now invite you to slip below the surface of our current primary cultural identity of Consumer. Enter the deeper waters of beauty and enchantment that this eternal field of possibility offers and that we respond to with heart and soul.

Our next step is an Archetype-appropriate introduction that explores some of the intimate connections the Lover can inspire. These include our relationship with nature's beauty, the sensual experience of being alive, music, self-image, intimate partnerships, the love of children, the exchange of gifts and goods, as well as inner felt harmony. The natural form for the Lover is poetry. As the Persian poet Rumi wrote in the 13th century, "In your light I learn how to love. In your beauty, how to make poems."

Notice if you can enjoy the emergent journey of this next poem, written by Richard as a homage to the Lover after a long slow evening walk in Spain. Can you relate to it? Can you see and enjoy the images as they arise?

Archetype-appropriate introduction

SEEING WITH OTHER EYES

A sunset walk along an Andalusian beach
Calls me to be – and to see with Venusian eyes.
I slow my mental pace, and my breathing,
Focus as my feet tread soft warm sand.
My body feels the caress of the heat

Which emanates from the sinking western sun.
I sensually open to my surroundings…

The beach-bar band is warming up,
jazzy scales tumbling through the waiting crowd.
"Cuando comienzan?" I quiz a passing barhop,
"When do they start?" He smiles at the question.
"They're musicians, they'll start when they are ready!"

I pass three youths, sitting by a cloth on the path,
Laid out with decorated shells and stones.
"Quieres uno?" the most confident one asks.
I choose and buy three that catch my eye.
We laugh at the exchange and I move on.

A young man embroidered with tattoos,
In calmly elegant, coolly worn clothes,
saunters gracefully, scanning the passers-by;
Open to some energy, something or someone
Worthy of attracting his bright-eyed attention.

At the shore a mother applauds her son
as he skims across the water on a skiffle board:
"Anda, guapo" she admiringly calls to him
cheering him on, as if he was a matador
Dancing with a sacred sea-crested bull.

A father stands with his teenage daughter,
Considering the luminescent beauty of her body.
His smile is a portrait of pride and sadness.
He knows that her heart will embrace another,
Move beyond family, some bitter-sweet day soon.

Another teenager charms her crush on her phone.
Dressed to entice, in a mauve and orange fantasy.
Her flirtatious laughter tinkles high and light,
Though she nervously bites her little-fingernail,
Still not sure of the catch she's yet to land.

I reach the small river that winds past the town
Before emptying itself into the sea beyond.
A beloved song, "The Ocean Refuses No River",
swirls around my mind as I enter the water
My paddling feet come alive to eddying rhythms.

I feel the flow of the sea pressing inwards,
the less urgent flow of the river the other way.
As they meet and mingle and merge together.
The small, warm inland soul surrenders gladly
To the vast ocean spirit where everything began.

Now, as the sun reaches down to the horizon,
I immerse myself, reverently, and float at ease,
Sensing the making of life through light and water,
I feel myself merging with all that is possible...
The ocean swallows the great golden orb.

I return to land and towel, enjoy the gentle friction
Of cotton on my skin, the scratch of still-warm sand.
I say farewell with a steady sun salute,
Paying homage to the unfolding apricot sky,
Then I head for home, my hands filled with treasures.

Did you enjoy the journey, see the images or imagine faces as they appeared, or did it put you off? Perhaps more to the point, is this the kind of musing journey that you would, or do, enjoy? Do you allow yourself to simply be open to what life offers as you move through it? To be regularly in such a space is difficult for most of us in our busy world. Do you make time for it occasionally, regularly, or rarely, if ever? The alternative is often one where we focus on the destination and miss the journey – where we think about where we are going rather than enjoying where we are, right here, right now. The Lover connects us to the simple presence and curious wonder that most of us had as children but often lose as the world of intentions, ambitions, outcomes and targets takes over.

We now move into a broader view of the gifts of the Lover Archetype, written in the first person. Many of us will inevitably have moments when we embrace some of the alluring possibilities described below. But are these qualities and preferences core to who we are, or more like borrowed clothes, just stepped into when it serves us, or for special occasions? The Lover seeks the special in every day.

Lover Gifts - subjective expression

I RELISH THE BEAUTY OF THE WORLD.
I DELIGHT IN OTHERS

I love life in its magnificent variety of riches and fullness. I long for beauty. I am naturally appreciative of harmonic depths as well as sensuous pleasure. I seek union, merging and one-ness. I yearn to be fully immersed in someone or something.

I am drawn to decorate and beautify; myself, those I love and the spaces I live and love in. I adore good music and fine art. I have a heightened sense of design aesthetics. I enjoy the effort it takes to look good and feel good. Dressing well exhibits my self-worth and demonstrates to others that I care. I can discern what is of the merely "trendy" fashionable moment from what has lasting worth and value. If something does not look good, taste good or sound good, I will not want it. I notice and appreciate others trying new styles, flavours and looks.

I desire the finer things in life, luxuries both big and small. I have a taste for delicious drinks, sweets and gourmet foods. Food for me is an art form, presented beautifully in perfectly proportioned quantities.

I have a sense of soulful connection to many I meet. I can be a Muse for others, inspiring them to be creative, make more of themselves, or simply dress up for a fun night out. I am happy exchanging "sweet talk" and compliments. I am willing to be vulnerable; to fall for someone new, or a beautiful vista, or a stylish product.

I know how to attract what I want and enjoy the art of seduction. I have a broad and engaged social network, many close friends and an ability to create almost instant intimacy. I share my secrets and enjoy hearing those of others. I fully support everyone's right to find love where they choose.

I am always ready to engage passionately with what attracts me. I love money and know how to accumulate net-worth. I enjoy the ease and freedom it can bring. I have a natural sales personality, willing to sell and be sold to. I enjoy exchange and barter to create relationship and meaningful, memorable contact with others.

I seek artful work and a career I love. At work I can "weave spells", creating images and communications that catch the eye and the attention of those we want to attract. I can summon the power of Eros and use it for creative inquiry, discovery and expression. I can lose myself in these heightened moments of energizing a desired future, when it feels as if a team in creative flow has become "one" in its co-creative capacity.

I am committed to living a passionate life.

The Lover works in many different ways in life and work. Few readers will feel that all the above fits, but hopefully you are getting a clearer sense of what parts of this Archetype you embrace and which others you tend to neglect or even reject.

We complete our immersion into the Lover with a poem that speaks of how this Archetype feels from the inside out, when it is working with us or working on us. Enjoy the words and the feelings they evoke and notice how often you might be aware of these or similar sensations in your daily life.

LOVE SONG

I am the song that settles in your head,
the canny hook line that plays incessantly.
I carry the sounds of the famished heart
and a deep, sweet keening from the well of need.
I can feed you, heal you, make you irresistible –
bring you spells of glamour and enchantment.

You'll love me, enjoy me, need me and want me;
I'll make you more charming, cooler and sexier.
Through me the looking-glass smiles its respect.
I add to the richness and quality of life.

Together we can reach for a better future,
the longed-for delights of a golden time –
a world transformed by line and proportion,
by texture and style, by the play of light –
by the beauty to be found in relationship.

I can bring you the pleasures of naming –
the brands and the logos, the secret signs
of those in the know, of the cognoscenti.
And I can fill the halls of desire –
bring fashion and taste, and wealth and reward,
the comforts of elegance and design.

More – I bring you the eternal distance,
the desert mirage that beguiles the soul –
that deeper, mystical, impossible longing
for the perfect, the ideal, and the unreachable.
The sadness that opens up after loving –
the yearning that tells you who you really are.

Not the arrival but the beckoning,
Not the safe harbour but the distant sail;
Never the answer but the unceasing question,
Not the achievement but the thirst for the Grail.

WILLIAM AYOT

49

So, having read and absorbed this Archetype, we invite you to respond intuitively below. Consider the Lover both in your personal life and in your work life and then either circle a letter for each or take notes as before. A fuller description of this intuitive assessment appears at the end of the Gifts of the Sovereign section.

My Core Archetypal Life Pattern

A = Leading Actor (natural favourite)
B = Major Supporting Actor (easy competency)
C = Minor Supporting Actor (earned competency)
D = More Offstage Actor (lesser used)

Lover

MY CORE ARCHETYPAL LIFE PATTERN			
A	B	C	D

My Core Archetypal Work Pattern

A = Leading Actor (required daily and used most)
B = Major Supporting Actor (often required)
C = Minor Supporting Actor (occasionally required)
D = More Offstage Actor (rarely if ever required)

Lover

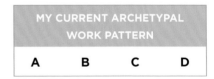

MY CURRENT ARCHETYPAL WORK PATTERN			
A	B	C	D

Reflections on the Realm of Relationship

Both Archetypes of Relationship work from and with the heart. The Nurturer is often more developmental ("What can I do for you?") where the Lover is more consensual ("What can we do together?"). The Nurturer tends to prefer a slow, patient and predictable pace that allows others to find their own way – except in a crisis or emergency, when they will find whatever speed or strength it takes to protect those in their care. The Lover tends to live spontaneously and can move incredibly fast to follow an emergent impulse or a current desire – though time will slow down for them when they give themselves to a particular moment, happening or person. They may also lose patience with those who do not meet their needs and be ready to move quickly on to new shores, new people, new social circles or new work they find a passion for.

So, which of these do you feel more connected to at this point?

CHAPTER 4

THE REALM OF

Creativity

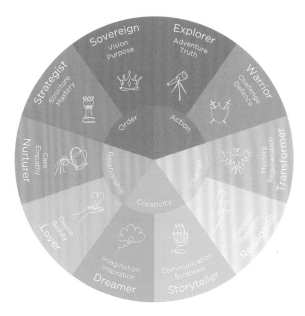

"Creativity is intelligence having fun."

ALBERT EINSTEIN

"If people are not within your midst who dream about tomorrow - with the capacity to bring tomorrow into the present - then the country might as well just recede back into the cave because that's where we're headed."

NEIL DEGRASSE TYSON

"Access to talented and creative people is to modern business what access to coal and iron ore was to steel-making."

RICHARD FLORIDA

"The things we fear most in organizations - fluctuations, disturbances, imbalances - are the primary sources of creativity."

MARGARET J. WHEATLEY

"Our dreams are first-hand creations, rather than residues of waking life. We have the capacity for infinite creativity; at least while dreaming, we partake of the power of the Spirit, the infinite Godhead that creates the cosmos."

JACKIE GLEASON

"The paradox of innovation is this: CEOs often complain about lack of innovation, while workers often say leaders are hostile to new ideas."

PATRICK DIXON

"Science requires speculation, creativity, and wild ideas."

DEBRA FISCHER

We now enter the Realm of Creativity, where the future first appears. Both the Dreamer and the Storyteller allow vital new possibilities to emerge into the world. Both are invested in moving beyond limits, beyond the confines of an "old story" of how something is, or should be, or how it should be done. Both are capable of changing lives and perspectives with their gifts – but they go about this is in importantly different ways.

The Dreamer is open to endless possibilities. They tune into emerging intimations of the new and the as-yet undiscovered. Their unique gift is a capacity to leave the material world of the known, tried and trusted behind them and journey into the ephemeral world of images and inspirations of everything that could be. They see the beginning of the future and intuit what is coming towards us. They can sit with the unknown with a patient curiosity through hazy beginnings until the images become clear enough. Then they find their own way of expressing these for the benefit of others and the sake of the emerging future itself. They may move slowly and follow several inspirations before they find the one that was calling to them.

The Storyteller creates a path into the future through coherence and narrative-structuring. They are looking for what connects the dots, what synthesis of emerging new ideas will best serve their current purpose. They may take a selection of apparently different and sometimes even contrasting new ideas and weave them cleverly together, until a new and coherent narrative emerges. They work towards sense-making and translation, able to take seemingly complex ideas and find simple enough ways to express them. They can then use intelligent wording and compelling images so that others will notice and pay attention to the desired future they are calling in. Their quick-thinking capacity creates sparky energy that draws others around, like children gathered and listening with bright eyes to a thrilling story.

The future does not emerge without the Dreamer, but it does not find form and traction without the Storyteller.

Gifts of the Dreamer
Imagination and Inspiration

"Creative people do not see things for what they are; they see them for what they can be."

JULIE ISRAEL

When was the last time you dreamed something big or seemingly impossible?

Do you seek out or enable creative environments for yourself and others around you? Or does it strike you as illogical that the "right space" could help you imagine the "right solution" to a pressing problem?

We start our in-depth inquiry into your relationship with the Dreamer with words most naturally associated with the essence of this Archetype, so please notice which of the following might feel true for you, on a good day.

KEY WORDS

Imaginative, Poetic, Sensitive, Idealistic, Compassionate,
Spiritual, Visual, Boundless, Imaginal, Believing

THE DREAMER IS INSPIRED BY

Fantasy, Symbols, Infinity, Mythology, Non-Dualism, Dreams,
Intangibles, Metaphors, Mysticism, Visions, Ecstasy, the
Transcendent, the Invisible, Art, Music, Archetypes, Lateral
Thinking, "Negative Capability", Emergence, Holding Paradox,
Possibilities, Altered States

The Dreamer has a myriad of avenues towards that mysterious place where the future begins, and only the most deeply invested Dreamers will use all of these listed. Most of us with ready access to the Dreamer will find our preferred access points and use these fairly consistently.

The Dreamer has a curiously mixed reputation in our times. On the one hand, we applaud and praise those who come up with imaginative solutions to complex problems. On the other hand, we often dismiss this capacity as unrealistic fantasy and day-dreaming. In addition, we now often delegate imaginative capacity to others, rather than claim it as our innate birth right. Just think of the evolution of children's games over the last 50 years. We regularly outsource entertainment to ever fancier technological creations, and very few of us sit around, daring to be bored, until our own inspiration gives us an interesting activity to pursue.

This Archetype tends to be under-rewarded by much of the current formal education system and by many parents who intend "sensible careers" for the young. They don't realize that in times that will require ever more imaginative solutions and evolutionary leaps, dreaming may be one of the most essential, valuable and important capacities we will need ahead.

When we do give ourselves permission to enter a different state of mind (at least in the developed Western world) it is often outside of our working environment. Dreamer access can be relegated to weekends and holidays, where it becomes a form of escapism and is often fuelled by substances, most typically alcohol or recreational drugs. In the counter-culture there is a huge increase in the demand for non-denominational spiritual practices and ceremonial medicines, often imported from cultures where the Dreamer is more validated as part of everyday life and work.

The next piece introduces you to this Archetype in an appropriate manner, crafted here as a screenplay for a short film about imagination arriving from the invisible worlds around or within us. The endless possibilities of film and its use of light, shade and image are natural resources for those interested in making imagination visible and fantasy real.

Archetype-appropriate introduction

SCREENPLAY FOR A SHORT FILM

FRAGMENTS OF THE DREAM
(working title)

BLACK SCREEN:
(O.S., Offscreen) A low tone is heard as if a long way off, then getting closer, being joined now by another note in harmony, then another, we imagine an unspoken Mermaid lullaby...

FADE IN:
Gentle pulses of dark grey across the screen, hard to see at first but then becoming more visible.

CROSS FADE:
EXT, Exterior Scene: THE OCEAN DEPTHS
We gradually become aware of our surroundings, as the grey cross fades to dark blue.

Sounds of the ocean depths merge with the lullaby...

A flash of light catches our attention, but before we can focus on it, it disappears.

CROSS FADE:
EXT: LONDON CIRCA 1600 AD
We emerge into grey skies above Elizabethan London. Occasional, intriguing glimpses of the old city below us. We are "a creative spirit" hovering in the air, seeking a host to inspire.

CROSS FADE:
EXT: THE OCEAN DEPTHS
Back to the ocean depths. Another flash and this time we see a hint of silvery flesh, swishing towards us and then swiftly away.

CROSS FADE:
EXT: LONDON – looking down from the clouds but lower now and just able to make out the rounded shape of the GLOBE THEATRE, as we float gently down towards it...

CROSS FADE:
EXT: THE OCEAN DEPTHS
Another flash and this time we see a hint of silvery words, glistening in the water – in Elizabethan script – some are clear and some are unclear:

A...IMA....INATION...

Interior Scene: WILLIAM SHAKEPSPEARE'S STUDY CIRCA 1600 AD

The sea is still there but we are now inside William's head.

(O.S.) Muffled – The Voice of Shakespeare's Muse (our off-screen Mermaid)
MUSE

...odies ...orth.. orms... ings... unown...

JUMP CUT:
Inside Shakespeare's head as his eyes open and we (and he) slowly focus on the white page swimming towards us from the wooden desk.

SHAKESPEARE'S P.O.V. – the quill on his desk, glowing luminous as his hand moves slowly towards it. He picks it up and begins to write...

(O.S.) The Muse speaks again, more clearly now but with an edge of the oceanic depth's soundscape still around. As we hear her, we watch William write:

MUSE (speaks softly)

And as imagination bodies forth
The forms of things unknown... the poet's pen
Turns them to shapes... and gives to airy nothing
A local habitation and a name...

CROSS FADE: The camera swims around William as the creative spirit envelops him.

CROSS FADE, CLOSE UP: Shakespeare's hand crosses out his working title:

The Adventures of Puck

and writes underneath:

A Midsummer Night's Dream

CROSS FADE: Back to the ocean depths.

SLOW FADE to BLACK as the sound slowly fades along with the light, until we are back in the darkness and the silence from which we began...

THE END

How was that for you? Did you follow the sequence of images? Did you allow yourself to see, and maybe even enjoy, the images described? Or was it an effort – did you lose patience with it?

We move now into the subjective expression of this Archetype. As we have already noted, there are many ways into the Dreamer and so what follows is necessarily more meandering than some of the more clearly definable Archetypes. Again, please notice which elements of the following piece you connect to or can claim as a natural capacity in your life at present. Which might you have connected to at an earlier time of life but are disconnected from now? And which, for whatever reason, have you never felt connected to?

Gifts of the Dreamer - subjective expression

IMAGINE WHAT IS POSSIBLE!

I am open to the as-yet unknown. I am visual and intuitive. My world is awash with images and I go with their flow. I wonder how things could be different. I allow emerging images to float around until they slowly form into pictures and patterns.

I trust in the unseen and the invisible. I have access to what poet John Keats called "negative capability", when one is capable of being in "mysteries, uncertainties and doubts, without any irritable reaching after fact and reason". I can explore future possibilities without getting dragged back by the needs of the present.
I can imagine the new story while living in the old. I tune into the zeitgeist, the spirit that is seeking to emerge in our time, and dwell there.

I am naturally sensitive to people, places and things. I know intuitively rather than logically what works for me and what does not. I am compassionate and often sense what others are feeling before they tell me. I am idealistic and trust in the good and the better. I live imaginatively, feeling my way into what to do next rather than planning it. I accept that others with a more logical, goal-orientated approach will find this disconcerting.

I like to operate poetically and artfully. I respond to an "as if" world and believe that you cannot become anything that you cannot first imagine. I know this as the true magic of creativity. I trust in the underground currents of life that subtly shape the surface. And I cannot explain what is happening while the sands are shifting, until they have settled again.

I enjoy metaphors and thinking about images that can describe aspects of life. I view the world symbolically, noticing what is happening as if it were not an accident but part of a mysterious unfolding story, as in a dream. I naturally develop an archetypal eye, able to see energetic patterns underneath the superficial reality of how things appear to be.

I am drawn to the mysterious and the mystical. My motivation is a yearning to tap into source, to be inspired, a word whose root, "inspirare", connects to the ancient idea of "being breathed into by the divine". I give my faith to where my beliefs take me, whether that be new or old ideas, things, institutions or people. And these beliefs will shift, eddy and change as I mature and flow through life. There is a part of me that wants to transcend, to move beyond the mundane things of life, and that can feel weighted down by gravity and the material world.

I give myself permission to go beyond boundaries and "through the veils". I engage with other realties and other worlds, whether spontaneously arriving in front of me or deliberately induced. I like to be inspired in many different ways. I may try a number of different techniques, including mind-altering pathways; drawing from meditation, breathing, dancing, creative, spiritual and shamanic practices, all the way through to indigenous hallucinatory medicines. These are ways to access the dreams that are seeking to emerge and not an end in themselves.

I have an inner sense of the oneness of all things, that ultimately there is no duality. This view is familiar to many NDE (near-death experience) survivors and to those sensitive to other worlds and planes of reality, like psychics, mediums and channels. I

also recognize this view in Carl Jung's notion of the Collective Unconscious, in Lynne McTaggart's description of "The Field" and in Rupert Sheldrake's discovery of "Morphic Resonance".
I know I am never truly alone. I am always part of and connected to a greater whole.

The Dreamer is always open and rarely closes down options, which is why there are so many possibilities in the above. How many of these have been active in your life to date? Please notice which ones you have an inner reaction or aversion to. Do you know why some (or most) of these may feel far away from who you are and what you do? Were there any decisions or circumstances in your life that either connected you deeply to this Archetype or led to it being avoided or maybe even dismissed?

As we share the final invocation, a beautiful poetic expression of the Dreamer at work in dawn's early light, just be aware of how and when you allow this energy into yourself. The Dreamer as a potential does not exist solely to be the starting point of a great idea. It does not always seek or need a point or a purpose to show up. It may arise just because... to live is to dream...

Poetic invocation

REVERIE Nº 365

"Imagination is more important than knowledge..."
ALBERT EINSTEIN

You wake at first light,
Sensing the stranger
Who stands in silence
At the foot of your bed.
You rise and follow him
Out onto the terrace.

(Continues)

(Continued)

It is dark and the chill
Of the night is upon you
But you know somehow
That all will be well.
The hillside falls away
And the lights below
Call from the darkness
To the morning star.
Everything is waiting:
The hidden world,
Its infinite possibilities,
Compassions and cares,
Signs and revelations;
Its endless imaginings
All become one. For
This is where he lives,
The stranger within you,
In the rose-pink,
Birdsong-haunted space
That opens between dawn
And the departing night.
The valley and the trees
And the rolling hills
Appear through a mist
As the new day unfolds.
You turn to speak
But there's nothing to say.
You are bathed in morning
And the stranger is gone.

WILLIAM AYOT

So, having read and absorbed this Archetype, we invite you to respond intuitively below. Consider the Dreamer both in your personal life and in your work life and then either circle a letter for each or take notes as before. A fuller description of this intuitive assessment appears at the end of the Gifts of the Sovereign section.

My Core Archetypal Life Pattern

A = Leading Actor (natural favourite)
B = Major Supporting Actor (easy competency)
C = Minor Supporting Actor (earned competency)
D = More Offstage Actor (lesser used)

Dreamer

MY CORE ARCHETYPAL LIFE PATTERN			
A	B	C	D

My Core Archetypal Work Pattern

A = Leading Actor (required daily and used most)
B = Major Supporting Actor (often required)
C = Minor Supporting Actor (occasionally required)
D = More Offstage Actor (rarely if ever required)

Dreamer

MY CURRENT ARCHETYPAL WORK PATTERN			
A	B	C	D

As we segue into the Storyteller be aware of which of these two may feel closer to your core, or are they equally present or absent at this point?

Gifts of the Storyteller
Communication and Synthesis

"As the world we live in is so unpredictable, the ability to learn and to adapt to change is imperative, alongside creativity, problem-solving, and communication skills."

ALAIN DEHAZE

Have we got a great Archetype to share with you now! Are you paying attention?

You may not believe all that you are about to read, only because if it sounds too good to be true – it could be just that, truly good!

We humans are the ultimate storytelling animal, from those first early cave paintings at Lascaux and other sites, we left our mark on the world through pictures that tell a story. Then as we invented language, we learned to encapsulate sequences of events into narrative structure and began to share these as both bonding tales and early learning tools. Once the magic of written text was developed, stories could be shared far beyond the mouths that first spoke them. Legends and myths were born that passed down the generations as a gift from the past to the future.

We can make a story out of anything and everything – a day, a month, a year, a decade and a life; an animal, a person, a couple, a family, a community, a tribe, a nation and a species. We can live by stories, and as the history of religious wars tells all too clearly, we can die by them as well. Story is ubiquitous, it is everywhere in history and it is what will lead us into our future.

See which of the following words you think of as core to who you are and how you express yourself in the world...

KEY WORDS

Communicator, Translator, Mediator, Synthesizer, Advertiser,

Conceptual, Critical, Versatile, Adaptable, Agile, Trickster,

Mercurial, Quick-Thinking

THE STORYTELLER CONNECTS WITH

Ideas, Metaphors, Information, Multiple Perspectives, Puzzles,

Juggling, Multi-Tasking, Wit, Details, Logic, Intelligence, Making

Connections, Creating Narratives, Clever Articulation

The connectivity of the Storyteller is essential to effective communication and meaning-making, two deeply human gifts. The ability to assimilate different threads of ideas and images and weave them together to make a coherent whole is an art as well as a craft. As the world around us fills with information and often opposing sets of "alternative facts", mindful discrimination becomes ever more important. In a time of information overload, knowing what to listen to and how to communicate its essence becomes a crucial task for all those who want to make a difference.

Our next level of study is an introduction in the style and manner of the Storyteller. This involves a TV newsroom, flashing headlines and roving reporters. Could you work in and enjoy such an environment? Or would you be more likely to find it too scattered or distracting?

Archetype-appropriate introduction

INSIDE STUDIO 3 AT CHANNEL 5 TELEVISION STUDIO IN LOS ANGELES

BREAKING NEWS!

A RAPID SEQUENCE OF NEWSPAPER HEADLINES SPIN INTO SHOT:

THE DAILY MESSENGER: *"WHEN IS A STORY NOT A STORY?"*
THE HERALD: *"HOW TO LIVE IN A POST-TRUTH WORLD"*
THE TELEGRAPH: *"IT'S ALL IN THE STORY"*
THE POST: *"TRUTH IS NOT TRUTH!"*

ANCHOR - EVE:

Story is back in fashion folks, so light the campfire and gather around!

Today we bring you a report from the frontline of narrative research. Over to Jennifer in London:

JENNIFER: (IN FRONT OF LONDON CITY SKYLINE)

From kindergarten to the boardroom – and some say there is no telling which is which sometimes! – the value and necessity for storytelling is in the throes of a big revival. Over to Storyteller and founder of the Centre for Narrative Leadership, Geoff Mead, running a group in Wiltshire...

GEOFF MEAD: (SITTING BY A CAMPFIRE IN FRONT OF A GROUP OF DRESSED DOWN EXECUTIVES)

Human beings are natural storytellers. We grew up listening to stories and we tell stories to our children – so why when we go to work do we suddenly stop being a Storyteller and become a Number Cruncher? Human beings live by stories – and that means that any shift is incredibly difficult to contemplate, unless we can find a new narrative to support it. Did you know that there is a tribe in South America whose word for "human" when literally translated reads "Featherless Storytelling Creature"?

ANCHOR – EVE:

And now to John in Mercury, Nevada...

JOHN: (AT A SUBURBAN GRADE SCHOOL)

I am speaking with Natalie, a seven-year-old first-grader – can you tell me about your favourite teachers, Natalie?

NATALIE: (AGED 7)

I love the teachers best who tell good stories – they make me want to listen and learn.

ANCHOR – EVE:

And finally, founder of Storyworks.com and internet philosopher, Abdul Genus:

ABDUL (IN A ROOM SURROUNDED BY SCREENS WITH DIFFERENT IMAGES):

Stories help us make sense in an increasingly confusing world.

A key reason for the remembering of narrative in our times is the slow dissolution of the old story that we have been living with since the Industrial Revolution. And that kind of stuff is freaky scary to most people – unless or until we create a new narrative that gives it a context. Remember Holocaust survivor Viktor Frankl's paraphrase of Nietzsche: "Humans can take almost any 'what', as long as we know the 'why'...?" A compelling story gives you the "why"!

CUT TO ADVERTISING BREAK...

Did you feel in tune with the style, the content and the pace of this – or did it feel too much, too soon? Were you ready for the next slice of the story or was there too much information to take in, too many different contexts to integrate into a digestible piece for you? Again, no right or wrong reactions to this, just a gentle test of a natural Storyteller's capacity for quick thinking and synthesis.

Either way we will move swiftly into the subjective expression of this Archetype's gifts. Keep noticing what you relate to, which of the following genuinely live in you, which you can lean into occasionally, and which are remote and distant.

Storyteller Gifts – subjective expression

I CONNECT, I SYNTHESIZE, I COMMUNICATE

I have an innate ability to find and make connections; between things, people and especially ideas. I naturally tell good stories but insist that these are supported with relevant information. Facts are important and details matter. I am well referenced, well read and draw from a wide range of sources and resources.

I enjoy communicating in a number of diverse ways. I reach the minds and touch the hearts of my chosen audience to leave a memorable impression. I enjoy wit and word play. I know how to adjust my style to reach whoever I am talking to. I am clever, often using word play and metaphors. I paint pictures with words. I apply image, analogy and similes subtly yet surely to enhance memorable impact. I relish answering tricky or difficult questions. I know the impact of words and that what we say really matters. I appreciate the value of the "bon mot". I remember clever phrases that catch the essence of an idea; witness Victor Hugo's insight:

"Nothing is more powerful than an idea whose time has come."

I am a critical thinker and will challenge others' ideas to better understand them. I avoid repeating un-reflected opinions. I discern between tight and flabby ideas. I do not mind if others see me as sceptical. It helps me think sharply and see through attempts at deception. I have a well-developed "bullshit detector" and can tell when others are "blagging".

I am agile and versatile. I have excellent analytical skills: I can take things and ideas apart in a logical way. I do not get overwhelmed by the increasing complexity of modern life. I monitor the constant flow of information intelligently and stay on top of it. I look for the jewels in the mud and can easily sift these when I find them. I can study several subjects simultaneously and juggle multiple pieces of information, until I see their useful connections. I can then create a new synthesized and coherent idea, often greater than the sum of its parts.

In life, too, I can multi-task, adapting quickly from one job or interest to another without losing stride. I am naturally good with logical games and puzzles. I can easily learn different languages. I am good at "sleight of hand", prestidigitation, "léger de main". Metaphorically and perhaps literally, I make a good close-up magician.

My thinking is so naturally quick that I often have to consciously slow down to allow others to catch up. People find what I talk about compelling which makes me good at advertising and being a "way-shower" for others. I know how to frame a concept or a product so that it has appeal.

I can talk my way out of bad situations, de-escalate conflict and talk others down off the ledge. I am an effective mediator. I am curious and interested in finding other ways of looking at any issue. I listen to different points of view and can help others understand how to bridge the gaps between them. Greater understanding leads to mutual benefit. As I give to others as their go-between, I receive the gift of greater understanding myself.

As a natural messenger, I can deliver difficult messages without causing offence. I find the right way to speak of that which others dare not. I can name the unnamed without becoming confrontational. I can speak truth to power.
I can story the future.

Storytelling being such a rich part of ancient life, and communication being such an obvious necessity in modern life, all of us will do some of these. But, do a majority of these attributes feel close to you and easy to access on a day when you are feeling powerful, on fire and in some kind of flow? Or is it more of an effort to get this skillset going – but easy enough when you put your mind to it? Or would you rather delegate it to others; the communications department at work or the chatty ones at home, in family and friendship circles?

We bring this to an end with a poem about an individual storyteller. Notice if, in your circles, this would be you or one of your good friends – and if not, would you appreciate and value a person like this, or would you more likely think of them as a bit of an annoying show off?

Poetic invocation

TRISMEGISTUS

He's the one who'll make them understand,
take an idea and, like a radio,
plant a seed in their imaginations.
He was born to tell stories, to spread the word,
to persuade and compel, to amuse and teach.
His bright-eyed, fast-talking wit and humour
brings them along, then gives them the facts.

You can feel the synapses tingle when he talks,
see the way they respond to his speed and crackle;
watch the spark of his thinking set them alight –
a maven creating a forest fire.
Yet it's not about him. He's not showing off.
He loves to conflate and to synthesize,
to take new thoughts and rub them against things;
to bring high-flown conceptions together,
then get down and dirty with the detail.
He's a puzzler, a joker, a juggler, a fool,
and yet he's Coyote, the trickster personified.
This is his genius, his gift to the world –
agile messenger, the eternal adept.
Don't try and hold his magic in the bottle.
Just take out the stopper and let him fly.

WILLIAM AYOT

So, having read and absorbed this Archetype, we invite you to respond intuitively below. Consider the Storyteller both in your personal life and in your work life and then either circle a letter for each or take notes as before. A fuller description of this intuitive assessment appears at the end of the Gifts of the Sovereign section.

My Core Archetypal Life Pattern

A = Leading Actor (natural favourite)
B = Major Supporting Actor (easy competency)
C = Minor Supporting Actor (earned competency)
D = More Offstage Actor (lesser used)

Storyteller

MY CORE ARCHETYPAL LIFE PATTERN			
A	B	C	D

My Core Archetypal Work Pattern

A = Leading Actor   (required daily and used most)
B = Major Supporting Actor (often required)
C = Minor Supporting Actor (occasionally required)
D = More Offstage Actor   (rarely if ever required)

Storyteller

MY CURRENT ARCHETYPAL WORK PATTERN			
A	B	C	D

Reflections on the Realm of Creativity

The Dreamer tends to start slow, often in silence and empty space, waiting for inspiration to strike. The Storyteller sprints from a standing start, thinking, talking and filling the space with ideas and concepts until the spark is lit. The Dreamer has the first images of the future, but the Storyteller delivers the compelling message about what it is and how to get there. The Dreamer is abstract, and at early stages of the creative process sometimes incomprehensible, trusting in the mystery of imagination. The Storyteller is conceptual and coherent, almost always laying a trail of thoughts that others follow to a logical conclusion. The Dreamer is open to universal possibilities and may follow one thread of these until they feel its essential nature, which may remain inside themselves or private, for a while or forever. The Storyteller will weave together a rich mix of old and new ideas to form a new pattern and express this intelligently, so others appreciate and see it too. The Dreamer works from Soul or Spirit, focusing on image, the Storyteller more from Mind, translating thoughts into words and language. Together they create the future.

CHAPTER 5

THE REALM OF

Change

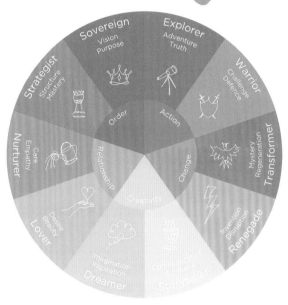

"Never doubt that a small group of thoughtful, committed, citizens can change the world. Indeed, it is the only thing that ever has."

MARGARET MEAD

"Those who are crazy enough to think they can change the world usually do."

STEVE JOBS

"You never change things by fighting the existing reality. To change something, build a new model that makes the existing model obsolete."

BUCKMINSTER FULLER

"If you think you're too small to make a difference, try going to bed with a mosquito."

ANITA RODDICK

"The changes we dread most may contain our salvation."

BARBARA KINGSOLVER

"Leadership is about creating change you believe in."

SETH GODIN

"The past can teach us, nurture us, but it cannot sustain us. The essence of life is change, and we must move ever forward or the soul will wither and die."

SUSANNA KEARSLEY

Change happens, that's clear, whether we plan for it, intend it, or not. Both Archetypes in the Realm of Change, the Renegade and the Transformer, will help us deliver change; whether in ourselves, families, local communities, at work or in the larger global systems in which we interact and connect. Both are motivated to see and live beyond the status quo, not to settle but to see what else could be and what else might work better. Both tend to see the world as a work in progress, as a never-ending process of the new becoming old, the fresh becoming stale and therefore requiring rethinking, retooling, renovating and rejuvenating. In contrast to the Realm of Order, these Archetypes are comfortable with not knowing the new until near the end of the transition. If the Realm of Creativity allows us to see the future as possibility, the Realm of Change enables us to "Act-It-In" and live it in reality.

The Renegade does this in an instinctive, almost rebellious way, as if thumbing their nose (or lifting a middle finger) to what existed previously. They can move like a lightning bolt, often taking others by surprise, shaking up the old with a radical new approach, design or system. Think of all the disruptive technologies that did not exist 10 or 20 years ago – and the entire "status quo" industries that have either been made redundant or had to frantically scramble to keep up with fast-paced, agile Renegade entrepreneurs. Renegades tend to be early adopters of any new system and technology that can accelerate the shift into a new way of thinking, being or living.

The Transformer works more slowly, taking time to notice first what is wrong with the current systems. Where the Renegade might start with prototype solutions, the Transformer is more likely to start with penetrating questions. What's wrong? What is the present system missing? What has been neglected, forgotten, excluded or denied that may need to be remembered? What is stuck, ailing or wounded by the current way of doing things? Transformers will seek a deep inquiry into the symptoms before they diagnose the cause, let alone prescribe the cure. The Transformer is a guide for a rite of passage into a rebirth, patiently attending the mini deaths and births along the deep journey of Transformation.

Gifts of the Renegade
Invention and Disruption

"*I alone cannot change the world, but I can cast a stone across the waters to create many ripples.*"

MOTHER TERESA

Let's not beat about the bush here. When was the last time you deliberately disrupted yourself, did something radically different from your norms, or broke a rule you had followed for years? If you have to dig deep into the memory banks, you are not a natural Renegade.

But for those who might need a little more information to make up their minds, here is that now (all too predictable) list of...

KEY WORDS

Intuitive Disruptor, Eccentric Inventor, Liberator, Rebel,

Provocateur, Maverick, Unique, Has Epiphanies, "Eureka!"

THE RENEGADE THRIVES ON

The Zeitgeist, Freedom, The Future, Disruptive Technologies,

Revolution, Uniqueness, Structural Collapse, Surprise,

Revelation, Flashes of Insight, Emerging Ideas, Brilliance

Yeah, probably *not* you, right? There are not many around who have fully outed themselves as Renegades, and those that have are often off the grid, going it alone or in networks connected to radical causes and ideas. Many with a youthful capacity for this have learned to tone it down or suppress it in order to fit in with the crowd and/or to hold down a paid job in a big organization – unless the boss is a Renegade too.

We tried to come up with a set piece that would give you an Archetype-appropriate introduction to the energy, but, frankly, anything too set is not the point, so here's what emerged from our research attempts...

TRANSCRIPT OF RECORDED ZOOM CALL,
22 SEPTEMBER 2019

OK. We're recording... What should we call this one? * **"Ideas for Renegade Intro" – maybe subtitled: **"Star Date 22/09/19"**. * Nah, Trekkies are hardly cutting edge **and** you can't put that weird Brit date on it, the Yanks won't get it * Isn't this one about breaking rules? * Yes, but in a unique way, don't be so obvious. * Fine... what about a rap song * Hardly on the zeitgeist, too consciously cool and too much money in it now, no? * But you might create a new style, "Crap Rap"! * I think that's been done. * What other scenes or genres would be in character? * How about a guy who's lived in his garage for 250 days, playing with advanced technology, tuning into sounds from outer space and then realizes Aliens are communicating with him? * Hmmm, interesting – the natural Renegades would get it, but you might lose everyone else... * Then just be wacky, use a dada poem or a fridge magnet idea. I'll google one. Everyone's walked past a fridge and moved magnets around,*

*trust me, they'll get it... Here we go: "investigate the cat wandering between song and moon". It's a haiku * Yes, but to express the Renegade gift doesn't it need to make sense but in a different way? * You can do that later in the chapter * So what's the essence we need to get to? * Breaking tradition – not just being a rule-breaker but doing it in a rule-breaking way, not talking about it, doing it – "backwards writing, example for" – you could do that * I don't know... * Wait, I found a "Fridge Magnet Generator", I'll try one now and send it, then you write "Spotted on a friend's refrigerator" and no one will ever know * Sure Laurence * I've emailed it * PAUSE * Got it... Oh shit, I deleted it by mistake! * Better work on your tech skills Richard! I'll resend it * Don't, I've just had an idea... * What? * Just send me the recording...*

So, that's us bending the norm and breaking the rules (a little bit); how do you do it – if you do?

The subjective expression lays out some more of the territory and covers different Renegade angles. Even fully signed up Renegades are unlikely to do all of this, because if they did, they would be just like all the other Renegades – and that would never do!

"And now for something completely different..."
MONTY PYTHON

I thrive on radical change. I don't let the norms limit my ability to stretch and break boundaries and traditions. I often feel as though I am looking at things from above, emotionally detached but intuitively engaged by what's possible. I love "changing things up" in a rapid turnaround.

I see how things really are long before others catch on or catch up. This can feel lonely but usually I feel lucky that I can see through the bullshit that others choose to believe in. I cannot and will not blindly follow where things are supposed to go. I speak up forcefully about alternatives and other ways to move forward.

I can be a conscious rebel and start trends and movements that others get attracted to later on. I am spontaneously intuitive and can tune into the collective unconscious easily. Insights then appear on my radar screen like lightning bolts and instant hits – a rapid succession – flashes of insight – electric! Making connections, networking, idea-sharing, idea "hacks" – Open Source Everything!

And stuff comes through me, I have little or no ego attachment or need to claim ideas. I know they aren't "mine". It's about sourcing the next thing and creating a radically different future, rather than about money or possessions.

Zero pre-judgement, no labels, skin colour, faith etc – none of that matters. I see others as human beings first, part of a species. Endlessly curious. Aware that we are all grains of sand on the beach and each unique too. I am interested in both how we connect and synergize and how we are uniquely different and individualistic.

I recognize that humanity needs some rules to maintain basic order, but I don't internalize these. I believe in the power of the collective and that all of us are smarter than any one of us: Collective Wisdom. We are only just beginning to tap into the potential of the world mind and I want to liberate and accelerate anything that can help – especially advanced technological innovation. I can see the possibilities of the enhanced human and embrace the intelligent application of artificial intelligence.

I find different ways of connecting and tuning into others, both peer-to-peer and to my "tribe" – those who share the radical thinking required to break out of fixed and outdated paradigms. I love global networks of the forward-thinking and will organize around common interests much more than neighbourhood proximity. I can be happy alone in my "electric incubator garage" or in a leading-edge multinational – size does not matter – only scope.

I break through the old to accelerate the emergence of the future. I break the old rules for the right reasons.

See why it's often impossible for natural Renegades to thrive in traditional organizational structures? And, to some extent, in traditional family or community structures too? When we map leaders, teams and departments around all 10 Archetypes – with the exception of hi-tech naturally disruptive technology companies and activist campaigner groups – the Renegade is almost always the least represented. (The Lover is the next currently "least owned" Archetype in leaders.) But when we hear what leaders and HR departments are wanting, the expressed need is often exactly for radical thinking and quick pivots to meet the complex reality that for many is the new normal.

Often Renegades will be hired to solve a pressing problem, but they rarely stay for long. There is an inherent difficulty in creating a work environment that welcomes the Renegade and is not too counter-cultural for others. The attempt often creates resistance and resentment – and many Renegades we know have been ejected from the system they were brought in to turn around. Many others have self-ejected, having felt either undervalued, lonely or oppressed, especially by traditional working cultures. Of course, one way through this "implant rejection" is for others to learn to embrace this energy more in their own lives and working practices (which we will get to in Part Two, Archetypal Development – Expanding Your Repertoire).

For now, we invite you to notice which, if any, of the traits, interests and natural passions above feel close enough for you to step into them occasionally, even if not regularly.

The final piece offers a poetic description of what happens when you have a Renegade at work. Notice how you respond to people like this in your environment. Are you curious about what they bring? Do you welcome their different point of view? Or do you resent the way they have to question and change everything?

"TROUBLE AT MILL"

Instagram grabbed her early on –
before that, Kindle and a bundle of apps.
She adored the way they flipped things over,
put bright and shiny spanners in the works;
forced the old suppliers, the creaking giants,
to face new landscapes, and realities.

There's a thing in the way an edifice gives,
a while before the monolith collapses –
before the crack, the crumble, and the fall,
the rubble and wreck of worn-out systems.
It's the subtlest of ripples, a trembling
of the web, a loosening in the Zeitgeist
that sets up a tingle of insight in her.
Between this moment and any outcome
opens a broad space, filled with provocations,
a birthplace of quick and fruitful disruptions,
of lightning bolts and Eureka moments...
This is the space from which she operates.
You'd think she was a nerd but it's a choice,
like her delight in springing gentle surprises.
And the way she dresses – another challenge,
oranges and purples, scarves and jumpers;
charming you, like a bomb in a teddy bear.
Then there's her smile of gleeful revelation –
In a child, you'd say it was mischievous –
her air of knowing, of holding all the cards,
which she lays down with a conjurer's flourish.

This is the way she will find your future –
though the Old Guard will be uncomfortable,
call her a rebel, and "trouble at mill".
But she is happy to let them grumble,
accuse her of arrogance and even worse,
because in the end this great disruptor
is the woman who will make them all free.

WILLIAM AYOT

So, having read and absorbed this Archetype, we invite you to respond intuitively below. Consider the Renegade both in your personal life and in your work life and then either circle a letter for each or take notes as before. A fuller description of this intuitive assessment appears at the end of the Gifts of the Sovereign section.

My Core Archetypal Life Pattern

A = Leading Actor   (natural favourite)
B = Major Supporting Actor (easy competency)
C = Minor Supporting Actor (earned competency)
D = More Offstage Actor   (lesser used)

Renegade

MY CORE ARCHETYPAL LIFE PATTERN			
A	B	C	D

My Core Archetypal Work Pattern

A = Leading Actor   (required daily and used most)
B = Major Supporting Actor (often required)
C = Minor Supporting Actor (occasionally required)
D = More Offstage Actor   (rarely if ever required)

Renegade

MY CURRENT ARCHETYPAL WORK PATTERN			
A	B	C	D

So that's it for now, folks. How close is this Archetype to you, at this point in your life? As we move on notice which, if either, of the Archetypes of Change you feel more naturally comfortable with.

Gifts of the Transformer
Mystery and Regeneration

*"I want to beg you as much as I can to be patient
Toward all that's unsolved in your heart,
And to learn to love the questions themselves,
Like locked rooms,
Or like books that are written in a foreign tongue."*

RAINER MARIA RILKE

WARNING!
If you take this Archetype seriously, it will change your life.

Transformer energy creates the space where the magic of healing happens, and often involves, metaphorically or literally, the mysteries of birth, death and rebirth. This is serious business and requires a serious investment of time and psychic, emotional energy – which is also why it is often avoided in modern culture, until or unless a personal or professional crisis forces a turn "into the dark". Why go through a difficult "initiation" if we can simply turn on the latest super-hero movie and feel better – for a while?

It is the Archetype of depth and contains a power that is usually shocking to those who meet it unprepared. For those who embrace it, it becomes a lifelong friend and close confidant, one you naturally turn to in the times of greatest need.

KEY WORDS

Magician, Healer, Regenerator, Change Agent, Deep, Powerful,

Psychological, Magnetic, Intense, Inexorable

THE TRANSFORMER HONOURS

Renovation, Roots, Research, Transitions, Upheaval, Total

Change, Power, Deconstruction, Transformation, Secrets,

Death and Rebirth, Breaking Down to Break Through, The

Underworld, Mystery, Hidden Gold

So how did you respond to these words? Which feel close and which furthest away from how you see yourself?

The next piece, the Archetype-appropriate introduction, is cast in terms of a psychological report. The Transformer requires a degree of vulnerability and exposure when what is hidden is brought to the surface. This is not, of course, always made public and the raised awareness within the individual, the team or the system facing the challenges may be as far as the information goes. Most initiations remain private or shared with a close circle, but in the interest of our inquiry here, we chose to write up parts of Richard's own "live case study" as an objective expression of his experience of the Transformer. As you may notice, this impulse also contains a search for meaning within experience and embodied learning.

Archetype-appropriate introduction

CONFIDENTIAL
PSYCHOLOGICAL REPORT

The subject, R, was born in Brighton, England, into a famous acting family with two successful actor parents. His primary care-taker for the first five years was a strict German nanny who became the person he trusted most. When she left, he was not given the chance to say goodbye. His early sense of rejection was reinforced.

He later started acting out his resentment and anger on the paid care-takers who were around and, as a result, was sent to a strict school that used the cane to enforce good behaviour. At age 10 he was sent to a more liberal-thinking boarding school. He still felt rejected by his parents. He developed a nice and funny persona in public but would withdraw to play invented games in private. He hid his true and deeper self but attracted the malicious attention of older boys. He endured psychological bullying between the ages of 10 and 13.

His only subjects of note were English and Drama. At his father's express wish, he applied for Oxford University but failed to get in and was later accepted into the UCLA Theatre Arts Department. This felt failure turned into a blessing in disguise. The distance from home freed him from the previous persona, while the freedom of the Californian culture allowed him space to explore other realms. This included wilderness walks, spiritual teachings, and the exploration of altered states.

He received a first glimpse of his future calling while studying Theatre History. The origins of theatre were not just entertainment and cultural mirroring. The first actors were priests and shamans who enacted numinous stories to give their community identity and meaning. This began a quest for R into the sacred purpose of theatrical practice and how it can help others.

Before leaving America, R met and married a woman who had done 10 years of transformational development work. She became his partner and "Medicine Woman", guiding him towards initiation. Returning to the UK, they had a child, and soon after his own father died. Within a month of the funeral he heard American Poet Robert Bly talking about initiation. Bly said, "Nowadays it is almost impossible for a man to be initiated until the day his father dies".

R followed this call into the emerging men's movement in the UK, formed a small men's support group and then entered Jungian analysis. Meanwhile, he pursued his first career intention: to be a successful theatre director. He was initially looking for a "quick fix" that could help him heal his past and get back into "real life". He discovered that healing work was in fact the life that he was looking for – and it gradually become a new career path.

He became more interested in the educational properties of theatre and less in public performance. He transitioned from theatre director to a personal and professional development practitioner and consultant, using powerful theatrical techniques. For the next 15 years, R explored the uses of theatre as an embodied educational tool, rites of passage in various cultures, Systemic Constellations, Group Process and other theatrical tools for development.

At mid-life, aged 50, R took a six-month sabbatical which kick-started a five-year review of his life and work. This included two profound Vision Quests, based upon First Nation American wisdom traditions. He saw that his public performance as a speaker was still an homage to his father's career as an actor. He decided to slow down and wait for insights.

Gradually, his occasional work with Laurence Hillman, based on the planetary Archetypes, called him to explore them further, and R re-entered Jungian dream analysis to process what was rising from his inner depths. This combination of deep archetypal reflection and creative inquiry over the last four years has created a series of events and possibilities that R finds especially intriguing and inspiring (including the book for which this report is written).

At present, he is feeling both freer of initial parental patterning and more grateful for all his formative experiences, which have equipped him to do the work he now believes he was born to do.

END OF REPORT

Maybe not so *confidential* anymore now... but we trust you to keep it to yourself! Please notice your reaction to the piece. Were you interested in the Transformer-inspired stages of the journey into meaning and purpose? Does this kind of thinking and approach feel familiar? Was your reaction something along the lines of, "Of course, after tough times you go to therapy"? Did it leave you curious about what is unexplored in your own past? Do you have any inner judgements about the process involved? Was there perhaps a sense of, "It's all right for him, but I would never do that"? Or perhaps more simply, "What's the point!"?

Your reactions are part of your meta-archetypal patterning – and there is no right or wrong reaction, only what feels true. Notice if your sense of aptitude for the Transformer is reinforced, increases or decreases as you read and contemplate the next piece.

Transformer Gifts – subjective expression

I DELVE INTO THE DEPTHS – I BRING BACK A GIFT

I believe in profound healing. I research and work with the cycles of life, death and rebirth. I seek to understand the mysteries along the way. When involved in change, I look to the past first and notice what needs to die. I help organize ritual events in which the past can be, symbolically or literally, buried. I know that this is necessary to clear space for future birth and rebirth.

I search and research the subjects that call me, willing to dig deep into their roots. I patiently investigate the deeper truth that emerges with the determined pursuit of a cause or subject.

I look beneath to understand the deeper workings of a person, a thing or a system. I will not be taken in by surface appearance. I am aware of the shadow behaviours that can invisibly run people and systems. I work to bring these to awareness and enable appropriate remedy.

I am fascinated with many kinds of power, including personal, collective and sexual power. I study how it can be used, manipulated and/or transformed. I have the ability to sense when power and authority are being abused. I stand against inappropriate behaviour. I am not afraid to name "the elephant in the room" that others avoid. I hold my own power.

I understand how to let things go. I will not hang on to the "status quo" because it feels more comfortable. I am a powerful agent for change, and I do not suffer fools gladly. I point out when others jump to simplistic conclusions and fail to consider the actual depth of the problem.

I embrace apparent failures as important lessons and signposts on the road. I know that without the willingness to fail there is no true risk and therefore no true success.

I see change as a fundamental part of life's unfolding. I honour transitions. I make the unconscious conscious through the process of deconstruction and reconstruction. I accompany others on their passage to the Underworld, whether in long life transitions, in therapy, in rites of passage, or in shamanic journeys.

I hold that pain and grief are not symptoms to be swiftly cured but rather a deep experience to be honoured. I know that sometimes a "little bit of poison" is the antidote. I recognize that sometimes the only way to "break through" may be to first "break down", and I hold others through this.

I am grounded, connected to the earth and the soil. I feel the importance of healthy roots. I have an intuitive knowledge of the riches within and below. I know that all life begins in darkness – whether in the womb or the earth. I am equally aware of the power of death and know it as an essential part of life.

I offer true regeneration.

So, how was that? Obvious, sensible enough, a little scary – or downright terrifying? In all ancient cultures that we know about, there were people delegated into Transformer-type roles. These people were hugely valued. It was their job to help keep the culture healthy and to restore equilibrium and harmony when things got out of balance. Today, in a "quick fix" world of instant gratification, many of us lack the patience to give the Transformer the energy and time it needs. It usually feels easier not to open that can of worms – but sometimes the worms are the only thing that can regenerate our soil for future productivity.

Might there be something in your life or work right now that really needs to be looked at? Perhaps something to be transitioned away from and that may even need to "die" and be buried? If there is and you recognize that you are resisting this, is there someone you know and trust who could give you some Transformer advice about your situation? Our closing poem might give you a clue about what to look for in a potential Transformer ally.

Poetic invocation

THE MEDICINE MAN

Out there – in a grey room down a corridor,
hidden as much by choice as necessity –
he's awaited the call since he saw the need.
Not exactly shunned but never welcomed,
he's the silent one you may have avoided;
instinctively treated with utmost respect
but left there – out there – because you knew.

At the meeting he's the last one to speak,
his slow words dropping like autumn leaves
as he itemises causes, and prescribes
the total medicine of his changes –
changes that begin with naming what must die.
And this is how he goes to work – slowly,
relentlessly, digging through the layers,
getting at the source, exposing the root
of all that's wrong, to find the hidden gold. (Continues)

(Continued)

Unafraid of tears on the fearful journey
to the Underworld where things are reborn,
he knows the way. He's been there before.
Having met his demons and his twilit ghosts,
he returns to recast and re-forge the broken;
strong arms working like an ancient smith
to beat out the new on the anvil of the old.

It's been like that since the dawn of time –
the noiade, sangoma, wise-woman, shaman,
waiting patiently at the edge of the village;
warlock, healer, midwife of the mysteries,
despised by those who failed us in the past
but turned to in need, gingerly embraced
and finally recognised at their departure –
though somehow lost in all the excitement
that surrounds the squalling infant of the new.
So, when you meet the mysterious stranger
on the awayday, or maybe in the mirror,
don't be afraid to look him in the eye –
just ask the question that's been eating you.

(Noiade = Sami shaman
Sangoma = Zulu healer)

WILLIAM AYOT

So, having read and absorbed this Archetype, we invite you to respond intuitively below. Consider the Transformer both in your personal life and in your work life and then either circle a letter for each or take notes as before. A fuller description of this intuitive assessment appears at the end of the Gifts of the Sovereign section.

My Core Archetypal Life Pattern

A = Leading Actor   (natural favourite)
B = Major Supporting Actor   (easy competency)
C = Minor Supporting Actor   (earned competency)
D = More Offstage Actor   (lesser used)

Transformer

MY CORE ARCHETYPAL LIFE PATTERN			
A	B	C	D

My Core Archetypal Work Pattern

A = Leading Actor   (required daily and used most)
B = Major Supporting Actor   (often required)
C = Minor Supporting Actor   (occasionally required)
D = More Offstage Actor   (rarely if ever required)

Transformer

MY CURRENT ARCHETYPAL WORK PATTERN			
A	B	C	D

Reflections on the Realm of Change

Both the Archetypes of change can be of immense use for any kind of transition but recognizing which you need more is important. The Renegade is intuitive instinct and hands-on capacity to make things happen quickly – a sharp mind that often looks for what is different and what could be different. The Transformer connects to other worlds and other levels of reality – reading the signs in nature, dreams, life and work – getting a felt sense of what is wanting to be born and what needs to die. The Renegade is likely to be an initiator of process with an entrepreneurial spirt that is visible and willing to lead from the front. The Transformer will be more likely to walk alongside or even behind the change, working as a guide and a holder of the process. They may prefer to remain out of the limelight and be an advisor to those more obviously on the frontline of change.

Which of them are you closer to, if either?

CHAPTER 6

THE REALM OF
Action

"Let your performance do the thinking."

CHARLOTTE BRONTË

"You miss 100% of the shots you don't take."

WAYNE GRETZKY

"There is only one proof of ability – action."

MARIE VON EBNER-ESCHENBACH

"Often we are caught in a mental trap of seeing enormously successful people and thinking they are where they are because they have some special gift.
  Yet a closer look shows that the greatest gift that extraordinarily successful people have over the average person is their ability to get themselves to take action."

ANTHONY ROBBINS

"An organization's ability to learn, and translate that learning into action rapidly, is the ultimate competitive advantage."

JACK WELCH

"It's easy to feel helpless – like you can't fight the tide. But remember: small actions can have a huge impact, and one person like you can inspire others to action."

CELESTE NG

"You don't have to be great to start, but you have to start to be great."

JOE SABAH

Overview

Finally, into Action! Welcome to the realm where Actions really do speak louder than words – even if we have to write about it and you have to read about it first!

Both Archetypes of Action move out into the world with courage and determination. The Warrior does this with a fierce will to be first, to be best, to win. Warriors thrive on competition and hone skills to maximize impact and achieve measurable success. The Explorer looks for the new and the undiscovered country; they want to get to the bottom of things (in their quest for Truth) and also to the top of things (in their trek up a mountain). Yes, they do want a lot, and they often get it too. They prize what is new and true over what is first and best. The Warrior will work on the practical where the Explorer ponders the philosophical, the Warrior looks at the finishing line, while the Explorer seeks the next horizon. Generally, the Warrior prefers using known successful strategies to meet new impressive goals, whereas the Explorer prefers to lean into the unknown, letting go the ways of the old territory to meet the new with fresh eyes. Which one might be your favourite mode of Action?

Gifts of the Warrior

Challenge and Defence

"A life of reaction is a life of slavery, intellectually and spiritually. One must fight for a life of action, not reaction."

RITA MAE BROWN

Warriors don't waste words. We aim to keep this Short, Sharp and Sweet.

KEY WORDS

Champion, Spearhead, Amazon, Defender, Trouble-Shooter, Brave, Fierce, Passionate, Forceful, Decisive, Fearless, Surgical, Leads from the Front

WARRIOR'S DRIVE

Competition, Challenge, Action, Direction, Tactics, Risk-Taking, Seed-Planting, Making Things Happen, Adrenaline, Competitive Advantage

Does this sound like you on a good day? If so, you will probably recognize much of the following from your life and working practices, including regularly updated – and regularly completed – "To-Do" lists.

Archetype-appropriate introduction

THE 9-STEP PEAK PERFORMANCE WORKOUT PLAN
(For individuals and teams)

1. **Determine your target**
   Choose a goal that will stretch you but that is achievable. Don't be soft on yourself. Do not let fear of failure stop you from going for something big.

2. **Assess your skills**
   Be honest. What have you got? What do you need? Measure the gap accurately. Decide on equipment and training needs to effectively bridge that gap.

3. **Get, check and test the right equipment**
   Get the best you can afford. Get advice from those who have achieved similar targets before you. Test it, multiple times.

4. **Train to become future-fit**
   Take it seriously. Remember, prepare well, or risk failing. Measure improvement regularly. Do not stop when you hit a plateau. Keep motivated and you will keep moving.

5. **Develop discipline to break bad habits**

   Do not slip back into old negative patterns. Keep a grip on yourself. Focus on the end goal. Find a coach if you need one. Who do you need to be to hit that target? Become it!

6. **Take the first step**

   Go for a quick win. Pick "low-hanging fruit" to build motivation. Log the success.

7. **Keep going when it gets tough**

   Build momentum. Record regular updates on progress. When progress slows down, recheck the strategy. Are there alternatives? Scan possible shortcuts that could accelerate results. Otherwise, be patient but determined. Let no one think you will ever give up. Persevere. Grit your teeth and buckle down. You will never regret the efforts you make, only those you fail to make.

8. **Achieve the target**

   Make sure there is a victory at the end of the line, even if the target has shifted from the original goal. Calibrate your learnings. Celebrate the win (but not for too long).

9. **Repeat from Step 1** – with a new target.

Notice your response to this Action Plan. Do you recognize this approach to goals and targets? Taking it as a metaphor for getting stuff done, does it feel normal and self-evident? Do you respond to all of it positively or only parts? Or does it feel a bit much, maybe too set for you, too fixed in its intentions? At this point, where would you imagine the Warrior in your overall archetypal pattern; nearer the top, middle or bottom of your favourites list?

   The Warrior is an Archetype that often polarizes people into attraction or aversion. So, we want to give some brief context before we move on. We are living at a time where the Warrior Archetype is being questioned and re-visioned perhaps more dramatically than at any other time in recorded history. Mankind's *Terrible Love of War* (as James Hillman's

2004 book title sums it up) has reaped an unimaginable toll on countless innocent victims as well as on millions of those complicit in its execution. At the time of writing there are approximately 50 wars and unresolved violent conflicts occurring around the world. Meanwhile, some of the most notable skills associated with martial characteristics throughout history, such as "being a predator", "penetration" and "seed-sowing", once absolutely essential to the survival of early humans, are being seriously and rightfully questioned.

After so much systematic use, over-use and abuse of these energies (particularly the overwhelming abuse by men in positions of power) it can be tempting to think that the core drivers of the Warrior have long outlived their usefulness. However, it is important to realize that the essence of an Archetype does not go away, even if a growing majority recognize and shun its worst excesses. But it can be re-purposed and reimagined to meet an emerging need in a new time.

When a student stands in front of a tank in Tiananmen Square and puts a flower in the gun, when the #MeToo movement rises to defend rights and reveal abuse, or when *Rainbow Warrior* Greenpeace activists abseil into a large corporation's shareholder meeting to challenge unacceptable behaviour, these can be seen as newly emerging and appropriate expressions of the Warrior. They are subtly evolving those same traditional Warrior skills by "turning the predator into the prey", "penetrating" public opinion and outdated mindsets, and "sowing seeds" for a more sustainable future.

So, for those readers who may have good reason to distrust Warrior energy, we invite you to give it another chance as you read on. Could there be something lurking in this universal energy pattern which you have not yet appreciated, which might actually help you move forward with greater determination and, therefore, more chance of success?

Warrior Gifts – subjective expression

I TARGET, I ACT, I ACHIEVE

I motivate myself and others. I model high energy and stamina. I am decisive. I distinguish between urgent and important tasks. I am direct and I look people in the eye. I speak only when necessary and what is necessary.

I have the courage to stand up, make a point, fight for a cause. I can feel the fear and do it anyway. I can assert authority forcefully, without aggression. I drive myself and others to make things happen. I set stretch targets to achieve goals. I enjoy sparring and healthy competition (with self and others). I am disciplined "on and off the pitch". I always seek to improve performance through training, practice and instruction.

I will train up the willing weakest links to make a stronger chain. And I will dispose of bad apples to protect others. I will "show the sword" when helpful but can discriminate how and when to use it.

I build trust by acting honourably ("do as I do") and will not tolerate hypocrisy ("do as I say, not as I do"). I enjoy serving a worthy cause and will sacrifice comfort to serve it well. I am willing to take a hit for the team.

I can fight fires with calm and clear inner strength. I do not wobble under pressure. I keep mentally and physically fit and ready for action.

I fearlessly pursue victory, often against the odds. I do what it takes to win, but not at all costs – and only if the circumstances are extreme, "by any means necessary". I am linear and logical in pursuit of a target and willing to take shortcuts, if the reward is worth the risk. My naturally high energy often includes a high sex drive, but I own this appropriately and responsibly. I know how, when and where to plant creative seeds.

I prepare the ground for future success. I lead from the front by preference but not by need. I can step back and delegate when it will serve the end game better. I will aim for win-win outcomes, whenever possible.

I Act-In the desired future, until it is achieved.

Of course, very few with Warrior as their Leading Actor will do all of this, even on an exceptionally good day. However, to have a range of these qualities and aptitudes available will inevitably have a positive impact on our ability to execute. If we have the right order, relationships, creative impulses and necessary transitions in place, then making them deliver on their promise often falls to the Warrior.

As we complete our Warrior immersion, see how this poem lands with you. Do you recognize and admire people like Joe? Do you feel kinship with them, or do they feel very far away from who you are and how you currently choose to operate?

Poetic invocation

BEING JOE

*She thought of him as a mercenary thug
but soon discovered that she'd got him wrong.
The tyrants of her past and the schoolyard bullies
had clouded her view and cast him as a brute –
until they had that meeting with Endico,
when it all got personal and she was attacked
by some jerk who thought he could belittle her
for being a woman, or new, or both.*

*She'd never seen anything quite like it –
the clarity, the precision of Joe's response;
the fierceness of him – she thought of a falcon
that stooped on its prey from a hundred feet –
and the way he called it, exactly as it was,
demanded a retraction, but still closed the deal.* (Continues)

(Continued)

From then on, she watched him, like a hawk,
and like a young hawk she learned by doing.
What came was a brand-new way of behaving,
kindled by him – fiery, competitive,
purposed yet passionate and up for the fight –
setting things alight and quick to get the win.

And being Joe, he saw he had a playmate:
a potential eagle, a taker of risks,
perched on her clifftop and ready to fly.
Within a year they'd formed an alliance,
to shake the firm and re-boot the energy,
reshape the market and take on the world.
Meetings were shorter, clearer and sharper,
what mattered to her now was to get things done.

And that was how she became CEO,
re-forged her life and realised who she was.
Later she told Joe how he'd started it –
remembering the bozo who put her down.
Joe didn't say much – didn't really need to –
he just smiled, and turned to the next big thing.

WILLIAM AYOT

So, having read and absorbed this Archetype, we invite you to respond intuitively below. Consider the Warrior both in your personal life and in your work life and then either circle a letter for each or take notes as before. A fuller description of this intuitive assessment appears at the end of the Gifts of the Sovereign section.

My Core Archetypal Life Pattern

A = Leading Actor (natural favourite)
B = Major Supporting Actor (easy competency)
C = Minor Supporting Actor (earned competency)
D = More Offstage Actor (lesser used)

Warrior

MY CORE ARCHETYPAL LIFE PATTERN			
A	B	C	D

My Core Archetypal Work Pattern

A = Leading Actor (required daily and used most)
B = Major Supporting Actor (often required)
C = Minor Supporting Actor (occasionally required)
D = More Offstage Actor (rarely if ever required)

Warrior

MY CURRENT ARCHETYPAL WORK PATTERN			
A	B	C	D

So, as we stride into our final Archetype, notice how you might respond differently to the essence of the Explorer than you did to the Warrior. Which is your preferred way to step into Action?

Gifts of the Explorer

Adventure and Truth

"We do not need, and indeed never will have, all the answers before we act... It is often through taking action that we can discover some of them."

CHARLOTTE BUNCH

A huge welcome to the Explorer! It took you a while to get here, but now it's time to spread your wings and have an adventure! We hope you brought a backpack and supplies, as you will likely need them where we are going...

KEY WORDS

Enthusiast, Adventurer, Teacher, Optimist, Wide-Ranging, Striding, Honest, Philosophical, Expansive, Jovial, Multicultural, 'Can-Do' Attitude

THE EXPLORER SEEKS

Progress, Knowledge, Truth, Nature, Justice, Joy, Hope,

Abundance, Ascendance, Oneness, Success, Big Ideas

How many of these words would you likely use to describe yourself on a good day? All, most, many, about half, a few, a couple or none?

The next piece is designed to take you further into the Explorer mindset. It takes the form of a travel guide with a philosophical twist. It combines this Archetype's two great passions in search of the larger order of things: the outer quest into the "brave new world" with the inner quest for truth. You may find one of these paths more appealing than the other, both about equal, or neither to your liking.

Archetype-appropriate introduction

THE JOURNEY TO THE MOUNTAIN
(A philosophical travel guide)

A)   Preparation

Begin from where you are. It is the only starting place you really have. Access your journey needs with care; you do not want to be overloaded for the trip. Consider giving up some old familiar comforts that will only weigh you down on the road. Bring only what is essential – good shoes, a hat, a walking stick and a rucksack to hold water, snacks, map, compass, binoculars and a journal. The binoculars are to see what is further out, beyond you, the journal to write down what is true, deeper inside of you.

Leave your affairs in good order. You do not know where life will lead you and when you will return, if ever. Who knows what excitements, enticements, risks and even dangers await? Such unknowing is part of the joy of discovery.

B) Stepping Out

Lao Tzu said that "the journey of a thousand miles begins with a single step" – so fix your eye on the horizon you are heading towards and take that step.

Allow your eyes and senses to open as the landscape unfolds around you. Remember that nature is more than something you travel through en route to a pre-determined destination. Open to the immense possibilities of each moment and each step. Let each thing that catches your attention entertain you, just as you entertain it, for whatever time is right. Be in companionship with the journey.

C) Teachable Moments

The world is your teacher now. Everything and everyone that you encounter will offer a unique and unrepeatable opportunity for connection and exploration, enjoyment and education. Trust that any exchange could be a gift or a teaching for the other as well, so be generous with your sharing.

Strangers meet and neither knows the other's past. During such encounters, you can drop all preconceptions of yourself. You are not limited by what you have known so far. Nothing that you have previously done and no part of who you have previously chosen to be need get in the way of the pure joyful exploration of what you do and who you choose to be now.

Every moment on this journey is a discovery, an uncovering of a deeper truth. Feel the liberation. Enjoy the freedom that is so hard to experience in the confines of a tight schedule and goal-orientated busyness.

D) Go Off-Piste *(not to be confused with the English phrase, "going off pissed", although there are likely to be parties and laughs along the way...)*

Be willing to leave the beaten path, it is the best way into the unknown that you are seeking. Notice what is the right level of risk to break out of old patterns – and then take the next bold step. As philosopher–poet David Whyte says: "Remember, if you can see more than one step ahead on the path in front of you, it is not your path!"

Open your mind, heart, body, soul and spirit to the quest. Beyond

*the Journey to the Mountain, life too can be a joyful pilgrimage, if
we only let it lead us where it wants us to go.*

E) **At the Peak**
*Give yourself permission to enjoy the peak moments. Be joyful and
grateful for them. Take photos, write about these moments as they
can become guides and teachers for you and others in the future.
You will enjoy sharing your adventures later with good friends and
fellow travellers. Now, when you are ready, take out those binoculars
and scan the horizon for the next peak...*

So, take a moment to notice how this piece lands, particularly its mix of
inner and outer quests. Is this, metaphorically at least, how you operate?
What is your general attitude to adventure; is it a major part of your life
and leisure time, relatively minor, perhaps a thing of the past now "best
left to the young", or could it be your blind spot – the road less travelled,
the risk left untaken? As we move into the subjective expression one last
time, see if this feels more or less familiar – and if less, are there valuable
potentials in it, pieces that might help you stretch positively in future?

Explorer Gifts – subjective expression

I SEEK, I DISCOVER, I QUEST AGAIN

*I have a broad-minded, wide-ranging view of life and its myriad
possibilities. I could go anywhere and want to go everywhere. I can
feel at home wherever I am, though I may not want to stay in any
one place for too long.*

*I am an active learner and will often set myself to study a new
subject, especially an as-yet unexplored territory. I am tenacious
in the pursuit of discovery and revel in unveiling new truths and
possibilities for others. I am naturally curious and can experiment
in almost any area of endeavour, from a research lab to a refugee*

camp (and most places in-between). To me, the world is my oyster and I want to connect to as many facets of it as I can.

I have an innate sense of justice and what is right. I actively seek to right wrongs and protect the exploited. I stand for social justice. I can be a vocal champion for those who do not have their own voice due to circumstance. I know the world can be a better place tomorrow than it is today, and I strive to make it so.

*I enjoy sharing knowledge and teaching others what I know and believe in. I create a collective 'can-do' attitude and ignite positive energy. I lead and teach by example, drawing people into my orbit with ease. I am honest with myself and those around me. I relish mentoring others to live into a bigger potential than they might otherwise settle for. I recognize that my more introverted colleagues and acquaintances occasionally see me as larger than life. But life is to be lived, it is **not** a rehearsal!*

I am inspired by bigger and better possibilities. I am a natural optimist. I greet each day with enthusiasm, good humour and a joie de vivre that is infectious. I enjoy expressing myself fully and being the jovial centre of social gatherings. My active sense of humour can lighten a heavy meeting or gathering. At funerals, I will tell the tall tales that sweeten others' sorrow.

I give generously, in all areas of life, knowing that I will receive back in return as much or more than I need. I honour the ways of exchange and reverence. I feel empathy with those I have met briefly on my travels, however far away they may be now. I see us all on simultaneous, interconnecting journeys.

I often believe that "bigger is better" but not at the expense of others or the environment. I feel closely connected with animals and nature. Those who impact these negatively, I judge harshly. I speak my mind when I see others treat the Earth with casual disdain or contempt or treat her purely as an exploitable object.

I know that every step out there is also a step "in here". Others can judge me as running away from the real world, but I know I am going deeper into it. I quest my own truth. I only believe something that I have tried out myself. I want to meet the deepest part of myself, wherever that search may take me.

Carl Jung said: "Many of us are walking around as if in shoes too small for us." I do not tiptoe, I stride; I do not reduce myself, I expand; I do not settle, I probe the unknown.

So, how was that for you? The Explorer is naturally broad-minded and their interests are vast. You will almost certainly be drawn to some of these more than to others. Nature, philosophy, humour, justice and teaching is about as broad a spectrum as you can have. But this spread, too, is part of the character pattern. So even a sense of having different interests in different fields and at different times in life could be a clue that this Archetype is a key player on your stage.

As you read this final poem of the Archetypal Gifts, notice if it describes familiar elements of your personality. If not, are you drawn to others with such characteristics, or not so much?

Poetic invocation

JOY-BRINGER

"No one wants to be led by a pessimist."

BILL CLINTON

He's got a smile that makes you want to join him
In crossing any wilderness he'd care to name.
Big man, arms wide – speaking for a multitude.

"You can do it."

He deals in big words like justice and honesty.
Broad-shouldered, carrying everyone with him,
He wants to build an empire, of opportunities.

"We can do it."

(Continues)

(Continued)

Large hands open, uplifting, accessible,
For him it's about sharing, the gift and the giving,
The fullness and plenty that flows from knowledge.

"I know we can do it."

Long legs stepping out, showing everyone how,
leading from the front and forging ahead
but leaving a footprint so you'll know the way.

"We can all do it."

Eyes alight, still sparkling at the end of day
Chin lifted up – half prayer, half aspiration...
This is what he brings us – hope, success and joy.

"Fantastic – we did it!"

WILLIAM AYOT

So, having read and absorbed this Archetype, we invite you to respond intuitively below. Consider the Explorer both in your personal life and in your work life and then either circle a letter for each or take notes as before. A fuller description of this intuitive assessment appears at the end of the Gifts of the Sovereign section.

My Core Archetypal Life Pattern

A = Leading Actor (natural favourite)
B = Major Supporting Actor (easy competency)
C = Minor Supporting Actor (earned competency)
D = More Offstage Actor (lesser used)

Explorer

MY CORE ARCHETYPAL LIFE PATTERN			
A	B	C	D

My Core Archetypal Work Pattern

A = Leading Actor　　　(required daily and used most)
B = Major Supporting Actor　(often required)
C = Minor Supporting Actor　(occasionally required)
D = More Offstage Actor　　(rarely if ever required)

Explorer

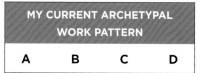

MY CURRENT ARCHETYPAL WORK PATTERN			
A	B	C	D

Reflections on the Realm of Action

Both Archetypes of Action will get things done and break through boundaries. Both will take risks and sacrifice personal comfort in pursuit of a meaningful result. The Warrior maintains energy through personal will and drive and often focuses on short-term measurable impact. The Explorer gets their energy from curiosity and enthusiasm, often focusing on a longer-term pursuit that may be part of an even larger systemic inquiry. The Warrior goes from target to target, the Explorer from mountain to mountain, truth to truth. Which are you closer to, at this point in your life and work?

Next steps

And that, dear reader, brings us to the end of the chapters of extended introduction to the Archetypes. We have been asking you at regular intervals to assess your reaction to the 10 Archetypes contained in the Five Realms of Order, Relationship, Creativity, Change, and Action. For all those readers who have not yet done a more detailed self-assessment either online or during a workshop, we invite you to do that next (see the following chapter). If you are already familiar with your current archetypal patterning, you may want to revisit it now, or jump to the chapters on archetypal Shadows.

INTERMISSION:
Self-Assessment

Now that you have a more detailed understanding of the 10 Archetypes, we invite you to assess your archetypal patterns, both for your core personal life ("My Core Archetypal Life Pattern") and your current working situation ("My Current Archetypal Work Pattern").

Please remember that each of us can draw from all 10 Achetypes, but our unique life and work situations will call on them in different ways at different times. Some may always be prevalent, and some may almost always be distant. We would emphasize that even if you have a preferred pattern that appears fixed, this may not be a disadvantage. If everything is going well in life and work, your current archetypal patterns may be exactly what you need. It is when you face a new challenge or situation in which your habitual responses are no longer effective that you can usefully consider bringing a new character onstage. How you can do that is the subject of Part Two of this book.

Some of us favour certain Archetypes consistently throughout life, while others enjoy exploring different patterns at different times. So, as you engage with this self-assessment, you might also reflect whether you would have answered differently 10 years ago.

A REMINDER OF THE ARCHETYPAL GIFTS

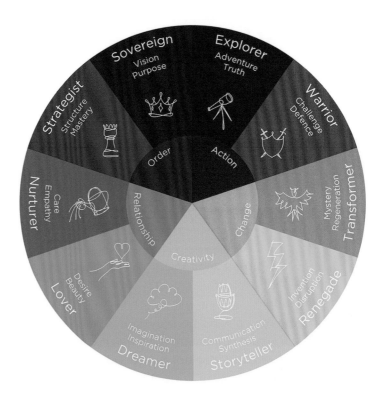

Archetypal Gifts Wheel

You have already had an option to do an intuitive self-assessment after each Archetype immersion in the last five chapters. We are now inviting you to put your intuitions and reflections together to create a complete pattern assessment for life and work (separately).

We remind you of the key words for each Archetype below. You may be sufficiently familiar with them to go straight to the assessment below. You can also use this list as you need during the assessment.

LEADERSHIP GIFTS – KEY WORDS (REVIEW)

Sovereign

Royal, Ruler, Visible, Heroic, Luminary, Generative, Playful, Heartful, Magnanimous, Loyal, Present, Spacious, at the Centre of Things

Radiates: Purpose, Generosity, Courage, Will, Self-Confidence, Vigour, Strength, Vision, Vitality, Charisma, Ambition

Strategist

Structured, Rational, Principled, Ethical, Pragmatic, Organized, Controlled, Mature, Contained, Precise, Deliberate, Measured

Respects: Time, Focus, Rules, Mastery, Limits, Discipline, Duty, Hierarchy, Boundaries, Tradition, Wisdom, Objectivity, Goals, Capital, The Establishment, Law and Order, The Truth in Numbers

Nurturer

Supportive, Caring, Reassuring, Protective, Responsive, Instinctive, Parental, Trusting, Nourishing, Sensitive, Empathetic, Receptive, Cosy

Values: Relationships, Potential, Growth, Feedback, Togetherness, Time to Reflect, 'Keeping the Hearth', Legacy, Conservation, Emotional Intelligence, Natural Cycles, Tending Gardens, Feeling at Home, Full-Body Listening

Lover

Alluring, Sensual, Sociable, Desirable, Charming, Passionate, Seductive, Creates Longing, Acts as a Muse, Accumulates Self-Worth and Net-Worth

Adores: Design, Style, Luxury, Money, Pleasure, Relationships, Beauty, Fine Art, Fashion, Decorations, Harmony, Song, Fantasy, Enchantment

Dreamer
Imaginative, Poetic, Sensitive, Idealistic, Compassionate,
Spiritual, Visual, Boundless, Imaginal, Believing
Inspired By: Fantasy, Symbols, Infinity, Mythology, Non-Dualism,
Dreams, Intangibles, Metaphors, Mysticism, Visions, Ecstasy,
The Transcendent, The Invisible, Art, Music, Archetypes, Lateral
Thinking, Negative Capability, Emergence, Holding Paradox,
Possibilities, Altered States

Storyteller
Communicator, Translator, Mediator, Synthesizer, Advertiser,
Conceptual, Critical, Versatile, Adaptable, Agile, Trickster,
Mercurial, Quick-Thinking
Connects With: Ideas, Metaphors, Information, Multiple
Perspectives, Puzzles, Juggling, Multi-Tasking, Wit, Details, Logic,
Intelligence, Making Connections, Creating Narratives, Clever
Articulation

Renegade
Intuitive Disruptor, Eccentric Inventor, Liberator, Rebel,
Provocateur, Maverick, Unique, Has Epiphanies, "Eureka!"
Thrives On: The Zeitgeist, Freedom, The Future, Disruptive
Technologies, Revolution, Uniqueness, Structural Collapse,
Surprise, Revelation, Flashes of Insight, Emerging Ideas,
Brilliance

Transformer
Magician, Healer, Regenerator, Change Agent, Deep, Powerful,
Psychological, Magnetic, Intense, Inexorable
Honours: Renovation, Roots, Research, Transitions, Upheaval,
Total Change, Power, Deconstruction, Transformation, Secrets,
Death and Rebirth, Break Down to Break Through, The
Underworld, Mystery, Hidden Gold

Warrior

Champion, Spearhead, Amazon, Defender, Trouble-Shooter, Brave, Fierce, Passionate, Forceful, Decisive, Fearless, Surgical, Leads from the Front

Drives: Competition, Challenge, Action, Direction, Tactics, Risk-Taking, Seed-Planting, Making Things Happen, Adrenaline, Competitive Advantage

Explorer

Enthusiast, Adventurer, Teacher, Optimist, Wide-Ranging, Striding, Honest, Philosophical, Expansive, Jovial, Multicultural, 'Can-Do' Attitude

Seeks: Progress, Knowledge, Truth, Nature, Justice, Joy, Hope, Abundance, Ascendance, Oneness, Success, Big Ideas

Core Life Assessment instructions

1) Please think about which of the four categories each Archetype is most likely to be in:

Leading Actors

These Archetypes embody your favourite natural gifts. They give you a joyful sense of purpose on your best days. They feel like trusted and go-to inner advisors.

Major Supporting Actors

These Archetypes are favoured back-ups. They are easy competencies you can draw on at will, even if you don't enjoy them as much as your Leading Actors.

Minor Supporting Actors

These Archetypes have qualities and behaviours you can access when you have to. They are earned competencies that you can step into, but you generally choose not to until you need them.

More Offstage Actors

These Archetypes are less favoured and less used. You may feel uncomfortable with them or about them (for numerous reasons). You may judge them as being of little or no value.

Our experience is that the vast majority of those who have self-assessed so far have found that they have a minimum of two and a maximum of three Archetypes in each category.

2) Please divide the 10 between the four categories and assign a minimum of two and a maximum of three in each category. Write down the order in the template provided below or make your own notes separately, as you prefer.

3) For the Leading and Major Supporting Actors there is space for you to write a couple of the key words (from the list above) that you are most proud of for each. This gives you a clearer sense of which gifts fit you best.

4) For the Minor Supporting and More Offstage Actors there is space for you to write down one or two Gift words from these Archetypes which you would like to access in future. This will give you a first idea of what you might want to develop in Part Two.

Current Work Assessment instructions

For the Current Work Assessment, you can choose whether to assess your working role generally or specifically. You can choose to apply this to the general requirements of your current role, or to a specific priority at this time. If you have a number of different projects that require different approaches, we invite you to select the most urgent or the most important of these to assess your pattern.

1) Repeat the same process as you used for Core Life Pattern above, now for your Current Work Pattern, but with the following different filters in mind:

Leading Actors

These Archetypes represent key and non-negotiable parts of your current work. You need to access these gifts daily.

Major Supporting Actors

These Archetypes represent a needed part of your current work. You need to use them regularly, although not as much as the Leading Actors.

Minor Supporting Actors

These Archetypes have qualities and behaviours you draw on occasionally. They can be a useful support but are currently not used regularly.

More Offstage Actors

These Archetypes are rarely if ever used by you at work. They can feel redundant to your current role or responsibilities.

2) Write the Archetypes in your preferred order with 2–3 in each category. Then write down the most relevant key words for you: for your Leading and Major Supporting Actors this is what is most required of you; for your Minor Supporting and More Offstage Actors this is what might be useful to bring in more.

SELF-ASSESSMENT: ARCHETYPAL GIFTS

MY CORE ARCHETYPAL LIFE PATTERN	MY CURRENT ARCHETYPAL WORK PATTERN

Archetypes and key words that reflect what I am most proud of:

Archetypes and key words that reflect my current working reality:

Leading Actors (2-3)
(natural favourites)

Leading Actors (2-3)
 (required daily and used most)

1) _____

Key words: _____

_____

1) _____

Key words: _____

_____

2) _____

Key words: _____

_____

2) _____

Key words: _____

_____

3) _____

Key words: _____

_____

3) _____

Key words: _____

_____

Major Supporting Actors (2-3)
(easy competency)

Major Supporting Actors (2-3)
(often required)

1) _____

Key words: _____

_____

1) _____

Key words: _____

_____

2) _____

Key words: _____

_____

3) _____

Key words: _____

_____

2) _____

Key words: _____

_____

3) _____

Key words: _____

_____

*Archetypes and key words that
I would like to have access to:*

Minor Supporting Actors (2-3)
(earned competency)

1) _____

Key words: _____

_____

2) _____

Key words: _____

_____

3) _____

Key words: _____

_____

*Archetypes and key words that
could be useful at work:*

Minor Supporting Actors (2-3)
(occasionally required)

1) _____

Key words: _____

_____

2) _____

Key words: _____

_____

3) _____

Key words: _____

_____

More Offstage Actors (2-3)
(lesser used)

1) _____

Key words: _____

_____

2) _____

Key words: _____

_____

3) _____

Key words: _____

_____

More Offstage Actors (2-3)
(rarely if ever used)

1) _____

Key words: _____

_____

2) _____

Key words: _____

_____

3) _____

Key words: _____

_____

Gifts Assessment - reflections

Notice the similarities and any differences between Core Life and Current Work patterns, especially in your Leading Actors and More Offstage Actors. If the differences are extreme, there are two ways to reflect on this:

a) If the personal and professional sides of your life are quite different and you feel that the mix creates a good balance for you, it could be an excellent pattern at this point

   Or

b) If the difference is causing inner tension over an extended period of time, it could be a sign that your working life is not aligned with who you really are – in which case you may consider exploring other options that feel more "on purpose" and fit your core archetypal pattern.

People who lead their own companies or follow a portfolio/"gig economy" career are likely to find work that fits their Core Life Pattern whenever they can. Others feel they cannot afford the luxury of doing what they love. They may prioritize career paths that use more of their competencies than their passions, but which can fund their Leading Actors to be more centre stage in their spare time, hobbies and holidays. There is no right way to be, only what feels good enough or true enough for you, at a given time.

However, in the more extreme cases of mismatched patterns, there can be trouble ahead. If your favourite Leading Actor is most offstage at work, you will probably feel unfulfilled or somehow "not best used". If your More Offstage Actor in life is the most required Leading Actor at work, you will likely feel uncomfortably stretched or stressed. In these cases, you have a couple of very different options. If you can afford the risk, you can look for different work that fits more of your Leading Actor's core pattern, which will create more meaning and purpose in your working life. Or if taking such a risk is not realistic, you can develop added expertise in the required More Offstage Actors, so you reduce your discomfort and increase your competency. We have coached many people through both options in our Archetypes at Work™ coaching practice.

For the majority of the remaining chapters we will focus on your Leading Actors and your More Offstage Actors. These are likely to have the most impact on your Shadows of Too Much and Too Little. In this and the following assessments we also include your Major and Minor Supporting Actors as this can give you a subtler understanding of your inner resources.

At this point, you have assessed your current archetypal patterns and reflected on what Gifts you are most likely to be using on a good day. Now, when you are ready, we are going to look at what might be equally true of you, on a bad day...

CHAPTER 7

ARCHETYPAL SHADOWS OF
Too Much

We hold the Archetypes to be ever-present patterns in human nature, whether we are conscious of them or not. For most of us, there will be many good days when we access a favoured Archetype's Gifts with ease and achieve exactly the impact we desire. And, there will be bad days too, where we will be guilty of overplaying a favourite Archetype. You can have too much of a good thing, and the Archetypes are no exception. For clarity, you are much more likely to activate the Shadows of Too Much in your two to three Leading Actors and two to three Main Supporting Actors than the others. In contrast, less favoured Archetypes are liable to activate the Shadows of Too Little, which we describe in Chapter 8.

The illustration below offers an overview of the Archetypal Shadows of Too Much.

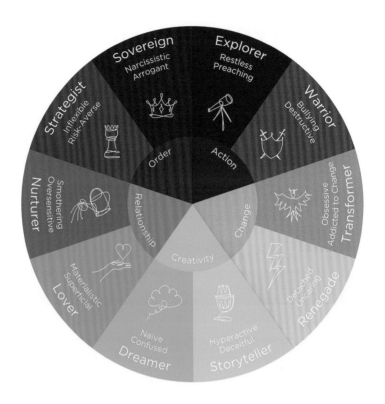

Archetypal Shadows Wheel – Too Much

Headline overview

Too Much Order: The Sovereign can become Narcissistic and/or Arrogant and the Strategist Inflexible and/or Risk-Averse.

Too Much Relationship: The Nurturer can become Smothering and/or Oversensitive and the Lover Materialistic and/or Superficial.

Too Much Creativity: The Dreamer can become Naïve and/or Confused and the Storyteller Hyperactive and/or Deceitful.

Too Much Change: The Renegade can become Detached and/or Uncaring and the Transformer Obsessive and/or Addicted to Change.

Too Much Action: The Warrior can become Bullying and/or Destructive and the Explorer Restless and/or Preaching.

So, what are the differences between accessing a favoured Archetype's Gifts and slipping into the Shadow of Too Much? First, you are likely to experience mixed results from your efforts and a positive outcome becomes difficult to predict. Secondly, there is a difference in how it feels. On a good day, you will probably sense that you are being an effective instrument, using or channelling Archetypes and their gifts well and with ease. On a bad day, it may feel that a particular energy has *you*; as if you are in *its* grip rather than the other way around, almost as if you have become possessed by it. On these days the impact on others is likely to be more negative than positive. Given the Classical roots of archetypal psychology with its pantheon of gods and goddesses, a phrase Laurence often uses with clients is, "Either you do the gods or the gods do you!" On a good day you are an instrument, "doing the gods", and on a bad day you are gripped and "the gods are doing you".

This chapter is designed to raise awareness of key dangers for you, so that you can then choose to manage these more effectively. We use the word *Shadow* partly as defined by Jung to describe those parts of ourselves that we either cannot see or may not choose to see. This includes certain attitudes and behaviours that we actively shy away from and may even repress. Shadow also refers to simple terms of light. Many of us in a task-focused and high-achieving world tend to see ourselves as full of light: gifts and potential. We don't focus on our blind spots and Shadows: the less well-lit parts of ourselves, where we may not live up to our preferred self-image.

How Shadows of Too Much develop

The most obvious way these Shadows develop is by "habit of nature", the repetition of what feels like an innate capacity. It is easy to over-use behaviours that come naturally to us, particularly those that get us what we want and/or feel good. The sense of "this is how I am" is a great reinforcer of habits and attitudes. This is called "internal validation".

Another route can be etched into our psyche from "external validation". Most of us are coded from an early age to seek approval from others, especially those with the power or means to meet our basic needs. So, as we grow up, we develop practices, skills and ways of being that we are both proud of and that those powerful "others" appreciate and reward. Naturally, we then tend to do more of what gets a good result.

Both internal and external validation can create a self-reinforcement loop. Unless we find environments that support and stimulate self-awareness, we might fail to recognize when we slip down that gentle slope from expressing a Gift to activating a Shadow of Too Much.

Other, more complicated, reasons can originate in our formative years. The Shadows may have become ingrained parts of our character; things we learned to identify with, especially those ways of being that served us in earlier life – and not just at home. Some are reinforced by our neighbourhoods, peer groups, faith groups and even national cultures. Initially, such attitudes may develop from a felt need to adapt to our circumstances. But after years of repetition they feel so normal that we fail to notice their negative impacts and limitations. The earlier felt need creates an assumption of their innate utility that goes unchallenged.

When we internalize parental or cultural voices in this way, it will often lead to us over-relying on some ways of being in the world at the expense of others. A classic example that reinforced gender stereotypes for far too long claimed that "girls should be nice" and "boys don't cry". This type of parental and societal messaging directed boys to emulate Warrior-type behaviours (being tough and taking risks) and girls to strive for Nurturer behaviours (being kind and putting others first). Then, as grown-ups, that woman may compulsively put others first and do Too Much Nurturing at work, while that man might not recognize others' stress levels and push them too hard: Too Much Warrior.

One of the most complex beginnings is when a habit has developed as compensation for something that did *not* happen early on. When there is an obvious deficit of some necessary or desired energy in early years, some of us will grow up believing that it is our function in life to overcome that deficit for others. We may then end up offering too much of what we did not get enough of early on. A typical example of this would be a person who grew up in a home with little or no care and who then becomes a compulsive care-taker later on in life: Too Much Nurturer.

While simpler causes of Shadow behaviours can be remedied fairly easily – and even reading this chapter may do it for some – more complex causes are likely to be remedied only with care and over time. Others, in our experience, often benefit from expert guidance from a coach, mentor or therapist to help them decode habitual Shadow patterns of thought, feeling and behaviour.

Once a basic understanding of our own Shadows is in place, we are more likely to develop awareness of what we react to in others. This is especially useful for effective team communication and productive feedback loops in work, social or community groups.

It is therefore important to know not just *which* Archetypes you are accessing, but also *how* you are accessing them and *why* you are accessing them in the way that you are.

Now going deeper

For this analysis we shift from the first-person subjective expression "I" to a more objective, third person "They". This is because the Shadow of Too Much is rarely identified and owned by the individual themselves. For example, obsessed Warriors are more liable to think of themselves as forcefully assertive rather than as an aggressive bully. In addition, it is generally true that when people learn about their Shadows they are more likely to change their behaviours than to brag about them. You rarely hear the Warrior say, "Oh yes, I am a bully!" Rather, someone else is liable to say, "Be careful, they bully others when under pressure!" Others typically notice the negative impact of the Shadows of Too Much first.

Whether these others feel the individual in question is ready to get honest feedback about their observations is another issue. It usually depends on the psychological maturity of those involved as well as the system they belong to. Does the individual involved appreciate feedback? Does the Shadow-spotter feel empowered to speak up? If the answers are negative, nothing will change, which is one reason why so many Shadow behaviours are visible in the world.

One advantage of doing this archetypal diagnostic work as a team or a cadre of leaders is that the shared language can lead to the creation of responsible feedback loops. People can use the language of the Archetypes to deliver effective requests and feedback without others taking it personally. For example, it is much easier for a Nurturer in an archetypally aware group of Warriors to say, "Could we ask the Warriors to bear with us while we discuss the emotional needs of our new employees? We will decide on actions promptly." This, can serve as a pre-emptive request that can avert a more typically unconscious Warrior outburst, "Stop wasting our time with personnel issues, we have work to do!"

Becoming aware of how you can get in your own way on a bad day – as well as the likely negative impacts on those around you – are essential steps on the path to psychological maturity.

Too Much Sovereign
Narcissistic and Arrogant

As you read the introductory poem, please notice your reactions. If your Sovereign is a Leading Actor, could this be how others see you? Very occasionally, obviously, on those very few, very, very bad days! If not, have you had a boss or a colleague like this at work or overtly visible in your local community. Or someone you notice on the world stage?

ECLIPSE

They should have a whip-round, buy him a crown,
Put him on a throne and call him Your Highness.
He thinks he's a king, so he puts you down.
He's a stranger to common grace or shyness.
If he can steal the limelight or the credit,
He will – he's the centre of his universe –
And anything smart, he's sure to have said it.
His overblown ego's become a curse.
He likes to think that he's one of the guys
But meetings turn ugly if he starts to sulk;
And as for push-back – well nobody tries –
If you're really unlucky you meet The Hulk.
The fact is his reign should not have been allowed.
Things are getting dark here. Sun's behind a cloud.

WILLIAM AYOT

When the Sovereign gets carried away, their ego inflates and they come across as narcissistic and grandiose, "It's all about *me*!" They become overly selfish, bigger than life, liable to boast about accomplishments, yet blame others for failures: "I don't make mistakes, it must be someone else's fault". We may be able to detect in these people the "tyrant in the high chair" who got their way early on by making a lot of noise and still throw a temper tantrum when denied their way. On a bad day, their pride and arrogance become ostentatious and obnoxious, especially to those with more natural humility.

The driving motivation of this Sovereign is not a Vision that others could serve but a need to feel elevated and be served by others. When the Shadow Sovereign arrives in the spotlight, they want to stay there and are rarely willing to yield centre stage to others. They often have a compulsive desire for attention, adoration and applause. They therefore find it difficult to bless others to grow and flourish under their leadership or authority. They may even put or keep down potential rising stars with real talent. The message they unconsciously deliver is, "Your offering is not as good as Mine!" Those without genuine ideas of their own may lay claim to the good ideas of others. In the long run, if these behaviours are not appropriately named, addressed and changed, talented colleagues will leave for a more generative and/or democratic environment where they can spread their wings.

The Shadow Sovereign has a tendency to believe that, "They can't do it without me". Yet they will often deflect real responsibility and refuse to face critics. They may humiliate bearers of bad news and want to "kill the messenger". They will often surround themselves with "yes people" and overtly sycophantic friends, colleagues and fans, who feel good basking in the reflected power of a big ego who makes them feel valued, even though they will only ever be in the shade of the shining Alpha leader.

Sometimes the Shadow Sovereign is actually a façade, like the eponymous character in the *Wizard of Oz*, born from a deep felt need to project the appearance of strength and power. In reality, they are protecting themselves from a deeper feeling of being small and powerless. People motivated by this need draw from the authority and limelight that others project onto them to compensate for their own lack of self-worth. In other words, even if I don't feel good about myself, if those around me see me as powerful, it helps – and maybe it makes it true! Some live in constant fear that their façade will be seen through and someone will say, "The game's up!" This pattern is recognized in leadership development as *impostor syndrome*.

At this point, just notice if this rings any bells, whether for yourself or as a reflection on others around you. A small warning here: the Narcissistic personality is notoriously difficult to give feedback to, unless they are genuinely open to growth and development. If not, one likely reaction is rejection, sometimes not just of the feedback but of the person attempting to give it. Another is collapse. Here the ego deflates and they regress into feeling the smaller person inside (often learned as a young child) that the façade is designed to cover up. At this point it is literally like their balloon has been popped and, much like a small child, they feel terrible, until they figure out how to puff themselves up again. Any attempt to give feedback to others should be carefully thought through. In regards to yourself, if you are still reading, that's a good sign that you are interested in development! The later chapters will give you some clear ideas and actions to take when you are ready.

Too Much Strategist
Inflexible and Risk-Averse

What could possibly go wrong with the Strategist? Don't we always need to frame, structure and focus our activities, tasks and life? Yes – and no... See how you fare with this poem; does it provoke memories of any of your bad days, or those of others you have worked with or around? Though they can appear on the world stage, you are less likely to know them or remember them as they take up less space and are less charismatic than the Shadow Sovereigns.

GALL AND WORMWOOD

Like a sad, overworked old Labrador
She sinks down into her seat at meetings.
A leaden-eyed, logical detail-bore
Who's clearly taken one too many beatings.
Oh, she can still do it, but her eyes are cold,
Harsh and inflexible, single-minded –
Using her position to maintain her hold –
She's lost perspective, become bitter, blinded.
When she tells us not to reinvent the wheel,
Or trots out her bile, or kills a good scheme,
Snarls that a risk is our Achilles heel,
It feels like she's taken a knife to the dream.
Her sadness infects everyone in the room.
We want to succeed, not drown in her gloom.

WILLIAM AYOT

Anyone you know?

Let's broaden our awareness to include some of the other most prominent dangers of the Strategist Shadows, summed up below:

1) **Risk-Averse, Rule-Bound and Closed:** preferring the known and the safe. Not open to anything new which does not fit into current accepted practice. Often overstating the potential risks of change in order to keep the status quo. Overvaluing the carefully built existing structures and the way things are done. "Don't reinvent the wheel!"

2) **Over-Controlling and Micro-Managing:** keeping a tight rein on all tasks and outcomes. Believing that there should be no variance from the initial plan. Judging harshly those who bend or break the rules or the cultural norms. Looking over people's shoulders, constantly correcting any deviation from how they would have structured the task they supposedly delegated to others. "Do it the way I showed you".

3) **Perfectionist:** nothing is ever quite good enough. They want things 100% right and don't recognize when 90% would get the job done. They apply the same over-rigorous standards to everyone in their sphere of influence.

4) **Rigid Scheduling:** whether an agenda timed to the minute or a project plan over six months, they can get obsessed with timelines and punctuality, not recognizing that projects invariably change.

5) **Inflexible, Unyielding and Narrow-Minded:** stubborn in sticking to what has been previously agreed to. Unwilling to contemplate a change of mind or direction. Setting limits too tight and not allowing room for imagination, expansion or the radically new. Unwilling to champion unproven ideas.

6) **Rank-Focused:** believing that those in more senior positions must be right and need to be respected. "They got where they are for a reason".

7) **Depressive and Pessimistic:** exuding a leaden energy that drags others' positive spirits down. Always prioritizing the problem over the opportunity. Seriously doubting unexpected success – especially against the odds.

8) **Stagnant and Inert:** maintaining old energy in a system, not allowing any fresh or younger energy in. Preferring stasis over movement, methodical, predictable inching forward over quick leaps and bounds.

9) **Obsessed with Numbers:** remaining over-reliant on figures. Unable to understand the human cost of their rational decisions. They would not compute the note above Einstein's desk at Princeton: "Not everything that counts can be counted and not everything that can be counted counts!"

The Shadow Strategist can originate from simply being well organized at school and then keeping this effective habit going. Being recognized for careful risk management and effectively balancing budgets at work reinforces early habits. Taken to an extreme, in senior roles this same gift becomes over-controlling. Risks are restricted to what the Shadow Strategist personally decides is safe enough, limiting the space and time for others to explore more expansive options.

On a deeper level, this tendency could be generated by a Shadow Strategist parent who made focus and structure the only things they would reward in their child. So, the child grows up believing this is the only way to get ahead and to get approval and be loved.

We have also coached Shadow Strategists who had the reverse experience – unstructured, Bohemian parents who let their kids run wild with no limits. That adult child then seeks to impose the inner need for order, yearned for earlier in life, on the world around them later on.

Could any of this point to a Shadow potential for you?

Too Much Nurturer
Smothering and Oversensitive

Have you ever worked with someone who was so caring and empathetic that you got to the point where you couldn't quite take it anymore?

A LITTLE BIT OF FEEDBACK

Oh, for goodness sake! Just leave me alone!
Your incessant caring is creeping me out.
And as for your "chats" on the telephone –
Endless sharing is not what it's about.
I get that you need to feed us all up,
That "cake" expresses your "deep conviction"
But have you noticed that a bottomless cup
Of tea and more "munchies" feeds your addiction?

We all love to love, and like to be mothered,
But you want us to be Santa's little elves.
It's not so much caring as being smothered –
Sometimes they need to do it for themselves.
So forget the treats – I'll eat on the run –
Spare me your emotions and get something done!

WILLIAM AYOT

The Shadow Nurturer becomes a compulsive care-taker, loath to let others look after themselves. They will often "over-share" and unload their emotions on others. On a bad day, they can turn any meeting into a therapy session. They tend towards being intrusive in their wish to hear about colleagues' private lives and may not recognize the focused work environment others may need. They can be overprotective to the point of smothering and stifling those around them, sometimes infantilizing them. The Shadow Nurturer often feels that something terrible will happen to "their flock" unless they take care of everyone and everything: "They will always need my help. They can't really do it for themselves".

They can be addicted to feeding others, metaphorically or literally. They may over-eat, using comfort food to absorb some of the many emotions they tend to carry.

Their deep wish for everyone to be a happy family can prompt them to smooth over key differences between colleagues: "Why can't we just all get along?" They prefer to avoid conflict and fail to recognize when courageous conversations, or even confrontations, might lead to a clearer resolution. They prefer to give positive feedback and may skip the negative, thereby enabling a complacent working environment where little is challenged effectively.

The Shadow Nurturer may also have a hard time letting go of the past. There may be boxes stored away, stuffed with every possible memento and photograph: "You never know when you will need it". The attachment to the past is rooted in deep nostalgia that can interfere with effectively being present in the current moment, day or year.

Some compulsive care-takers started by simply being a great friend early on and offering a good shoulder to cry on. The trust and appreciation gained from this capability felt good enough to initiate a lifelong habit. Others were cast as necessary carers early on, gaining approval for looking after ill or younger family members. People required to step into this role as a child often unconsciously look for the next person or group to serve in a similar way later on in life. Some others will have suffered from a childhood that lacked care and affection and then grow up compensating for what they missed by over-caring for others.

Do you recognize any of these patterns, or any of these possible initiating events, in yourself or in others close to you?

Too Much Lover
Materialistic and Superficial

We will start differently with the Lover, to set a little context. With most Archetypes we are likely to slip into the Shadow after accessing the Gifts; in other words, we often tend towards doing something well before we do it Too Much. As we noted in the Lover's Gifts introduction, however, the Lover has been substantially hijacked over the last century by the increasing emphasis on a consumer culture and its over-valuing of materialistic buying power. We could say that the Shadow Lover has been embraced by society as a whole, usually as a "good thing", and so it is all too easy for many individuals to be seduced by Shadow Lover habits, with little or no access to the positive Gifts. On a good day, the Lover helps us soulfully connect with life, on a bad day, we may not notice that we have sold our soul.

The media typically portrays the Lover in a simplistic and superficial sexualized way at the expense of the deeper sense of inner beauty and loving intimacy it also holds. There are countless industries and brands promoting status symbols that promise fulfilment; whether a designer wardrobe, gold and jewellery, a trophy partner, luxury car, big house or an offshore fortune. And since buying something outside to feel worthy is usually less effort than developing self-worth inside, many get seduced by the Shadow Lover. This is not only true for those with means, much of the current global finance industry is complicit and all too willing to lend money at high rates of interest that keep the consumer in debt for many years. Often this consumption is an unsuccessful attempt to fill a hole inside, where self-love might otherwise reside. But once the initial buyer's high has passed, the need reasserts itself and all too soon another thing to possess comes to the top of the wish list. As social philosopher Noam Chomsky wisely said, "You can never get enough of what you don't really want."

Does this poem remind you of anyone you know?

WHAT'S IN A NAME

The moment he entered the room you knew –
Here was an executive who loved his stuff,
Though as his list of acquisitions grew
The joke took hold that he'd never get enough.
Not just the firms he brought into the fold
But the watches, the bracelet, the priceless ring;
The house in the country the oligarch sold,
His flaunting of the glitz, the air of bling.
What did for him was the looseness of his tongue
The cruel asides, the flirting, the baloney.
The enemies he'd made, and those he'd stung,
Turned on him and branded him a phoney –
His salesmanship, his style, his effortless ease,
All came down to nothing. He was Mr Sleaze.

WILLIAM AYOT

The Shadow Lover is often greedy, accumulating money or possessions without any sense of limit. Some people in the grip of this may give themselves permission to do whatever it takes to get rich. Others enjoy flaunting wealth. Some buy their way into positions of power and influence to be seen in the right places and with the right people.

The Shadow Lover can get obsessed with superficial appearances, believing that how things and people look is more important than their essence. They may think themselves irresistible and attempt to attract or seduce others with what they have, rather than with who they are, as if they believed that true love and happiness can be bought or sold.

On a bad day, the Shadow Lover can come across as sleazy and oozing charm that many around them distrust. They can manipulate others for personal ends. They will exaggerate, oversell and even lie to get what they want. They can be spiteful and jealous, use words to hurt others or spread unfair gossip. They have the potential to deliberately set friends against each other to protect the special relationship they seek with one or both parties. In social networks they may show a compulsive need to be the most popular. Less discerning friends may be attracted by the superficial glamour and get caught in the web of gossip and intricate social complexities.

Other than cultural norms, parents exhibiting Shadow Lover values can pass these on to their offspring. So, children brought up by vain adults are often taught to prioritize outer appearance and social climbing over inner worth and true friendship. Conversely, some children are influenced by painful early experiences of poverty. They can feel humiliated or lesser than others who display greater resources and then develop an inner mantra along the lines of: "When I grow up, I'll show them..."

Too Much Dreamer
Naïve and Confused

LOST...

It starts with a tiny ripple in the mind
An enticing thought, something enthralling;
Misty and nebulous, vague and undefined,
Yet always in the background, always calling.

It entices her through a door in the wall
Where she dreams new worlds of cosy illusion;
Escapes the unpleasant moment, till the fall
That spirals her down and back to confusion.
Better the unreal than the commonplace.
Who'd want to live in a world so mundane?
Better to avoid reality's embrace,
To opt out and imagine "Castles in Spain".
Unbounded, ungrounded, unable to think,
Her addiction's a curse, as bad as the drink.

WILLIAM AYOT

Too Much Dreamer and nothing much gets done. They become unable to bring any ideas to earth and to make practical things happen. The numerous intimations of the future are all fantastical and unrealistic. Heads stay stuck in clouds building "pies in the skies". Shadow Dreamers escape into different worlds. They may be happy enough there, but others see them as gone or simply unfocused, as the Irish say, "away with the faeries".

The Shadow Dreamer may enjoy drifting through life as though floating semi-submersed on turquoise waters in a dreamy lagoon, where time seems to be slowed down. They forget that in this altered state they are unaware of practical realities and can become shark bait. Their sense of idealism can also render them highly gullible and prone to accept a wide variety of teachers and teachings. Especially when any of these resonate with their current set of fantasies. There can also be a slowly building resentment that the world is not recognizing the value of their imaginings.

Another danger lies in the Shadow Dreamer's inability to make a decision – or to stick to one when made. The Shadow of being open to all possibilities can make any choice seem like a limitation and therefore unsatisfying. Whichever path the Shadow Dreamer takes, they agonize over how much greener the grass could be on the other side. Eventually, this can alienate others, who lose trust in their ability to come up with a workable idea or deliver on a commitment. The dream can become a nightmare.

The Shadow Dreamer can be born in the artistic, imaginative child who loves day-dreaming and/or senses things that others do not – whether sounds, images, imaginal figures or spirits. It often feels like a destiny

143

rather than a choice. Pursuing big dreams often has a real-world cost and only works out for a lucky few. In others, the Shadow Dreamer can be a reaction to a reality that was, for any number of reasons, not healthy. The child can learn to escape from an unsafe world and, in extreme cases, disassociate. In contrast, an over-structured early life with no room for imagination can lead to a compensatory impulse to be free of constraints and limitations later in life.

Any of these scenarios can lead some Shadow Dreamers towards substance abuse and addiction. The yearning for a shortcut to other worlds and extreme states can be fulfilled short term through an over-reliance on alcohol, drugs or other mind-altering substances. Then the spirit of creation gets replaced by the spirit in the bottle; the yearning to go higher turns into a need to get "high" as often as possible.

Too Much Storyteller
Hyperactive and Deceitful

SLY

With a head full of tales that can't be ignored
He's a one-man, walking mythopedia,
But living by the sword you die by the sword,
And he's going to die by social media.
The deceit's more apparent with each new post
And his fakery will be his undoing,
But it's the contempt that galls us the most.

He's no longer trusted. There's trouble brewing.
The truth is his thinking's all over the place;
He's a meddler, erratic and capricious.
He may be quick, but he hasn't got the grace
To admit he's addicted to the fictitious.
Like a kid high on sugar, he's always wired.
If he can't grow up he really should be fired.

WILLIAM AYOT

Too Much Storyteller and there is a danger of "hyper-drive": being scattered, overly busy, disorganized and spread too thin. The Shadow Storyteller constantly gathers new trivia, fun facts, gossip and other tidbits of information to juggle. The need to be both informed and informer leads to too much talk and inappropriate sharing of confidences; their definition of a secret is "something you only tell one person at a time". They have the gift of the gab but not the matching filters to recognize in the moment what is appropriate to say and what is not. Others' eyes may start to glaze over with TMI (Too Much Information); they will want to hold up their hands to stop the incessant chatter, but the Shadow Storyteller does not notice and pauses only for breath. For others, the quick and versatile thinking becomes hyperactivity, the constant changing of topic and focus unpredictability. Continuous mind-changing can make others nervous, coming across as unreliable or fickle.

The overplayed Storyteller will exaggerate and stretch the facts at will. They may even ignore the original evidence and start peddling tall tales, fake news or lies. They will cleverly select evidence and spin reality to seal the deal and suit their own ends or those of their paymasters: "No, we are not invaders, we are peacekeepers". They can change the story from one telling to the next, which in a community or team creates confusion and incoherence. If the need to be liked is strong, they will underplay or edit out the parts their audience would not want to hear. They may choose a time to release news when others are distracted elsewhere; what politicians refer to as "a good day to deliver bad news".

Sometimes the Shadow Storyteller gets lost in the sheer volume of their own ideas and is then unable to finish anything or go to any depth. Think of a writer who starts endless novels but never completes.

Social networks can be addictive for such a person. They can be involved in multiple conversations around the globe at all times, so they never have to stop communicating. Some will veer towards the hyper-critical, repeatedly putting down others' ideas. Some become uncritical, forming quick opinions to pass on without any real thought, sharing every rumour and new theory. Either way, they prefer the juicy tidbit to the substantial. So, the quantity overrides the quality and serious issues are given little or no time to settle and be integrated into life. The Shadow Storyteller yearns to be seen as a player full of youthful zest – others may see them as a childish trickster and not take them seriously.

Such tendencies can begin when a child is rewarded for being bright, telling good stories and connecting easily with others. It can also come from a facility for banter that got attention back then. It may even have provided an escape route from punishment: the ability to talk oneself out of trouble. In conflicted families, it may have been generated by a need to mediate, perhaps by engaging others in a light-hearted way so as to divert conversations from more negative paths. Alternatively, an incurious or narrow-minded family of origin could trigger the compensatory route towards an ever-expanding knowledge base and deep curiosity. The Shadow Storyteller then prides themselves for developing a larger, savvier and more complex world view than the simplistic one they escaped.

Too Much Renegade
Detached and Uncaring

ROBOT

If not quite crazy, he's certainly weird,
Cold and aloof, still preaching revolution.
His tragedy is he was once revered
For his insights and his contribution.

Now he just drops in a differing view;
Sits in meetings, haughtily opining.
He's sure his promotion is long overdue,
That his techno-fixes just need refining.
The truth is he's always two degrees out –
He misses the moment and can't connect.
He's losing respect along with his clout
And his leadership skills have died of neglect.
When it comes to emotions, he's just not there.
You'd get more from a robot. He doesn't care.

WILLIAM AYOT

The Shadow Renegade is aloof and can exhibit a detached ideational arrogance, believing they alone see what needs to change and that others are blinkered and slow. Their refusal to participate in the collective and remain in their own world gives them an excuse not to have to defend their wacky stories. The compulsive eternal revolutionary knows exactly what is wrong with the world but has no practical ideas to fix it in the short term, only complaining about what is.

They may spend a lot of time alone but when in company the Shadow Renegade has endless opinions to share, usually more as a monologue than a dialogue, and often a rambling lecture of unproven facts. They can also show up as the misfit eccentric genius who is difficult for others to relate to. They can fit the stereotype of the nerd, with an unhealthy obsession for technology and an inability to notice or care about their unmatched socks.

To this Renegade being contrary can become essential and therefore hugely tiresome to co-workers, family members or partners. "I just don't fit in!" becomes an easy excuse to stop trying, because finding a compromise is seen as capitulating to the rotten system and "giving in to the man". Conspiracy theories are likely to arise here, often about the largest spheres, including cabals and secret world governments. This is partly because on a good day a Renegade will see unhelpful limitations of societal norms way before others do, but on a bad day their Shadow compulsion for radically alternative explanations can generate absurd, beyond-the-pale conjectures.

The Shadow Renegade is often emotionally disengaged from what they do, even when they are brilliant at it. They indulge in technological research or experiments without any regard for ethical or moral considerations. The end justifies the means even if it unleashes technology that cannot thereafter be tamed.

On a bad day they can become "rebels within their own cause" and sabotage their best ideas to change the world, often ignoring the need for any rules or structures that such an enterprise would require.

Alongside the genuinely innovative thinkers and future-wise geniuses destined to change the world, Shadow Renegades can be formed in childhoods steeped in non-conformity, where primary care-takers rejected societal norms. Such children are often raised to question and subvert authority and refuse to accept anyone else's rules on principle. The converse is also true: those constrained by excessive rules and imposed conformity early on will often decide that they will never be similarly constrained again. They then go out of their way to rebel against structures and the status quo as soon and as often as they can.

Too Much Transformer
Obsessive and Addicted to Change

DEATH WISH

Half of us think she's as mad as a hatter
The rest have her down as the pop-psych queen.
One day she's lost in some trivial matter,
The next she's a harpy, vindictive and mean.

Apart from her tiresome addiction to change,
Her vengeful edge and yearning for power,
Her behaviour is bordering on the strange –
She's growing more paranoid by the hour.
She sees folk watching her behind every door,
Imagines they wish her nothing but harm.
She's winning her battles but losing the war,
Distressing her friends and causing alarm.
Like a dictator she's harsh and unkind –
Worse, as a leader, she's ruthless but blind.

WILLIAM AYOT

The Shadow Transformer is obsessive, manipulative and can be power-hungry. They can use their deeper insights into the processes of life, death and rebirth to control situations and people. They will often mistrust others who have power and imagine all the harm that could be done, causing them to be like an "internal affairs detective", constantly digging deeper into others' psyches, motivations and drives. When they decide someone has betrayed their trust, they can become a powerful and punishing enemy.

In shadow, their ability to penetrate to the depths can become relentless and dictatorial. Once they have made up their mind they can stop listening to others and impose their will on all around them. They can miss the subtle signs of resistance and "double down" on their drive, often imagining unflattering comments are signs of disloyalty, or even a conspiracy against them.

Once they are set on a course of action, they move heaven and earth to make it so. They see no harm in stopping their old story in order to more effectively inhabit a new one. This can include departing from previously productive areas of work and study or even selling everything they have to get what they simply must have now. This can apply to both the most recent mystery they are compelled to explore and intense loving and/or sexual relationships.

Fascinated by change and obsessed with constantly questioning the ongoing value of what they just built up, they fail to understand why nothing seems rich or deep enough for long. However, they will not sit around and mope, but activate their inner drive to look for a new mystery, activity or person to investigate deeply – and so starts the cycle again.

The Shadow Transformer can become a compulsive navel-gazer, endlessly exploring their own psyche. They may go so deep into their inner world of pain and attempted healing that they find it hard to commune with others they judge as living brighter or more superficial lives. Thus, they can end up as the visiting shaman who lives outside a connected community, only engaging when there is deep healing required or a meaningful symbolic ritual to be held.

Paranoia can be an expression of the Shadow Transformer as well, obsessively thinking about who might be out to get them or take their power away. They assume they have unique insights into the psychology of what is going on under the surface. They believe that the naïve fools around them simply don't have the depth to see what weighs so heavily upon those doomed to carry the burden of insight.

Transformers are often wounded healers who have done their own work to heal themselves and now feel called to heal others. In their family and community of origin they may have understood the deeper and darker dynamics of what was going on. Such insights could have come at a cost to themselves because they didn't have the psychological acuity to process their experiences as they were exposed to circumstances way beyond their age. Conversely, a childhood which was relentlessly practical and externally action-focused, with no time or value given for inner work and the mysteries of life and death, may create the longing to dive deep in later life.

Too Much Warrior
Bullying and Destructive

OVERDRIVE

*"All tyranny needs to gain a foothold
is for people of good conscience to remain silent."*

EDMUND BURKE

*Hardly surprising they dubbed him Darth Vader,
That their office joke should become a given.
He was their Dark Lord, the Space Invader –
He drove them, hurt them and left them riven.
Some call brutality a lack of class,
Others see tyrants behind every desk –
But in the end, they couldn't let it pass,
His cornered fury was simply grotesque.
His need to win, to make losers squirm,
Caused endless departures and dismissals.
You reap what you sow when you lead a firm
And he left them with a harvest of thistles.
They say that a hammer sees nothing but nails.
Bully your people and everything fails.*

WILLIAM AYOT

Fire! (Ready, Aim...). When things don't work out as planned, the Shadow Warrior reacts quickly, and often with overwhelming force. If it does not fit, get a bigger hammer; when you are behind, step on the gas; when you sense a potential threat, strike first. Subtlety and disciplined action go out the window as the Shadow Warrior charges for the target, unconscious of the collateral damage they leave in their wake. They have a tendency to dehumanize the pursued as detaching from empathy allows them to give everything to the hunt. They can exploit opportunities without care for the human cost; ploughing the soil turns into careless natural resource destruction. Everything is about winning. However, the concept of win/win does not compute; they feel better when someone else visibly loses.

Under pressure, the Shadow Warrior can also become the bully who gets angry when things go wrong, picks on those apparently weaker and/or compulsively challenges others. They can be hard task-masters and constantly demand improved performance, without recognizing the demotivating effect this can have. While effective Warriors make for outstanding team players, Shadow Warriors compete against their own team. When asked to help colleagues, they think, "What's in it for me?" If the compulsion to win is extreme, they can even set others up to fail and/or actively sabotage them. They will jockey for position to get the best possible outcome for themselves, without any empathy for others who might deserve or need it more than they do.

The honourable defender can become an unscrupulous mercenary, willing to do whatever it takes to get the maximum reward, including cutting corners on safety and ethics. They can cheat because being first is more important than playing fair. Their reach usually exceeds their grasp. Living in overdrive, fighting on too many fronts simultaneously with an inability to know when to slow down, or how to stop, they can live on coffee and adrenaline – and may risk burnout. Yet Shadow Warriors rarely, if ever, ask for help and often demean others who do, judging it a sign of weakness. They therefore rarely notice when others get overstretched or overstressed.

This Warrior is often obsessed with developing fitness and exhibiting physical strength. Some have a significant sex drive and in relationships may prefer the thrill of the hunt to the intimacy of a long-term commitment.

The Shadow Warrior can emerge in a naturally competitive child proud of early visible high achievement who then applies that early learning to every area of later life. This can, of course, be reinforced and ramped up by competitive parents who implicitly or explicitly deliver the message that, "If you are not first, you are nothing!" The compensatory route can also be compulsive, often birthed by unambitious and unmotivated parents, who never seem to make anything happen for themselves. So, the child then either compulsively defends their family or strikes out on their own, determined to be successful no matter what.

Too Much Explorer
Restless and Preaching

MR MEGASTAR

Has anyone ever succeeded like Sonny?
His endless superlatives roll off his tongue.
His kids are sharper, more hip, more funny
Though his colleagues always remain unsung.
Boastful as a Viking in Valhalla
His bragging is always a little too loud –
He's quicker, he's braver, he's full of valour;
He's always the star with his audience wowed
While no one could dispute his vitality,
His zeal or his fervour, his lust for life,
There's a preachiness and a venality
That in the end breeds resentment and strife.
He's heading for a reckoning, there's no doubt.
When his bubble bursts we'd better watch out.

WILLIAM AYOT

The Shadow Explorer will take up too much space; they can be overbearing, loom over you, or just talk too loudly. They will have big ideas about the world and firmly believe that they have access to "The Truth". On a bad day, this can lead to preaching without listening. If not a particular religion, they are likely to be touting some philosophy or "ism" they feel called to spread widely, often inspired by a Thought Leader or Teacher they have studied. When an idea has them, they embrace it with a bear hug and don't let go – unless a bigger and better one comes along.

Shadow Explorers are endlessly restless, always scanning the horizon in search of something bigger and better. "Wondering through wandering" could be their motto. While questing, they may abandon all other commitments, including to family, friends and/or work colleagues. They prioritize their need for adventure over others' needs for stability and consistency. Perhaps, over that hill yonder, beyond that mountain, they will find the promised land. They give themselves endless permission to change their mind and go with the flow of the next adventure that calls them, often ignoring the emotional needs of those left behind.

"A rolling stone gathers no moss", and the Shadow Explorer lives (at least metaphorically) with a packed rucksack by the door, just in case... They can be compulsive "flitters", potentially ending up as a jack of all trades and master of none. They paint big pictures with a broad brush and often overlook the details. Then others have to take care of the details on their behalf and look out for the pitfalls that the Explorer does not see.

The Shadow Explorer can be tactless and inflate themselves with a grandiose sense of the importance of their ideas. They can be completely oblivious to another's pace and take over conversations without even noticing. They often boast and tell tall tales in a pompous way, exaggerating their adventures for impact. They may be relentlessly jovial, not noticing when others need a quieter space or tone in a conversation. They are prone to over-consume, and can expand their waistline along with their horizons, feeling unsatisfied no matter how much they take in. When "grow or die" is your motto, and it is taken literally, a person can end up huge. "Bigger is better!"

Next steps

At this point you should have a fairly clear idea of how you are likely to show up to others on a bad day. If you are still struggling, may we humbly suggest you phone a friend – or ask your family? They will usually be happy to help if you are struggling to come up with anything. When you are ready to face the music, in a self-reflective and gentle way of course, we invite you to fill out the self-assessment coming up next...

INTERMISSION:
Self-Assessment

We hope that your introduction to the Shadows of Too Much was insightful but not too painful. Now that you have a more detailed understanding of how all 10 Archetypes can show up when they are overplayed, we invite you to assess their likely impact on your Core Life and Current Work patterns.

A REMINDER OF THE SHADOWS OF TOO MUCH

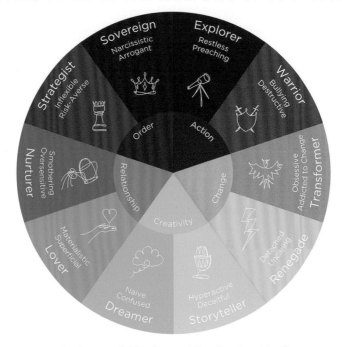

Archetypal Shadows Wheel – Too Much

It is most likely that the Shadows that get in your way will be those belonging to your Leading Actors, however some people realize that the biggest risk comes from a Major Supporting Actor, so we will include these here for you to consider as well.

Here is a summary of the key words associated with Too Much as an easy reminder. Please refer to it if helpful to complete the assessment below.

LEADERSHIP SHADOWS OF TOO MUCH – KEY WORDS

Sovereign
Too Much: Egotistic, Self-Centred, Narcissistic, Grandiose, Overpowering, Childish, Selfish, Ridiculing, Proud, Arrogant, Ostentatious, Haughty, Putting Others Down, Compulsively Centre Stage, "They can't do it without me"

Strategist
Too Much: Narrow-Minded, Closed, Unyielding, Inflexible, Inert, Depressive, Pessimistic, Over-Controlling, Stagnant, Leaden, Rule-Bound, Risk-Averse, Rank-Focused, "Don't reinvent the wheel", "Don't rock the boat"

Nurturer
Too Much: Compulsive Care-Taker, Overshares, Oversensitive, Smothering, Overprotective, Food Addict, Unnecessarily Repetitive, Excessively Emotive or Emotional, 'Over-Feeds', "They will always need my help", "They can't do it for themselves"

Lover
Too Much: Materialistic, Superficial, Backstabbing, Greedy, Gossipy, Ostentatious, Jealous, Flaunting, Sleazy, Gaudy, Fake, Money-Obsessed, Overly Flirtatious, "I can sell anything to anyone", "Nobody can resist me"

Dreamer

Too Much: Unrealistic, Vague, Confused, Escapist, 'Lost', Gullible, Indecisive, Ungrounded, Naïve, Uncertain, Unbounded, Fantastical, 'Head in the clouds', 'Pie in the sky', 'Castles in the air', "So many dreams, so little time"

Storyteller

Too Much: Scattered, Unpredictable, Hyperactive, Heady, Fickle, Sly, Speedy, Busybody, Tells Tall Tales, Deceitful, Peddling Misinformation, TMI (Too Much Information), Creates 'Fake News', Never Grows Up, Addicted to Communication and/or Social Media, "You can't have too many ideas"

Renegade

Too Much: Detached, Intellectual Arrogance, The Eternal Revolutionary, Misfit Genius, Overly Opinionated, Emotionally Absent, Uncaring, Robotic, Overly Eccentric, Contrary, Technology-Obsessed, "I just don't fit in!"

Transformer

Too Much: Manipulative, Relentless, Obsessive, Totalitarian, Change Addict, Power-Hungry, Pop Psychologist, Fascinated by Death, Compulsive Navel-Gazing, Conspiracy Theorist, Paranoid, Self-Destructive, Vindictive, Sadistic, "To be alive is to suffer"

Warrior

Too Much: Bully, Impatient, Aggressive, Intimidating, Furious, Raging, Destructive, Vicious, Explosive, Reactive, Winning at All Costs, Sore Loser, Looking for a Fight, Too Quick to Act, Pre-Emptive Strike, "Fire, Ready, Aim!"

Explorer

Too Much: Restless, Tactless, Greedy, Overbearing, Zealous, Preaching, Inflated, Obnoxious, Boasting, Too Big, Too Loud, Overlooking Details, Oblivious to Others' Pace, "Grow or die!", "My truth is right!", "Bigger is better"

Shadows of Too Much Assessment instructions

For your 2–3 Leading Actors, look through the key words for Too Much and self-assess which 1–3 words are closest to you on a bad day or when you are under pressure. Or come up with your own words that you recognize more. Do this for both your Core Life and Current Work Leading Actors. Then write them on the assessment below (or on separate notes if you prefer).

Repeat this for your 2–3 Major Supporting Actors, where it feels relevant and true. Do this for both Core Life and Current Work. Feel free to leave some lines blank if you do not recognize these as being true for you on a bad day or under stress.

SELF-ASSESSMENT: SHADOWS OF TOO MUCH

MY CORE LIFE SHADOWS TOO MUCH	MY CURRENT WORK SHADOWS TOO MUCH

Archetypes and key words I recognize as being true on a "bad day" or under pressure

Archetypes and key words I recognize as being true on a "bad day" or under pressure

Leading Actors (2-3)
(natural favourites)

Leading Actors (2-3)
(required daily and used most)

1) _____

1) _____

Key words: _____
_____

Key words: _____
_____

2) _____

2) _____

Key words: _____
_____

Key words: _____
_____

3) _____   3) _____

Key words: _____   Key words: _____

_____   _____

And if relevant to you: **And if relevant to you:**

Major Supporting Actors (2-3)   **Major Supporting Actors** (2-3)
(easy competency)   **(often required)**

1) _____   1) _____

Key words: _____   Key words: _____

_____   _____

2) _____   2) _____

Key words: _____   Key words: _____

_____   _____

3) _____   3) _____

Key words: _____   Key words: _____

_____   _____

If you find this assessment more difficult than the Gifts, you are not alone. Looking at our less-than-optimal sides often takes a good deal of honest self-awareness, and some of us will have less experience with this than others. If you want to check out whether your self-assessment here fits you, you can think about sharing it with a friend, trusted confidant or coach and get their feedback. We all have Shadows but sometimes it is easier for others to see them than for us to recognize them. However, Shadows are often a major stimulation that our clients use to motivate their archetypal development intention. So, the good news is that whatever problems an overplayed Leading Actor may be causing now, there is a remedy, often in one of your lesser used Archetypes.

We turn now to the opposite pole, the Shadow of Too Little.

CHAPTER 8

ARCHETYPAL SHADOWS OF
Too Little

It is relatively easy to recognize that you can have Too Much of a good thing. It can be harder to recognize the cost of having Too Little. But, seeing with an archetypal eye, this also has a significant impact on life and work. Given that every Archetype has a unique set of Gifts and productive behaviours, when we have little or no access to a particular Archetype we show up with a gap in our potentially full spectrum of choice. This gap will manifest as another set of behaviours and attitudes, demonstrably different from the Shadows of Too Much. For clarity, there is much more likelihood of you exhibiting the Shadows of Too Little in your lesser used Archetypes – your Minor Supporting and More Offstage Actors. These Shadows tend to create a different blind spot from those of Too Much. With Too Much we will often imagine that we are still using Gifts that we are proud of and do not notice when we start over-using them. With Too Little we often do not recognize the Gifts that lesser used Actors could offer – and therefore do not call on them appropriately.

The overview of all 10 is below, with more details to follow.

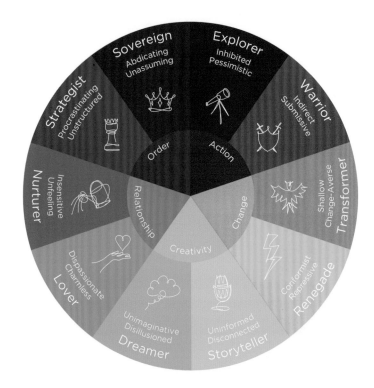

Archetypal Shadows Wheel – Too Little

Headline overview

Order: Too Little Sovereign will show up as Abdicating or Unassuming, while Too Little Strategist is Procrastinating or Unstructured.

Relationship: Too Little Nurturer will come across as Insensitive or Unfeeling and Too Little Lover as Dispassionate or Charmless.

Creativity: Too Little Dreamer appears as Unimaginative or Disillusioned and Too Little Storyteller as Uninformed or Confused.

Change: Too Little Renegade will tend towards being Conformist or Repressive and Too Little Transformer being Shallow or Afraid of Change.

Action: Too Little Warrior presents as Indirect or Submissive and Too Little Explorer as Inhibited or Pessimistic.

How Shadows of Too Little develop

The origins of these Shadows are similar to the Shadows of Too Much and the two are often complementary. For example, an excess of Warrior will often be complemented by a lack of Nurturer. Natural Gifts and rewarded behaviours that tempt us into the Shadows of Too Much in our Leading Actors also result in the Shadows of Too Little in our More Offstage Actors.

Initiating impulses for these Shadows also vary. Most obviously, some of us don't use certain Archetypes just because others felt "more like me" and were more personally rewarding in earlier life. This would be especially the case when these same Archetypes were externally validated by significant others.

In addition, a lack of modelling can lead to a similar outcome. For example, without positive experiences of Warrior energies that validate their useful application in life, we may assume that any direct attempts to assert ourselves are overly aggressive – and are therefore to be avoided.

Others among us will have had formative times in life where certain Archetypes were deliberately ignored or were judged negatively by authority figures. Some behaviours associated with specific Archetypes may also have been actively punished. For example, a child who naturally enjoys day-dreaming may have trouble focusing on maths homework. Strict parents may have punished this tendency, thereby inadvertently devaluing the Dreamer and potentially limiting their child's later access to it. A subtler version of such messaging can occur when a child witnesses another being punished for certain behaviours: "I had better not do any of *that*!"

An inner felt need to compensate can be another cause of the Shadow of Too Little. The originating impulse for a young adult to be meek and submissive could be a total lack of effective Warrior energy around them. It can also be a reaction to being around a visible bully, whether at home, in school or in local neighbourhoods. When we see and feel the negative impact of Too Much of a certain archetypal behavioural pattern, it is only a small step to make the inner decision to avoid those behaviours. That very determination to avoid Too Much then guides us (often unconsciously) into Too Little.

Now going deeper

To explore these Shadows further we will start each Archetype with a short poem to give a brief felt sense of the dangers of the lack. We follow this with some examples of possible impacts which may allow you to notice if these tendencies are true for you. And then some likely origins that may help you recognize if you had a similar or related experience in your upbringing. We use a combination of third-person sentences and first-person narratives. The latter offer examples of statements typically reflective of the mindsets and assumptions that keep certain Archetypes further away from your core.

In an intermission, we will invite you to assess these Shadows of Too Little and the potential costs to your life and working practices. This will be our final prompt to take us into the chapters on Archetypal Development.

Too Little Sovereign
Abdicating and Unassuming

FISHER KING

Dull-eyed and listless, he stares at the wall,
His kingdom taken and the crown of power
Rolling away into a corner – he moans –

Pay heed to me stranger… I lost my kingdom…
Worse, I was afraid of the king in the mirror…

WILLIAM AYOT

When we shy away from the Sovereign, we will tend to turn down opportunities to be centre stage and opt for supporting rather than leading roles. Such people often fear that they will not meet the expectations of a visible role and so prefer the shade. They have little obvious ambition, vision or purpose and often internalize a mindset that wonders, "Who am I to make a difference?"

These people are unassuming, seem to lack life force and can come across as dull, apathetic or lethargic. Their low energy is often matched by low self-esteem. For some, this is caused by a lack of will, for others by a lack of courage. Often these folks fear putting their head above the parapet, lest they become a target. They try to live quietly and under the radar. "Don't pick me" and "Don't pick on me" are subliminal messages they send into the world.

The Sovereign-less prefer to be followers rather than leaders. They can be prone to manipulation by others because they often attach themselves to someone else's power, hoping – often unconsciously – that this will empower them as well. Others may lead relatively solo lives, hiding their light and denying the world their true gifts.

One origin of these tendencies would be natural gifts associated with other Archetypes that require little or no visibility. Another could be formative years surrounded by people with little or no ambition. Conversely, if primary influences modelled entitled narcissism this could lead a child to Sovereign aversion in later life.

Too Little Strategist
Procrastinating and Unstructured

THE CRAZY WATCHMAKER

A hundred promises, every one broken,
And the crazy watchmaker adding to the wreck,
Ignoring the chaos of cogs and springs –

It's a bit of a mess... but I'm sure I can fix it...
Maybe tomorrow... It'll all come together.

WILLIAM AYOT

Remind you of anyone? How about this more extended first-person narrative, in the appropriate manner, as someone with Too Little Strategist talks on the phone with a friend before a trip:

"Hi there, no I didn't finish the visa application yet. Hey, no worries, I'll get to it eventually; life is too important to waste chasing deadlines. Look, I'm out of money again, I don't know how that happened, can you lend me some for the trip? Just need to remember where I put my passport before we leave... My next steps plan? Well, there are so many opportunities out there, it

seems too hard to pick only one, go with the flow, right? I'm sure my dream job will show up soon... I know I have said that before... OK, maybe a few times before... OK, maybe I have said it for years, but look on the bright side, one of these days it's got to come true! ... Nah, the finance training was so boring, I quit – well, I didn't exactly deregister but I did stop attending which is the same thing, surely?... What?! You think they're still charging me, the bastards! I'll sue 'em!... What contract? Hah, never keep those things, what's the point, it's not like I'm ever going to read it, all that small print is bad for the eyes. Just need to grab a doughnut... Nah, I stopped counting calories, it just put me off eating and where's the fun in that? Listen, the phone is running out of battery and I've lost my charger, got to go..."

As we move through this chapter, you may notice that the Shadow of Too Little of some Archetypes can present similarly to the Shadows of Too Much of other Archetypes, and sometimes a mix of several. For example, Too Little Strategist can show up similarly to elements of Too Much Dreamer, Storyteller or Renegade.

Those with Too Little Strategist will tend to prioritize freedom over structure, going with the flow over detailed planning. But when all of these become habitual, the lack of Strategist can exact a heavy cost. We may compulsively change paths before completing any route or task. We may simply not see how the lack of structure or rules impedes effective progress.

This habit will often start early in life, born perhaps from a natural enjoyment in doing our own thing or from a wilful rejection of others' structures. A disorganized home life or instinctively rebellious parents or neighbourhood can seed a later distrust of organization; as can an overly strict schedule and a rigidly imposed set of rules that are then rejected later on.

Too Little Nurturer
Insensitive and Unfeeling

ONWARDS AND UPWARDS

Thin as a rake, a bundle of energy,
She's running on empty yet diamond hard.
No give in this one, just raw desire –

Don't talk to me about needing anyone...
Feelings are for losers... I'm fine on my own...

WILLIAM AYOT

Too Little Nurturer can often turn into a perverse badge of honour in families where success is prioritized over intimacy and in organizational cultures that pride themselves on being lean and mean. Many leadership teams recognize this as a key development area if they are to continue success but avoid burnout. Having coached many successful leaders who identified this as a More Offstage Actor, we have found a general mindset that accompanies this stance. It is summarized by the sequence of sentences below, many of which have been spoken to us in coaching sessions over the years. If the Nurturer is a More Offstage Actor for you too, maybe you recognize a couple of these:

Feelings are overrated, they don't help me get the job done, they don't put money in the bank – so why bother?

I don't ask for help; I don't need to. When the going gets tough, the tough get going. I pull my own socks up and get on with it, no time to sit around feeling sorry for myself.

I'm fine by myself, a good movie or book will do me most nights, if I've got time to relax after all the work is done... which it never is by the way. I don't have time for lots of social events, all that endless and pointless chit-chat, talking to people you probably won't like and who you are never going to see again anyway, trying to figure out if they have got a better job or a bigger house than you, total waste of time and energy.

Sure, I go to occasional family gatherings, but they are only marginally better than a trip to the dentist, aren't they? All those childhood stories we know by heart, endless nostalgia about the good old times. And those songs they insist on singing, do they have any idea how off tune they are?!

And in the workplace, come on! Emotions only get in the way; we are here to do a job, not sit around and talk about how sad someone is. They are probably sad, frankly, because they are doing a shit job, because they spend all their time talking and whining about not being happy!

If I do feel sad, which is very rarely, I give myself a large drink and a good talking to, that pretty much fixes it. That or a trip to the gym to work off the stress. Look, I'm pretty busy, so can we cut this short...?

The lack of Nurturer often results from overplaying the Archetypes of Change and Action. It can also be a more general symptom of the fast-paced and externally focused world we currently live in. Other origins can include Action-biased care-takers whose priorities we internalized or, conversely, over-nurturing care-takers whose tendency to smother we later rejected.

Too Little Lover
Dispassionate and Charmless

CAPTAIN, O CAPTAIN

Ungainly captain of the awkward squad,
Cut off from beauty and her lovely sisters,
He has no magnificence, no style, no grace –

We don't do charm... No one likes me anyway...
When last I heard, this was still a business...

WILLIAM AYOT

The Shadow of Too Little Lover often appears as unfriendly and unresponsive, even cold and distant. These people find it hard to show affection and often have difficulty welcoming it from others. They may avoid eye contact and find it difficult to relax into a friendly hug. An old joke from Finland describes the massive difference between an introvert and an extrovert: "The introvert looks at their shoes when they're talking to you; the extrovert looks at *your* shoes when they're talking to you..."

Some with minimized Lover have few if any natural social graces to offer, while others refuse to turn on the charm to ease social interaction, believing it to be fake or superficial. Another visible manifestation of Too Little Lover appears in clothing and grooming choices. Some see themselves as sensible dressers, but others see them as styleless or unkempt. Unaware of fashion trends and unwilling to make an effort, even for special occasions, they argue, "I showed up, didn't I?"

Such people tend to be uninterested in gossip and downplay the value of tuning into the grapevine. They end up out of the loop on the many human undercurrents of relationship in life and work.

Too Little Lover and people tend to prioritize function over form. So, shopping becomes a necessary chore, a targeted hunt for a needed item, and browsing an indulgent waste of time. These folks often believe they cannot "sell" and distrust those wanting to sell to them. They may enjoy art only for practical learning and not for its own sake. Living spaces can be bare or cluttered with "useful" stuff, lacking style and taste. Food is fuel rather than a tempting offering. Money and wealth may be held in subtle contempt and luxuries frowned upon. In committed partnerships with little Lover access there may be more a feeling of sibling co-habitation than passionate intimacy. Work may also be fairly joyless; something that pays the bills but with little or no heart and soul in it.

Those brought up with a strict work ethic may find the Lover hard to enjoy, especially in its more subtle forms of appreciative consciousness and the relishing of beauty for its own sake. The habitually task-driven may not know when to lift their heads up and smell the roses. An austere childhood could ingrain this too, as could a reaction against extravagant, money-obsessed or over-sexualized parents.

Too Little Dreamer
Unimaginative and Disillusioned

DREAMLESSNESS

Dried out, empty, shoulder to the world,
A sad woman locked in a cold grey room,
Sifting the ashes of her unsung songs –

Don't talk to me of dreams or imaginings...
I tried it... Believe me... visions turn to dust...

WILLIAM AYOT

While the cost of Too Much Dreaming is not getting enough done, the cost of Too Little is often a life without imagination and/or inspiration:

> *Look, if I can't measure it, it's not real. I don't see the point in having any illusions in my life, I refuse to put credence in anything I can't touch, taste, smell or see.*

> *I know what I know, and I am not going to take someone else's word for it. I like to know where I stand, and I like to stand on solid ground, follow me?*

> *All that fairy tale superstitious nonsense peddled by religions and faith healers and the like; I mean, how gullible do they think people are? Mind you, the weak-willed fall for it every time; they can't wait to believe that someone else walked on water, and when they try it themselves and nearly drown, they blame themselves for "not believing enough" – gimme a break!*

> *When did poetry put food on the table? I wrote a poem once, at school, they made me do it for a creative writing class. I wrote, "My name is Billy and this is silly!", got a C and didn't get asked again.*

> *And what's it all got to do with work? I mean, coming up with alternative practical solutions to a problem is one thing, but creative imagination is just day-dreaming with a fancy name – total waste of time and energy.*

> *Life presents us with real problems every day and that's where I put my focus – on being practical, getting things done and getting through to the end of the day without making a bad mistake. Look, I've got a budget meeting to go to... I need to get on.*

A natural gift for logic and practical application can lead to a minimization of Dreamer access. This can also be reinforced when evidence-based learning is judged as the *only* valid way to form opinions worthy of consideration. Compensatory causes can include formative years around significant others obsessed with artistic or spiritual fantasies, or who over-consumed drugs and alcohol. Both may naturally lead one to a later reaction against pushing the edge beyond the sensible, the measurable and the real.

Too Little Storyteller
Uninformed and Disconnected

JACK THE LACK

A tad confused – like the lad in the tale
Who gave his magical beans away –
He stands at the edge of the conversation.

You go ahead... You're the clever one...
It's all a riddle... What d' you mean, beans?

WILLIAM AYOT

Those with little or no access to the Storyteller are likely to come across as uninformed, confused and not "switched on". They feel out of the loop and in our era of 24-hour news they can feel lost; like a deaf person who cannot read lips at a party.

Too Little Storyteller and people lack curiosity. They are unlikely to open themselves up to new ideas or theories, especially those outside of their comfort zone. They may take pride in being simple, straightforward and "down to earth folk" but fail to recognize the downside of mental apathy. As if the brain has been tuned only to one or two favoured channels and ignores the many others available. They may have skills and knowledge passed on from others and/or drawn from common sense but lack wisdom, subtlety and finesse. They can then come across as simple or blunt and heavy-handed, with little or no dexterity. Without a regular exchange of ideas, they become single-minded and inflexible, not because they are stubborn or particularly fixed but rather because they don't explore other possibilities or see other viable options.

Being uncritical in their own thinking, they are unlikely to rigorously analyse the thoughts of others, simply accepting them as Right (if they fit their pre-formed opinions) or Wrong (if they differ). Such people often ingest the opinions of those they give authority to; whether parents, peer group, bosses, religious or political figures.

Lacking the ability to logically and objectively analyse the opinions and motivations of others, the Storyteller-challenged can be duped. They make easy prey for the clever trickster-type Storyteller who outwits them, spins them a yarn or fools them, whether into believing fake news, making unneeded purchases or unwise investments.

As always, causes will vary; perhaps a bruising education experience that left them feeling unintelligent, or a natural aptitude for physical ability that was favoured over mental agility. Perhaps uninformed parents or a small-town mentality with a constricted world view. A more compensatory origin could be a reaction against care-givers who had Too Much Storyteller: yarn-spinners, born liars or hyperactive tricksters.

Too Little Renegade
Conformist and Repressive

CONFORMIST

Afraid of change as much as the darkness,
He'll doggedly keep to the safe and narrow.
Ideas are dangerous to him, subversive –

Things were better in the good old days...
I don't want to know... What the hell was that?

WILLIAM AYOT

Those with Too Little Renegade tend to conform to how others see and shape the world and often lack a sense of their uniqueness. Their habituated voices of inhibition stop them from moving fast to seize unexpected opportunities. These people often fail to recognize when "The times they are a 'changin'" or see the need for occasional radical renewal when things get stale. If you ask them to contribute disruptive ideas to a project or a plan, you may get a blank stare, as if the very idea does not compute. Others may then label them "stuck in their ways" or even boring; "Don't rock the boat".

When something unexpected happens, and these things invariably do, those with Too Little Renegade feel unprepared, easily shaken and/or fearful. When things get too modern for them, in other words, when history progresses, especially at the ever-increasing rate of change of today, they can become reactionary. They may be overheard waxing lyrically over an old way of life seen through rose-tinted glasses: "It was so much better back in the day when..." These attitudes, however, are not in the service of preserving the essence of the past (which can be a gift of the Nurturer) but rather about resisting the essence of the emerging future. They therefore tend to lose touch and slowly fall behind when teams, institutions and society at large is in any kind of evolutionary leap – as appears to be the case in our time. As we witness the proliferation of the World Wide Web, social networking and artificial intelligence, it is clear to many archetypal thinkers that the 21st century has already been, and will continue to be, shaped by overt Renegade energy. Lack of access to the Renegade at this point in history may come at a heavy price. Yet, ironically, in the vast majority of leadership teams we have worked with, it is repeatedly a least favourite Archetype.

Little or no Renegade often goes hand in hand with some form of technophobia, as all technology evolves quickly and in tandem with the radical shifts in the zeitgeist. The Renegade-challenged may judge early adopters as over-eager to chase the latest fad and so they will wait as long as they can until reluctantly becoming, by default, "the adopters of last resort". And as in work, so in life...

So, causes? Over-Controlling care-givers and educators can train and sometimes even beat the "inner rebel" out of a child before its potential value is seen or recognized. Alternatively, early experiences of radical change or being around revolutionary impulses can unsettle a child so much that the rest of life is spent avoiding change and looking for that missing stability.

Too Little Transformer
Shallow and Change-Averse

SMALL CONSOLATION

Wary of the dark and mysterious stranger
with his air of melancholy, his whiff of death,
She clings to the consolations of the light.

Don't go there... Be careful... You could get hurt...
There's no need for change... Let sleeping dogs lie...

WILLIAM AYOT

Those who avoid the Transformer often do so to save themselves discomfort and effort in the short term but may sacrifice self-awareness, depth and access to life wisdom in the long term. If the mysteries of life, and death, regeneration and rebirth are consistently denied we can end up living a very shallow and self-protected existence.

I don't go in for much self-analysis – why would I want to go over to the Dark Side, I like the light just fine.

Sure, we all have problems, but I don't like to look into them much, just get on with the day job and forget about it. Something good will happen eventually so you won't have to think about the bad anymore.

Keep things simple and straightforward. Don't go digging in the past and picking at scabs. It's only going to get depressing, and what's the point of that?

And at work, all those feedback loops just get in the way; we all have our grumbles with fellow workers but no need to share it with the person directly. I usually keep it to myself and stay well away from those I judge as difficult. Or sometimes I have a good gripe about them around the coffee station at breaks or down the pub. Just letting off steam, where's the harm in that? No point in saying what I really think and starting a row.

I don't go to funerals much, I don't want to be around all that grief and distress. I prefer to remember people as they were when they were happy, and we were having a laugh and a drink together.

Onwards and upwards, that's my motto. As long as your parents put a roof over your head till you left home, they must have done a good job, no?

Arguably, the deepest thought we can have as human beings is that life ends in death, in ultimate transformation, and that everything eventually comes to an end. For those with More Offstage Transformers, this sobering fact rarely enters their awareness. The failure to embrace transitions as a natural part of life can lead others to see them as uninitiated and naïve. These people tend to see little or no value even in the concepts of change and transformation.

While at first glance this could appear as a happy enough, if narrow, life, this is not really true. Contained long-term innocence is rarely bliss. Those who ignore underlying motivations in self or others can become impulsive and naïve. Those who refuse to examine significant past emotional events can be easily triggered and fragile. With little capacity to read beyond the surface, they can fall victim to controlling predators of all sorts.

At some point in life, death will enter. Either in the literal sense, when a loved one passes on, or metaphorically when something we rely on ends, like a long-term job or relationship. At such times, the Transformerless are ill equipped to cope. Being pain-averse and challenge-avoidant they go through life much like a shallow boat drifts on the water without the benefit of a keel. With depth comes stability.

Growing up around others who were afraid of change and avoided the depths of things can lead us to internalize and replicate this in later life. Alternatively, early experiences of constant change and upheaval can teach us to avoid these later on. In some cases, children can be especially sensitive to mysteries and energy fields that their primary care-givers do not understand or even fear, thereby teaching the child to repress these early Transformer Gifts.

Too Little Warrior
Indirect and Submissive

MR NICE-GUY

Can't take the push-back. Won't play it straight.
A glance with an edge would blow him away...
Kind but defeated, he can't speak to power –

After you... I insist... No really, after you...
Never put your head above the parapet...

WILLIAM AYOT

With little or no Warrior, people tend to be ineffective – albeit harmless for the most part. They often present themselves (unconsciously) as an easy target, even a pushover for those with more capacity for assertion. Unlike a pacifist who has an active conviction that fighting is wrong, these folks have no fight in them. They feel weak, fragile and/or submissive. No matter how much they are stirred or provoked they do not stand up for themselves (or others) and offer little or no assertive response to the actual provocation. If they do say a straight "no", it will be a quiet one and others may sense they mean "not really" or "not yet". They do not appreciate being challenged to perform quickly, publicly or at consistently high levels. Any ambitious initiative put before them is likely met with a quiet sigh of resignation. They tend to be highly risk-averse. Like a hare that is perpetually alert to any possible danger, this person is quiet – yet you get the impression that you could startle them with the drop of a pin.

These fuzzy edges often translate into language and speech too, where the Warrior-less are unable to be sharp and to the point. They might talk around what they see as important, but decisiveness evades them. The lack of Warrior means the target is rarely their focus.

These people rarely put themselves forward to be the vanguard in big or important tasks. This is one reason why they are frequently passed over for promotion.

Some of us are born naturally quiet, but as the old bumper sticker has it (in response to the biblical tenet that "the meek shall inherit the earth"), "The meek won't want it!" Growing up around people in a submissive home, community or culture can imbed this habit through later life. Especially when those environs lacked means or courage to stand up and be counted in the face of a threat. On the other hand, over-aggressive Warrior energy closer to or even in the home will often foster a nascent pacifist mentality later on. Others may have been taught that "nice is right" and had more competitive or forceful impulses trained out of them, leaving them unable to recognize "the price of nice".

Too Little Explorer
Inhibited and Pessimistic

HOME-BODY

Mountains unclimbed and oceans uncrossed,
A thousand forests and prairies unseen –
She shuts her eyes and says "no" to adventure.

I don't think I could... I wouldn't enjoy it...
Call me old-fashioned but I like what I like...

WILLIAM AYOT

Those with More Offstage Explorers can live in an artificially shrunken world, with no reach beyond the trusted and the familiar. Such people tend to come across as small-minded and inhibited. They can feel constricted, both to themselves and to others, a shrinking violet in a small pot in the shade.

Apparent shyness can also mask a lack of happiness and no zest for life. There is little expansion, grandeur or joy. The Explorer-challenged can be closed, cynical, lack humour and generally refuse themselves the good things in life.

The Explorer-averse do not comprehend why others suggest that they are missing out on new lands, cultures, foods and/or ideas. These folks avoid experiences and education that might grow them. Usually more rooted in pessimism than depression, they do not believe that the grass could be greener somewhere else. They imagine negative consequences and want to stay put.

Some of us naturally grow up with smaller possibility spheres and more limited circles of expansion. Some are genuinely happy with what they have and where they are, choosing to stay in the town where they were born, or go into a family business rather than exploring a path of their own. Others have inherited this mindset which can be based on fear. Whether fear of the unknown, or of failure. Alternatively, some may have experienced so much restless exploration and endless quests in early life that all they yearn for is the settled and safe enough limits of a narrow horizon later on.

Next steps

Now you have the full set of Shadow potentials in your awareness, Too Much *and* Too Little. Both will affect you, your efficacy in life, and both have potentially negative impacts on others. The more you become aware of your Shadows, the more you can mitigate against them and choose to develop out of them. We now invite you to complete the Too Little Self-Assessment.

INTERMISSION:
Self-Assessment

Shadows of Too Little

We hope that your introduction to the Shadows of Too Little was thought-provoking. Now that you have a more detailed understanding of how all 10 Archetypes can show up when they are underplayed, we invite you to assess the likely impact of this both for your Core Life and Current Work patterns.

A REMINDER OF THE SHADOWS OF TOO LITTLE

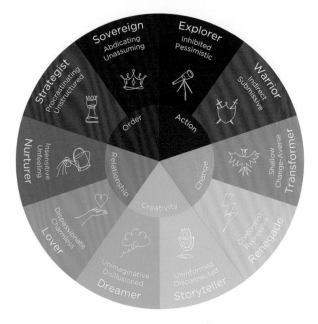

Archetypal Shadows Wheel – Too Little

It is most likely that the Shadows of Too Little that have a cost to you will belong to your More Offstage Actors, however some people realize that the biggest cost comes from not using a Minor Supporting Actor enough. So, we will include both here for you to consider.

Here is a summary of the words associated with Too Little. Please refer to it if it is helpful to complete the assessment below.

LEADERSHIP SHADOWS OF TOO LITTLE – KEY WORDS

Sovereign
Too Little: Apathetic, Weak, Uncentred, Dull, Dispirited, Unassuming, Lethargic, Lifeless, Low Energy, Abdicating, No Vision, Repressed Ambition, Low Self-Esteem, "Who am I to make a difference?"

Strategist
Too Little: Unrealistic, Impractical, Unstructured, Disorganized, Undisciplined, Scattered, Procrastinating, Always Late, Never Completes, Misses Deadlines, "I'll get to it eventually"

Nurturer
Too Little: Unfeeling, Insensitive, Lonely, Isolated, Numb, Undernourished, Unable to Slow Down, Lack of Self-Care, Emotionally Absent, Missing Instincts, "Feelings are overrated", "I don't ask for help"

Lover
Too Little: Styleless, Money-Phobic, Unaffectionate, Charmless, Unfriendly, Dispassionate, Frosty, Few Social Graces, No Eye for Beauty, Unresponsive, "I can't sell", "I'm not desirable"

Dreamer
Too Little: Unimaginative, Dry, Disillusioned, Dense, Dispassionate, Non-Believer, Limited Mindset, Unable to Visualize, No 'Inner Music', Can't Imagine Competing Views of the Future, "If I can't measure it, it's not real"

Storyteller
Too Little: Uncritical, Confused, Uninformed, Ignorant, Inflexible, Outwitted, Single-Minded, Lacks Mental Confidence, Feels Less Intelligent, Literal, Slow to Catch On, 'Out of the Loop', "Wait, I don't get it!"

 Renegade
Too Little: No Ideas, Conformist, Boring, Repressive, Change-Resistant, Afraid of The Unexpected, Lacking Creativity, Technophobic, Not Curious, Living in The Past, "There's nothing wrong with the old way!"

 Transformer
Too Little: Shallow, Change-Resistant, Uninitiated, Naïve, Simplistic, Gullible, Avoidant, Pain-Averse, Afraid of Death, Takes Things at Face Value, Unable to 'See Through', "Don't open a can of worms"

 Warrior
Too Little: Victim, Pushover, Weakling, Indirect, Quiet, Hesitant, Submissive, Undefended, Cowardly, 'Limp', Fearful, Too Nice, Risk-Averse, Low Energy, Playing It Safe, "I'm keeping my head down"

 Explorer
Too Little: Pessimistic, Inhibited, Hopeless, Constricted, Joyless, Cynical, Naïve, Narrow-Minded, Unfulfilled Potential, Missing The Big Picture, Stay-At-Home 'Local Yokel', "I'm only safe with what I know"

Shadows of Too Little Assessment instructions

1) For your 2-3 **More Offstage Actors**, look through the key above and self-assess which 1-3 words are closest to naming the cost to you for *not* having access to this Archetype. Or, come up with your own words that you recognize more. Do this for both Core Life and Current Work. Then write them on the assessment below (or on separate notes if you prefer).

2) Repeat this for your 2-3 **Minor Supporting Actors** if these feel relevant or true. Do this for both Core Life and Current Work. Feel free to leave some lines blank if you do not recognize any of these costs as being relevant or true for you.

SELF-ASSESSMENT: SHADOWS OF TOO MUCH

MY CORE LIFE SHADOWS TOO LITTLE	MY CURRENT WORK SHADOWS TOO LITTLE

Archetypes and key words I recognize as a cost to me for not using them (much)

Archetypes and key words I recognize as a cost to me for not using them (much)

More Offstage Actors (2-3) **(lesser used)**

More Offstage Actors (2-3) **(rarely if ever required)**

1) _____

Key words: _____

_____

1) _____

Key words: _____

_____

2) _____

Key words: _____

_____

2) _____

Key words: _____

_____

3)_____

Key words: _____

_____

3)_____

Key words: _____

_____

Minor Supporting Actors (2-3)
(earned competency)

1) _____

Key words: _____

_____

2)_____

Key words: _____

_____

3)_____

Key words: _____

_____

Minor Supporting Actors (2-3)
(occasionally required)

1) _____

Key words: _____

_____

2)_____

Key words: _____

_____

3)_____

Key words: _____

_____

If you find this assessment difficult you can share it with a friend, trusted confidant or coach and get their feedback. There is a cost to all of us when we do not have easy access to a particular Archetype. For some, this is simply a matter of having other priorities. It may be easily remedied as soon as we notice the absence and pay attention to it. For others, there may be an aversion to a particular Archetype that has become deeply ingrained over time – and this will take longer to overcome.

We have now completed our journey through Part One. When you are ready, it is time to turn towards Part Two. You may already have a sense of which parts of your current archetypal patterns could use a shift, or you may simply be interested to discover how you can develop Archetypes at a later date. Read on!

Part Two

EXPANDING YOUR REPERTOIRE

CHAPTER 9

HOW TO USE
Part Two

"It's easier to act your way into a new way of thinking, than think your way into a new way of acting."

JERRY STERNIN

Overview

Part One allows you to understand and access your current archetypal patterns in life and work. Part Two gives you the ways and means *to evolve your story, one character at a time*. It will help you expand your archetypal repertoire to become future-fit by changing your relationship with one or more Archetypes. We hope that you feel well grounded in understanding the Archetypes' Gifts and Shadows. We will now present multiple options for development: both *what* you choose to develop and *how* you choose to develop it.

You may already have an idea of what would be a useful development path for you, or you may want to wait until you have read all the options. Many people meeting the Archetypes for the first time look to their More

Offstage Actors as opportunities to expand their potential, the equivalent of "adding a string to your bow". Others are drawn to minimizing the impact of their Leading Actors' Shadows of Too Much. You can also choose to develop further gifts within a Leading Actor.

If, however, your current archetypal patterns are working optimally for you in both life and work, first, congratulations! Secondly, you may choose to use Part Two more as a helpful reference guide for the future, awaiting a time when an archetypal shift would serve.

In this chapter we will provide an overview of the development choices ahead. We explore the different time frames you can choose. We explain the background of the rehearsal practices that will activate these choices. We summarize the essence of all Part Two chapters and end by focusing on the methods contained in the chapters on Developing the Five Realms (Order, Relationship, Creativity, Change and Action).

Three development approaches

We will first make a distinction between *Horizontal Development, Horizontal Integration* and *Vertical Development*.

Horizontal Development is a move *across* the Archetype Circle from a Leading Actor to a lesser used one. This move can help you address and mitigate any of the Shadows that you have noticed get in your way. This tends to be the most popular approach and can get visible results quickly.

Horizontal Integration is a move *within* a Leading Actor that you are ambivalent about. If you noticed when filling out the Gifts Self-Assessment that you have easy access to some gifts of a particular Archetype but a reaction against others in that same Archetype, this could be an interesting inquiry and development approach for you.

Vertical Development is a move *upwards* to evolve a current Leading Actor in order to access its emerging potential. This move can help you refine your current gifts and discover their leading-edge benefits. This is more of a long-term inquiry and tends to suit those who have already done a lot of development and integration work in their lives to date.

For the rest of this chapter and the following five chapters on developing each Realm, we focus on the most effective methods to enable and enhance **Horizontal Development**. Horizontal Integration and Vertical Development are addressed more fully in Chapters 17 and 18.

A note on repetition

In Part Two there are several places where we repeat exact (or very similar) phrasings and words. This was an editorial choice because not all readers will read the book back to back but instead jump to areas relevant to their personal interests and needs. If, for example, the reader makes use of Appendix 3 and follows the development of a particular Archetype, if the repetitions had been omitted the reader would have ended up missing crucial information.

It is not necessary to read all the information in Part Two in one sitting or in a linear manner. It is entirely possible for you to pick only the material you feel drawn to at this time and then to return at different times to add more.

Horizontal Development – Acting-In your desired future

You may be tempted to wonder if it is really possible to develop an Archetype outside of your comfort zone. But we can assure you, after our combined 65 years of working with Archetypes, that it is only a question of *how*, not *if*. Essentially, using our theatre metaphor, you can learn to play any "character" (Archetype), as long as you are willing to rehearse it. Or, as we prefer to say, *Act It In*. By doing we become, by acting we make it real. Engaging in activities, practices and behaviours naturally associated with a less favoured Archetype enables us to develop more familiarity with it. This is the same process an actor uses to rehearse a new role. Eventually, we feel at home embodying the new attributes and behaviours that may have felt foreign or "not like me" beforehand. We can become what we intend *if* we are willing to rehearse and "Act It In". This is not so much about "faking it till you make it" but rather about practising to ready yourself for effective performance.

Please remember the basic premise that all 10 Archetypes are available to everyone as a human birth right. They combine to create the inner repertoire available to each of us. All of them will play a part in our lives, whether we appreciate them or not, and even though we will inhabit some more than others. Back in the Introduction, we referenced the Jungian concept that what you do not make conscious shows up in your life as fate. Taking responsibility for building conscious relationships with all 10 Archetypes over time is therefore a way to build your own agency and to be better prepared for whatever surprises life may offer you.

Combining Archetypes for effective Horizontal Development: Hybrid Roles

However, it is clear that old habitual patterns in people are likely to remain in place for a while, even after we recognize they may have outlived their usefulness. It is, for example, unrealistic to expect that someone who has spent 20 years as a driven Warrior can morph into a convincingly warm Nurturer by reading a few chapters in a book. After an archetypal development programme, even the most hardened Warrior may realize the value of looking after their people and generously decide to take a big bag of croissants into work the next day. The likelihood is that their people will take the croissants, wait till the Warrior has left the room, roll their eyes and say, "They've been on a course!" And then, "Don't worry, they'll get over it soon!" True to form, that Warrior is liable to cut everyone's lunch breaks as soon as the pressure mounts and they revert to type. This is because they have registered an intention but not rehearsed it enough and "Acted It In" in a way that enables the learning to stick.

We have found that realistic and effective Horizontal Development is therefore generally *not* about suddenly leaving behind a Leading Actor and quickly jumping into the territory of a More Offstage Actor, but rather by creating a new *hybrid role* to aspire to. This new role combines the old Leading Actor with the More Offstage one you desire to Act-In. In the example above, rather than our Warrior pretending to be a Nurturer and then regressing, it is far more effective that they set an intention – with actionable commitments – to become a more *Nurturing Warrior* over a realistic time frame. The commitments lead to practices that enable us to rehearse the new hybrid role, both in life and at work, until we have "made it our own". This new combination of more and less familiar Archetypes can then, over time, take the negative edge off the previous pattern. Many methods in Part Two will help you expand your repertoire in this and other ways.

Time frames

It is wise to consider the time frame likely to suit any development goal you set. The more substantial a shift you choose, the longer the development process will take. Is your desired shift going to require short, medium or long-term attention? We give a brief explanation of each time frame below, illustrated by a real-life coaching story from our Archetypes at Work™ coaching practice. In these examples you can notice the new combination of favoured and less favoured Archetypes that are being activated.

1. **Short term – quick win – 1 day to 1 month**

   Here you can identify an upcoming event or task in life or work that would benefit from a new and different archetypal approach from one you habitually use. You first identify which lesser used Archetype would help and decide on a new approach that you feel comfortable enough to apply quickly. Then plan a simple commitment or strategy to help implement the intention and try it out.

   Short-term development story

   The following is an example taken from a recent 5-day Archetypes at Work™ deep-dive with a large multinational team of engineers and scientists. Both parties in this example had previously identified two Leading Actors that dominated their leadership style:

   Karen (a visionary Storyteller–Explorer project leader) was finding her working relationship with Gregor (a brilliant Strategist–Nurturer research scientist) difficult and a cause of anxiety. This was partly due to working in different time zones but mainly due to what she felt as unhelpful demands on her time and attention, which often included a list of complaints she could do nothing about.

During a facilitated conversation based around their different archetypal preferences, Karen confessed that she would often schedule quick calls to try and limit the amount of information that could be passed across. For Gregor, this strategy misfired, as he would get frustrated not to complete the details, and so he would then start again on the next call. Karen would get impatient with Gregor's repetition of small details (Strategist) and would change the subject to the bigger picture that she preferred (Explorer), thus provoking further frustration.

After discussion of how both sides felt, they generated some short-term development commitments. Karen agreed to start scheduling more time for their project report calls (thereby entering Strategist territory) so she would not need to rush him into her faster pace. She also invited him to let her know specifically if she was cutting him off before he had finished going over the key details (entering the more empathetic Nurturer). In response, Gregor agreed to get clear before the calls about what was useful for Karen to know and committed to stopping his previous habit of naming ongoing concerns about some of his people (embracing Warrior decisiveness). A month later they both reported enhanced mutual understanding and a lessening of tension as a result.

2. Medium term – professional and task improvement – 1 month to 6 months

Here you identify a current work/life challenge or big goal and work on creating a new archetypal pattern to improve your performance.

Medium-term development story

Robert was a fast-paced Explorer–Transformer who was anxious to inject new products into his bespoke consultancy in order to combat a downturn in business. However, his insistence that the consultants on the team learn and apply new methods while still delivering the existing products was meeting resistance.

*During a facilitated team feedback session based on the
Archetypes, Robert received advice from a Nurturer colleague
that he needed to stretch into his own Nurturer if he was to bring
the collective along with him more effectively. He committed to
being more of a Nurturing–Transformer for the next 12 months.
He set up regular meetings and calls for the team to be briefed
on new possibilities and to mutually agree realistic time frames
for implementation. He also slowed down the pace of introducing
the innovations to clients to allow others time to catch up and
integrate what had already been introduced to the system. He
set up a prototyping lab where he could go at a faster pace than
some colleagues were ready for, so he could keep the Explorer–
Transformer engaged in the meantime.*

*The system has now settled into a more relaxed rhythm of
implementing change with less stress felt by the team generally.*

3. **Long term – enhancing greater life fulfilment – 6 months to 5 years**
   Here you identify an underused Archetype that you realize is
   causing an unnecessary and undesirable cost to your quality of life,
   and you commit to a long-term personal inquiry into how to best
   liberate that potential in yourself.

Long-term development story

*Chala was a successful designer who identified as a Lover–Dreamer
with Strategist furthest offstage. She came to coaching with a
stated intention of becoming more self-reliant. She reported that
as a child she lived in a fantasy world, getting so attached to the
imaginary "sets" she created that she would cry when dinner called
her out of her rich inner world. She later dropped out of school,
hating the rigid structures it insisted on.*

*She taught herself how to use her creative gifts and now, as a
sought-after interior designer, gave her Lover–Dreamer instincts full
rein. But she never got her drawings straight and never figured out
the details, needing others to whom she could "delegate the boring
bits". Her husband and her employees took care of practical matters
so she could keep dreaming. Everything seemed to work well until,*

now in her 40s, she felt a deep sense of internal disorganization and being "lost in my reveries".

In an early coaching session, Chala realized she had given the Strategist part of herself away to anyone else who was more organized. But now she felt an inner need for more structured independence. Over the next five years she gradually learned to put into place routines and structures that she genuinely appreciated. She recognized this to be a long and slow journey into the deeper issues of order in her life. Her parents had been obsessively organized and she had avoided this by entering her imaginal world.

A solo visit to Egypt proved a turning point. She put her experience into her own language: on a design level, seeing the discipline required to create the awesome beauty of the Pyramids. On a practical level, she took full responsibility for the details of her trip; making and sticking to travel schedules. "I thought that order and structure would feel limiting," she reported. "Instead it gives me a sense of freedom to be in the moment."

In a coaching session after her return she committed to develop a routine to structure her creative flow. She began to get up early, discipline her diet and take daily walks. She set specific goals and rewarded herself for reaching them. She volunteered to organize a niece's wedding. Now in her 50s, she sees her daily routines as "preparing the container": a way to create boundaries within which her creativity and imagination can flow like a riverbed that cradles the swirling waters.

Each time frame has its own benefits. While you are, of course, welcome to choose multiple development plans to implement simultaneously, our advice would be to prioritize one initially. Either the most urgent, for a quick fix, or the most important, to enable a bigger shift in professional effectiveness or personal fulfilment.

Getting ready for rehearsal

Our experience is that different people need different ways to activate their desired new Archetypes effectively. We have therefore created a wide range of options drawn from our combined areas of expertise in theatre practice, psychology, coaching and experiential learning. Our intention is that everyone will be able to find something that suits their needs.

Distinguishing between Outside-in and Inside-Out rehearsal styles

In effect, we are inviting you to think of yourself as an actor about to enter a period of rehearsal and, like many actors, you may have a preferred learning style. Most trained actors are aware of the two basic styles used to bring a new character to life, generally referred to as *Outside-In* and *Inside-Out*. Outside-In is a more traditional British acting style. Here, the character is first imagined as a persona very different from who you are normally. A variety of gestures, movement styles, tones of voices, behaviour patterns and costumes (often deliberately distinct from how you usually show up) are tried out and tested, until you find the ones that fit the character best. These are then repeated until they become comfortable and easy to inhabit, moving from an external "as if" play to a more internally felt reality (hence Outside-In). Once you have owned the new character in this way you can play it convincingly, as if it were really you. It requires performance energy and technique. The equivalent of this in sports psychology is when athletes who have never won a big competition imagine winning, and then act as if they have won, before they step onto the field.

Inside-Out is a more traditionally American style. Here, you notice and research the similarities between your own past experiences and those of the new character. You start with remembering times when you had similar experiences in your life as the character has in theirs. You remember in sensory detail how it felt "back then" and bring those sensed memories into the present moment. You then slowly begin to bring the character to life – from the inside out. Behaviours here are similar to how you normally show up – and are slowly expressed more fully until you find a real and believable way for you to inhabit the desired character (hence Inside-Out). This requires personal energy and emotional intensity – passion. In sports psychology, this is the equivalent of getting athletes to watch videos of the last competition they won, remember in detail how they felt and acted when they won, as preparation for the next competition.

Richard once sat in a lecture at UCLA given by the American actor Treat Williams who summed up the distinction simply: "The Brits have the technique but lack the passion, the Yanks have the passion but lack the technique." Of course, the best from all countries have both. A favourite tale from Richard's father, the late British actor Sir Laurence Olivier, highlights the difference. Laurence was on set in New York filming *Marathon Man* starring American actor Dustin Hoffman. They were shooting a scene in the story before which Dustin's character had been up all night, running away from pursuers. The day of the new scene Dustin came into the make-up caravan looking terrible and Laurence asked him what was wrong. Dustin replied, "I've been up all night to prepare for the scene." To which the Brit replied, "Dear boy, why don't you try acting?" Each to their own...

As a broad generalization, it is likely that those of you who enjoy taking risks and stretching yourselves will respond more to Outside-In, whereas those who prefer to manage risks and take smaller steps will respond to Inside-Out. You are, of course, welcome to try a mix of both styles and decide later which one suits you better.

Chapter Overview of Part Two: Archetypal Development

So, having laid out the groundwork and some of the theory behind what is to come, here is the order of play...

Chapters 10–14, Developing the Realms provide an in-depth selection of the best methods to rehearse and activate your less favoured Archetypes (more details below).

Chapter 15, Hybrid Roles: Combining Archetypes for Development. If you choose this approach, which Leading Actor and which More Offstage Actor do you wish to combine? We then offer a word-pairing exercise to help refine and fuse the energies from both.

Chapter 16, Meeting the Archetypes in Others provides cues to build rapport with other people, when one of their Leading Actors corresponds with any of your More Offstage Actors. Since each Archetype has a different attitude and mindset, when we meet such people we can think, "I just can't connect with them". We show you how to meet "the other" where they are and increase the chances of a mutually beneficial relationship.

Chapter 17, Evolving Your Core Strengths – Horizontal Integration. *Horizontal Integration* is helpful for those who have an ambivalent attitude towards a favourite Archetype (some Gifts are loved and others disliked).

Chapter 18, Evolving Your Core Strengths – Vertical Development. *Vertical Development* explores the evolving potential of the Archetypes. What are the leading-edge practices that are emerging at the boundaries of what we know about the 10 today?

A template for a personal **Archetypal Development Plan** follows to help you integrate Part Two and decide on final development goals.

Coda, Developing an Archetypal Eye completes Part Two with advice on how to use the Archetypes as an ongoing shorthand tool for decoding people, situations and events in your life.

Rehearsal Method Options and their archetypal flavours

The following five chapters on Horizontal Development provide a wide range of proven methods to Act-In each Archetype in turn. We include a relevant *archetypal flavour* as a guide to help you decide how you want to start. For example, if Strategist is a Leading Actor and you want to develop the Dreamer, you can choose a method with a Strategist flavour to start. And if you are looking for a bigger stretch, then maybe pick the Dreamer-flavoured method to activate the Dreamer! And you are welcome to try them all, of course...

Rehearsal Method Options – overview of choices

1. An ***Archetypal Gesture*** (and phrase). Embodying and speaking from an Archetype's perspective can give you a quick felt experience of a particular archetypal energy.
    (Archetypal flavour: A Sovereign/Lover approach – visible and sensory)

2. ***Activities and Practices*** to try out to get a deeper sense of the desired Archetype.
    a. *Locations and environments* likely to evoke the Archetype
        (An Explorer approach – going somewhere new and different)
    b. *Activities to rehearse the Archetype*
        (A Strategist/Warrior approach – planning and doing)
    c. *Creative Research*
        (A Transformer/Nurturer approach – research and conversations)

3. ***Inside-Out: Sense Memory and Active Imagination*** to gain access to less familiar Archetypes.
    a. *Sense Memory*
        (A Nurturer/Lover approach – remembering your past and accessing your senses)
    b. *Active Imagination 1 – imagining a real-life application*
        (A Dreamer/Strategist approach – imagination with a practical focus)
    c. *Active Imagination 2 – imagining an inner figure*
        (A Dreamer/Storyteller approach – imagination to create a story)

4. ***Outside-In: Rehearsal Cues*** to practise communicating in the manner of an Archetype in real life. This includes signature *Mood, attitude and mindset cues, Body language and physical cues, Voice/ Vocal tone, Typical words and typical phrases* of each Archetype
    (A Sovereign approach – rehearsal and performance)

5. ***Development Stories:*** we share real-life case studies of people we have coached to Act-In desired new Archetypes. We then invite you into a creative writing exercise to activate the power of intention.
    (A Storyteller/Transformer approach – narrative to describe effective change)

You may have noticed that the Renegade is the only Archetype that does not make an appearance above. The Renegade does not really respond to pre-set ideas and is much more likely to make up something spontaneously. So, if you have Renegade as a Leading Actor, and none of the above methods appeal to you, please feel free to make up your own and keep us posted… (By the way, the Renegade will make an appearance to support more future-focused development!)

As you move into the next five chapters you may wish to turn directly to those sections about your More Offstage Actors, or those you have already decided to develop. The format for all 10 is the same, the details for each Archetype is different. So please feel free to skip over Realms or Archetypes you have no particular interest in developing at the present time.

CHAPTER 10

DEVELOPING THE REALM OF

Order

1. **Archetypal Gesture**
2. **Activities and Practices**
3. **Inside-Out: Sense Memory and Active Imagination**
4. **Outside-In: Rehearsal Cues**
5. **Development Stories**

If you already know that you wish to develop the Sovereign or the Strategist, please notice which of the following you could imagine committing to as you read. Otherwise you can revisit the relevant Archetypes for you at any later time.

Developing the Sovereign

1. **Archetypal Gesture:** *"I accept; I radiate"*

    (A Sovereign/Lover approach – visible and sensory)

    An Archetypal Gesture is a simple way to remind yourself of the Sovereign Gifts (also available as a video and download from www. archetypesatwork.com/gestures). It is a symbolic gesture to practise in private, using Archetype-appropriate words as a quick memory tool for embodiment.

    Stand tall and hold your hands out above your head. Now imagine them moving slowly inwards until they grasp a crown the size of your head. Slowly bring the hands down until they touch and surround your head as you say the words: **"I accept"**.

    Now move the hands down so the tips of your fingers touch the middle of your chest. Slowly expand the hands outwards to embrace all in front of you as you smile and say: **"I radiate"**.

    Using this Archetypal Gesture is a simple way to evoke Sovereign energy in you, before an important meeting or presentation or anywhere else where you need to be visible. You can learn these simple gestures and phrases and practise them as often as useful.

2. **Activities and Practices**

    Below is a selection of ideas we have gathered over the years that have helped people gain more access to the Sovereign in life and work. It is by no means a full list and we encourage you to find your own variations if none of these feel quite right for you. We hope the following will give you ideas and inspiration for your own personalized Sovereign Development Plan.

a. **Locations and environments that are likely to evoke the Sovereign**

(An Explorer approach – going somewhere new and different)

Ornate spaces, Palaces, Versailles, castles, concert halls, Yosemite National Park, opulent structures and theatre spaces, being centre stage

b. **Activities to rehearse the Sovereign**

(A Strategist/Warrior approach – planning and doing)

- *Work on defining your sense of purpose*
- *Describe in one sentence who you are at your core*
- *Take an acting class or join an amateur theatre group*
- *Express your creativity – any way you choose*
- *Act as though you were Sovereign and let everything you say have royal gravitas*
- *Find a time to play – with children or by yourself*
- *Take on a board membership, non-executive directorship or volunteer as a school governor*
- *Work on ways to develop your self-esteem and become more visible in your life*
- *Speak from your heart*
- *Find a place in your life where you can truly shine*
- *Be generous – give something to someone you care about*
- *Practise speaking to the "why" in meetings, connecting people to the big picture; hold the vision*

c. **Creative Research**

(A Transformer/Nurturer approach – research and conversations)

Who do you admire that you assign Sovereign energy to? These can be people you know, people you admire from a distance (living or dead), or even fictional characters.

If they are available in your network, you could find time to be with them and notice how they act around others. Ask them about their sense of purpose and vision.

If they are well-known, look for articles, biographies, documentaries or films about them that you can absorb as you integrate what it means to embody Sovereign energy.

3. **Inside-Out: Sense Memory and Active Imagination**

These exercises are designed to give you inner access to the Sovereign. Please read through them and decide if you want to try one. If so, when you have time, we recommend that you find a private and comfortable space to work in, where you are not going to be disturbed. Have a notebook (or pen and paper) nearby. These exercises can be done alone or with a trusted colleague, friend or coach in attendance. If you prefer, they are also available as an audio download from www.archetypesatwork.com/guidedjourneys.

If you are alone, please read the relevant instructions for **a**, **b** or **c** below until they are familiar enough to start. Then close your eyes for anywhere from five to 15 minutes and allow yourself to enter the process as fully as possible. Be aware that you may feel as if you are moving in and out of the process at first. It may take a few attempts (perhaps three to five) for these exercises to feel comfortable – but you are stretching out of your previous comfort zone, so this is to be expected. When you are finished, make a few notes in a notebook about your experience.

If you have a companion, they can read the instructions below out loud in real time. For the Sense Memory exercise **a**, you can choose to remember in silence or speak the story of your memory as you relive it. For the Active Imagination exercises **b** and **c**, the instructions can be spoken to you, but your journey is best imagined in silence.

If you are using the downloads, play them and pause them as helpful as you go through the journey they describe. Repeat whenever useful.

a. **Sense Memory**

(A Nurturer/Lover approach – remembering your past and accessing your senses)

Allow yourself to drift into a place where you have easy access to your personal memory banks... Flick through a few memories, where you enjoyed being the centre of attention, however brief they may have been. Pick one scene to focus on and begin to recall it more fully. Where were you? What were you doing? Who was around you? How did you feel? Allow yourself to remember as fully as you can what you were experiencing then. See if you can now sense what enabled this brief entry into Sovereign territory. What part of you stepped forward and did you draw on? How did it feel being recognized or honoured as the centre of attention? What was it like to have people responding to what you were radiating?

When you are ready, come out of the memory and either take notes (if you are alone) or get feedback from your colleague. How did you feel and/or show up differently when you were accessing this memory?

b.   Active Imagination 1 – imagining a real-life application

(A Dreamer/Strategist approach – imagination with a practical focus)

Imagine yourself in a scene of your choice connected to your current life, where access to the Sovereign would be helpful. See yourself inhabiting this scene with full access to the Sovereign and their gifts. Observe yourself in your mind's eye as you engage with others being purposeful, poised, generous and magnanimous. Allow yourself to feel and sense the qualities that the Sovereign offers. Try to feel it in your body as an actual sensation and as an emotional response. How is this different from how you generally feel?

When you are ready, come out of the imagined scene and write down anything you want to remember. If you have a colleague with you, tell the story of your journey. You may wish to ask for feedback or to integrate the experience by yourself.

c.   Active Imagination 2 – imagining an inner figure

(A Dreamer/Storyteller approach – imagination to create a story)

Imagine yourself leaving the place where you are now and travelling through the air over varied landscapes until you land in a distant building that evokes Sovereign energy for you. (You can use the location prompts in 2a above if helpful.) Now imagine yourself preparing to meet a figure who will represent your Inner Sovereign. Wait until you are ready to be given audience by this figure. Know that you will be able to ask your Inner Sovereign an important question and that they will offer their wisdom in return. This may be a direct spoken answer to your question, or a symbolic gift that has some bearing on it, or both. When you are ready, imagine yourself entering the space where the Sovereign awaits. Allow the scene to unfold in front of you as you pay close attention to it: How does your Inner Sovereign look? What are they wearing? How do they hold themselves? How do they speak and what do they say? If a dialogue with them is appropriate, please imagine it unfolding. When the scene is nearing completion, allow this figure to offer you their gift or closing words of wisdom. Thank them for their time. With the knowledge that you can return here at other times, gradually exit this scene and imagine yourself travelling back through the air, over landscapes, and gently into the room you are physically in. Open your eyes slowly.

When you are ready, write down everything you can remember that may contain actual or symbolic clues about your Inner Sovereign, including any exchanges. If you received a gift, what was it? You might want to draw it or let your mind wander with free associations. What might this gift mean for you and your journey towards the Sovereign?

Any or all of these exercises can be repeated as often as you like. Then, when you are ready to try this out in a real-life situation where you wish to embody the Sovereign, take a minute to prepare. Remember the essence of your Sense Memory and/or Active Imagination journeys and the parts that felt most useful. What clues did they provide as to how you can confidently embody Sovereign energy? See if you can summon these into yourself and allow them to fill your being. Then, when you enter the actual scene, keep drawing on these to the extent that they are useful.

When you exit that scene, take a moment to notice if anything was different from how you might normally show up. If so, what was it? Did the preparation help you and, if so, how?

4. Outside-In: Rehearsal Cues

(A Sovereign approach – rehearsal and performance)

These are practical cues that you can use in real life, when you feel ready. You will probably want to rehearse them first – in private or with a trusted coach/colleague, and then in public, when you feel ready.

How to communicate as a Sovereign

These real-life attitudes, body language and voice cues, sample words and phrases are all resonant with the Sovereign. Please read through them and notice which might be useful for you to step into and rehearse for future use.

a. Mood, attitude and mindset

Upbeat, magnanimous, inclusive, passionate, naturally in charge, "I am an instrument", "I am willing to be seen", "I deliver the vision"

b. Body language and physical cues

Solid, unflappable, confident, present, benign, spacious, gravitas, magnetic, open gestures, feet firmly planted, open chest, standing at full height, shoulders easily rolled back, upright and long spine

c. Voice

Steady, firm, poised, calm, welcoming

d. Typical words of a Sovereign

Centre, identity, purpose, vision, core, heart, "I am", "We are", "I believe", courage

e. Typical phrases of a Sovereign

"Our vision is"; "Let us remember our purpose"; "I am here to guide us into the future"; "This is the central idea"; "Let's get back to our core"; "The heart of the matter is"; "We can be more than we have been"; "The reason why we're here is…"; "We have a long way to go and I am here to help us get there"; "Our best days lie ahead"; "You can rely on me"; "I want us to shine"

If the Sovereign is in your Archetypal Development Plan, please take a moment to reflect on the suggestions above. Which do you feel drawn to try first? You may need to experiment with different ways until you find what suits you best. The first few attempts may feel odd or "not like me", so we invite you to keep at it until they feel familiar enough. You might want to find a simple shift in body and voice that feels relatively comfortable as a first step and then extend it from there. The more you practise, the easier it will become to embody the Sovereign.

When you are ready, we invite you to bring what you have learned into a real-life situation, preferably one where you have a trusted ally present to give you feedback afterwards. When you are in that situation, draw on the spirit and actions of the Sovereign that you have Acted-In through your rehearsals. Notice if you think, feel and/or act differently from usual. When you exit that situation, either get feedback from your ally or reflect by yourself. What worked? What if anything would you do differently next time? Then, wait until the next opportunity presents itself – and repeat the process.

5. Development Stories

(A Storyteller/Transformer approach – narrative to describe effective change)

We complete our journey through rehearsal options with an example of Acting-In an Archetype taken from our own consulting practice. This mini case study describes how an individual successfully activated their desired outcome. This will also serve as an invitation and model for you to write your own future-focused story, one that describes the successful outcome of your own development plan.

a. Our coaching story

Stan was an executive at a large not-for-profit organization where he was in charge of fundraising. He had struggled with defining a clear sense of his own identity throughout his life. He reported that he never put himself first, suffered from low self-esteem, and shied away from the spotlight. In a coaching session, and now in his 40s, he self-assessed the Sovereign as his More Offstage Actor. When asked to describe himself, he could only say, "It's not clear. A foggy reflection, like I can only see the outlines."

When encouraged to talk about his sense of purpose at his job, however, his demeanour changed. As he reported his pride in standing up for the underprivileged population his organization served he radiated conviction and spoke from the heart. It was a different Stan altogether, sitting upright and exuding confidence.

When this visible change was fed back to him by his coach, he realized that he actually knew how to embody the Sovereign, albeit when it served others' rather than his own needs. Over the next few months he practised stepping into the Sovereign in other spheres. He began speaking to the organization's purpose at senior management meetings and got good feedback. He organized his first ever press conference to bring the organization's message to a wider audience. He carefully prepared his presentation to the press and practised the Sovereign Archetypal Gesture before each rehearsal with his coach and then before the actual press conference itself. The resulting coverage increased the credibility of the organization. Stan was invited to attend other meetings in the city related to the key issues his organization was dealing with. This extended his organization's influence further. His friends also noticed that he was more at ease being the centre of conversations at social gatherings.

b. Storying your future

A creative writing exercise to activate the power of intention, by creating a story to guide you into your desired future. We invite you to write from the perspective of that future you – as if you were looking back on your development having successfully completed it. This will take 30–50 minutes of quiet, uninterrupted time with writing materials or computer.

Guideline

Using the loose framework of our coaching story above, you will craft your own story as if it were your own real-life case study set at a realistic time in the future. From that future time, you look back and "reflect on your success", i.e. you create a narrative that describes *how* you activated the Sovereign, from this point forward.

Story prompts (a loose guide to follow if helpful):

i) *Presenting issue: What was it that motivated the desire to Act-In the Sovereign?*

ii) *Personal insights: What did you learn about yourself, your formative years, your primary care-givers' Archetypes that might have played a part in the presenting issue? (This part could be aided by an actual or imaginary coach or trusted confidant or be created from personal reflection or inner dialogue.)*

iii) *First steps and their results: What simple first steps did you take on your development journey? How did they help? What impact did they have? What did you learn – about yourself and/or the Sovereign?*

iv) *Next steps leading to integration: What else did you choose to do and over what time frame? How did these activations help? What was the felt difference in your life? What was the visible difference to others around you?*

So, that is the full collection of Rehearsal Method Options currently in our repertoire. In our experience, within this wide range of possibilities you will be able to find at least one way to effectively build a relationship with this Archetype. Then, with commitment and practice – and in a time frame that works for you – you will Act-In the Sovereign.

Developing the Strategist

1. **Archetypal Gesture:** *"I frame; I structure; I focus"*

   (A Sovereign/Lover approach – visible and sensory)

   An Archetypal Gesture is a simple way to remind yourself of the Strategist Gifts (also available as a video and download from www.archetypesatwork.com/gestures). It is a symbolic gesture to practise in private, using Archetype-appropriate words as a quick memory tool for embodiment.

   Stand still and straight with a clear focus on what is directly in front of you. Straighten your palms into two straight "blades" and lift them in a straight line until they are resting either side of your face. Now narrow your peripheral vision and say: **"I frame"**. *Then move your hands down, bringing one palm directly in front of the other in parallel. Your hands now move to indicate two steps forward – moving one hand at a time in front of the other each time – as you say:* **"I structure"**. *Now move your hands further forward until they are fully extended, keep your arms straight – bring your palms closer together like a funnel until the fingertips are nearly touching and say:* **"I focus"**.

   Using this Archetypal Gesture is a simple way to evoke Strategist energy in you, before any meeting or presentation where you need to be practical, logical and focused. You can learn these simple gestures and phrases and practise them as often as useful.

2. **Activities and Practices**

   Below is a selection of ideas we have gathered over the years that have helped people gain more access to the Strategist in life and work. It is by no means a full list and we encourage you to find your own variations if none of these feel quite right for you. We hope the following will give you ideas and inspiration for your own personalized Strategist Development Plan.

a.   Locations and environments that are likely to evoke the Strategist
(An Explorer approach – going somewhere new and different)
Square and geometrical structures, buildings with clear and clean lines, formal gardens, carpenter's workshop, construction site, watchmaker's studio, large-scale scaffolding, the Alps, the Pyramids, the Great Wall of China

b.   Activities to rehearse the Strategist
(A Strategist/Warrior approach – planning and doing)
- *Engage in future planning*
- *Hire a strategy coach and/or read books on strategy*
- *Develop a personal strategy and follow it through*
- *Commit to being on time for all meetings and commitments*
- *Learn strategic games – chess, bridge, Mah-jong and so forth*
- *Build a solid three-dimensional structure in your house or garden*
- *Find a Strategist elder or mentor to learn from and commit to following their sensible advice*
- *Mentor someone much younger than you to pick and stick to a chosen discipline*
- *Learn to work with figures or numbers – accounting or Sudoku*
- *Develop mastery in a practice or skill over time*
- *Practise minimalism by clearing clutter and reducing waste*
- *Toil harder than those around you and watch it pay off*

c.   Creative Research
(A Transformer/Nurturer approach – research and conversations)

Who do you admire that you assign Strategist energy to? These can be people you know, people you admire from a distance (living or dead) or even fictional characters.

If they are available in your network, you could find time to be with them and notice how they act around others, or even ask their advice about how they organize tasks to maximize effectiveness.

If they are well-known, look for articles, biographies, documentaries or films about them that you can absorb as you integrate what it means to embody Strategist energy.

3. **Inside-Out: Sense Memory and Active Imagination**

   These exercises are designed to give you inner access to the Strategist. Please read through them and decide if you want to try one. If so, when you have time, we recommend that you find a private and comfortable space to work in, where you are not going to be disturbed. Have a notebook (or pen and paper) nearby. These exercises can be done alone or with a trusted colleague, friend or coach in attendance. If you prefer, they are also available as an audio download from www.archetypesatwork.com/guidedjourneys.

   If you are alone, please read the relevant instructions for **a**, **b** or **c** below until they are familiar enough to start. Then close your eyes for anywhere from five to 15 minutes and allow yourself to enter the process as fully as possible. Be aware that you may feel as if you are moving in and out of the process at first. Also, it may take a few attempts (perhaps three to five) for these exercises to feel comfortable – but you are stretching out of your previous comfort zone so this is to be expected. When you are finished, make a few notes in a notebook about your experience.

   If you have a companion, they can read the instructions below out loud in real time. For the Sense Memory exercise **a**, you can choose to remember in silence or speak the story of your memory as you relive it. For the Active Imagination exercises **b** and **c**, the instructions can be spoken to you but your journey is best imagined in silence.

   If you are using the downloads, play them and pause them as helpful as you go through the journey they describe. Repeat whenever useful.

   a. **Sense Memory**

      (A Nurturer/Lover approach – remembering your past and accessing your senses)

      Allow yourself to drift into a place where you have easy access to your personal memory banks... Flick through a few memories of times in your life, however brief, when being structured and focused added real value. Pick one scene to focus on and begin to recall it more fully. Where were you? What were you doing? Who was around you? How did you feel? Allow yourself to experience as fully as you can what you were feeling then. See if you can now sense what enabled this brief entry into Strategist territory. What part of you stepped forward? What did you draw on? How did it feel when a logical and disciplined approach to a task or process achieved the desired result? What was it like to have your intention enabled through pragmatic organization?

When you are ready, come out of the memory and either take notes (if you are alone) or get feedback from your colleague. How did you feel and/or show up differently when you were accessing this memory?

b. **Active Imagination 1 – imagining a real-life application**
(A Dreamer/Strategist approach – imagination with a practical focus)

Imagine yourself in a scene of your choice connected to your current life, where having access to the Strategist would be helpful. See yourself inhabiting this scene with full access to the Strategist and their gifts. Observe yourself in your mind's eye as you engage with your life, projects and other people in a structured, deliberate and measured way. Allow yourself to feel and sense the qualities that the Strategist offers. Try to feel it in your body as an actual sensation and as a mental response. How is this different from how you generally think and feel?

When you are ready, come out of the imagined scene and write down anything you want to remember. If you have a colleague with you, tell the story of your journey. You may wish to ask for feedback or to integrate the experience by yourself.

c. **Active Imagination 2 – imagining an inner figure**
(A Dreamer/Storyteller approach – imagination to create a story)

Imagine yourself leaving the place where you are now and travelling through the air over varied landscapes until you land in a distant building that evokes a Master Strategist structure for you. (You can use the location prompts in 2a above if helpful.) Now imagine yourself preparing to meet a figure who will represent your Inner Strategist. Wait until you are ready to be given audience by this figure. Know that you will be able to ask your Inner Strategist an important question and that they will offer their wisdom in return. This may be a direct spoken answer to your question, or a symbolic gift that has some bearing on it, or both. When you are ready, imagine yourself entering the space where the Master Strategist awaits. Allow the scene to unfold in front of you as you pay close attention to it: How does your Inner Strategist look? What are they wearing? How do they hold themselves? How do they speak and what do they say? If a dialogue with them is appropriate, imagine it unfolding. When the scene is nearing completion, allow this figure to offer you their gift or closing words of wisdom. Thank them for their time. With the knowledge that you can return here at other times, gradually exit this scene and imagine yourself travelling back through the air, over landscapes, and gently into the room you are physically in. Open your eyes slowly.

When you are ready, write down everything you can remember that may contain actual or symbolic clues about your Inner Strategist, including any exchanges. If you received a gift, what was it? You might want to draw it or let your mind wander with free associations. What might this gift mean for you and your journey towards the Strategist?

Any or all of these exercises can be repeated as often as you like. Then, when you are ready to try this out in a real-life situation where you wish to embody the Strategist, take a minute to prepare. Remember the essence of your Sense Memory and/or Active Imagination journeys and the parts that felt most useful. What clues did they provide as to how you can confidently embody Strategist energy? See if you can summon these into yourself and allow them to fill your being. Then, when you enter the actual scene, keep drawing on these to the extent that they are useful.

When you exit that scene, take a moment to notice if anything was different from how you might normally show up. If so, what was it? Did the preparation help you and, if so, how?

4. Outside-In: Rehearsal Cues
(A Sovereign approach – rehearsal and performance)
These are practical cues that you can use in real life, when you feel ready. You will probably want to rehearse them first – in private or with a trusted coach/colleague, and then in public, when you feel ready.

How to communicate as a Strategist
These real-life attitudes, body language and voice cues, sample words and phrases are all resonant with the Strategist. Read through them and notice which might be useful for you to step into and rehearse for future use.

a. Mood, attitude and mindset
Serious, focused, timely, contained, on task, detailed, precise, clear, efficient, sequential, economical, ethical, respectful

b. Body language and physical cues
Authoritative, compact, solid, closed gestures, upright, steady, shoulders back, still, composed

c. Voice
Definite, rational, unemotional, calm, clear, concise, measured, instructive, respectful, efficient

d. Typical words of a Strategist
Goal, structure, points, plan, conclusions, background, agenda, rationale, facts (not fiction), order, agreements, understanding, contract

e. Typical phrases of a Strategist
"Our goal is clear..."; "The plan is simple..."; "I would like to advise you of..."; "The main points to consider are"; "The new structure will be..."; "The context for this is..."; "The objective of this meeting is..."; "The intended outcome is..."; "Our budget is limited..."; "The

research indicates…"; "What do the numbers tell us?"; "Let's look at the details first"; "We need to take a long-term view"

If the Strategist is in your Archetypal Development Plan, please take a moment to reflect on the suggestions above. Which do you feel drawn to try first? You may need to experiment with different ways until you find what suits you best. The first few attempts may feel odd or "not like me", so we invite you to keep at it until they feel familiar enough. You might want to find a simple shift in body and voice that feels relatively comfortable as a first step and then extend it from there. The more you practise, the easier it will become to embody the Strategist. When you are ready, we invite you to bring what you have learned into a real-life situation, preferably one where you have a trusted ally present to give you feedback afterwards. When you are in that situation, draw on the spirit and actions of the Strategist that you have Acted-In through your rehearsals. Notice whether you think, feel and/or act differently from usual. When you exit that situation, either get feedback from your ally or reflect by yourself. What worked? What if anything would you do differently next time? Then, wait until the next opportunity presents itself – and repeat the process.

5. Development Stories

(A Storyteller/Transformer approach – narrative to describe effective change)

We complete our journey through rehearsal options with an example of Acting-In an Archetype taken from our own consulting practice. This mini case study describes how an individual successfully activated their desired outcome. This will also serve as an invitation and model for you to write your own future-focused story, one that describes the successful outcome of your own development plan.

a. Our coaching story

Elena was the CEO of a niche marketing company that had been growing quickly until the recent unexpected loss of several important clients and vital revenue streams. She was a natural Dreamer–Storyteller–Renegade and often referred to as a creative genius. Well known for thinking outside the box with brilliantly novel approaches, she was also notoriously disorganized, missed appointments and gave conflicting instructions to her team. When she changed a plan mid-course, her team would get flustered and anxious, and some clients would back away from the creative mess that ensued.

In coaching, Elena identified the lack of Strategist as a current cost to her leadership. She recognized that she had previously hired an operations manager to play the Strategist on her behalf. This had helped organize the office and existing client list effectively, but the current expansion had inflated Elena's natural Renegade into the Shadow of Too Much. She admitted to breaking more rules and coming up with even more radical ideas that then exceeded the hired Strategist's capacity to build containing structures.

Seeking coaching as a remedy to the current downturn in clients and revenue, Elena saw clearly that she could no longer afford to externalize the Strategist. She had to find her own.

When prompted, she was able to identify the areas of her life where she was quite disciplined. For instance, she never missed a morning walk with her dogs and took the same 50-minute route every day; "I do my best thinking then." She was also never late for events and parent-teacher conferences at her children's school.

Seeing that she could access the Strategist in her home life when it really mattered to her allowed her to gain confidence to gradually own her innate Strategist. She started to organize the areas of client work where there was room for innovation and ringfence others that were best served by a more classic marketing approach. She even created a Thought Leader Forum, where other Renegades were invited into the office for a monthly evening talk and Q and A – to which existing and prospective clients were invited. Over the next year her organization gained more clarity and focus, and performance measurably improved.

b. Storying your future

A creative writing exercise to activate the power of intention, by creating a story to guide you into your desired future. We invite you to write from the perspective of that desired future – as if you were looking back on your development having successfully completed it. This will take 30–50 minutes of quiet, uninterrupted time with writing materials or computer.

Guideline

Using the loose framework of our coaching story above, you will craft your own story as if it were your own real-life case study set at a realistic time in the future. From that future time, you look back and "reflect on your success", i.e. you create a narrative that describes *how* you activated the Strategist, from this point forward.

Story prompts (a loose guide to follow if helpful):

i)   *Presenting issue: What was it that motivated the desire to Act-In the Strategist?*

ii) *Personal insights: What did you learn about yourself, your formative years, your primary care-givers' Archetypes that might have played a part in the presenting issue? (This part could be aided by an actual or imaginary coach or trusted confidant or be created from personal reflection or inner dialogue.)*

iii) *First steps and their results: What simple first steps did you take on your development journey? How did they help? What impact did they have?*
     What did you learn – about yourself and/or the Strategist?

iv) *Next steps leading to integration: What else did you choose to do and over what time frame? How did these activations help? What was the felt difference in your life? What was the visible difference to others around you?*

So, that is the full collection of Rehearsal Method Options currently in our repertoire. In our experience, within this wide range of possibilities you will be able to find at least one way to effectively build a relationship with this Archetype. Then, with commitment and practice, and in a time frame that works for you, you will Act-In the Strategist.

And that completes Developing the Realm of Order.

CHAPTER 11
DEVELOPING THE REALM OF
Relationship

Rehearsal Method Options

1. **Archetypal Gesture**
2. **Activities and Practices**
3. **Inside-Out: Sense Memory and Active Imagination**
4. **Outside-In: Rehearsal Cues**
5. **Development Stories**

If you already know that you wish to develop the Nurturer or the Lover, please notice which of the following you could imagine committing to as you read. Otherwise you can revisit the relevant Archetypes for you at any later time.

Developing the Nurturer

1. **Archetypal Gesture: *"I'm here for you; you matter"***
    (A Sovereign/Lover approach – visible and sensory)
    An Archetypal Gesture is a simple way to remind yourself of the Nurturer Gifts (also available as a video and download from www.archetypesatwork.com/gestures). It is a symbolic gesture to practise in private, using Archetype-appropriate words as a quick memory tool for embodiment.

    *Stand in an easy relaxed way with a friendly smile. Imagine there is someone you really care about standing in front of you. Place one hand on your belly and one hand on your heart as you say, in a rounded, warm tone: **"I'm here for you"**. Then extend both hands slowly out towards the imagined recipient of your care, as you say: **"You matter!"***

    Using this Archetypal Gesture is a simple way to evoke Nurturer energy in you. You can embody this gesture before any encounter you identify as benefiting from a caring, empathetic presence. You can learn these simple gestures and phrases and practise them as often as useful.

2. **Activities and Practices**
    Below is a selection of ideas we have gathered over the years that have helped people gain more access to the Nurturer in life and work. It is by no means a full list and we encourage you to find your own variations if none of these feel quite right for you. We hope the following will give you ideas and inspiration for your own personalized Nurturer Development Plan.

a. **Locations and environments that are likely to evoke the Nurturer**
(An Explorer approach – going somewhere new and different)
Comfortable gardens, cosy homes, well-kept shelters, family-sized greenhouses, hospitals, care homes, agricultural landscapes, cosy coffee shops, the home office, childcare facilities, small-scale fresh food plants, farmers' markets, hot springs or Jacuzzis, picnics, antique stores

b. **Activities to rehearse the Nurturer**
(A Strategist/Warrior approach – planning and doing)
- *Learn how to practise self-care*
- *Identify and explore what really feeds you*
- *Volunteer to help those in need*
- *Protect others' feelings in a conversation or meeting*
- *Tell a young child a meaningful story*
- *Make a picture book with fond memories*
- *Plant a garden and watch things grow*
- *Speak your feelings*
- *Support others at work*
- *Create cosy spaces at your workplace to relax in*
- *Honour the founders and the origins of your organization*

c. **Creative Research**
(A Transformer/Nurturer approach – research and conversations)

Who do you admire that you assign Nurturer energy to? These can be people you know, people you admire from a distance (living or dead) or even fictional characters.

If they are available in your network, you could find time to be with them and notice how they care for others. Ask them about their relationships and their reflections.

If they are well-known, look for articles, biographies, documentaries or films about them that you can absorb as you integrate what it means to embody Nurturer energy.

3. **Inside-Out: Sense Memory and Active Imagination**

These exercises are designed to give you inner access to the Nurturer. Please read through them and decide if you want to try one. If so, when you have time, we recommend that you find a private and comfortable space to work in, where you are not going to be disturbed. Have a notebook (or pen and paper) nearby. These exercises can be done alone or with a trusted colleague, friend or coach in attendance. If you prefer, they are also available as an audio download from www.archetypesatwork.com/guidedjourneys.

If you are alone, please read the relevant instructions for **a**, **b** or **c** below until they are familiar enough to start. Then close your eyes for anywhere from five to 15 minutes and allow yourself to enter the process as fully as possible. Be aware that you may feel as if you are moving in and out of the process at first. It may take a few attempts (perhaps three to five) for these exercises to feel comfortable – but you are stretching out of your previous comfort zone so this is to be expected. When you are finished, make a few notes in a notebook about your experience.

If you have a companion, they can read the instructions below out loud in real time. For the Sense Memory exercise **a**, you can choose to remember in silence or speak the story of your memory as you relive it. For the Active Imagination exercises **b** and **c**, the instructions can be spoken to you but your journey is best imagined in silence.

If you are using the downloads, play them and pause them as helpful as you go through the journey they describe. Repeat whenever useful.

a. **Sense Memory**

(A Nurturer/Lover approach – remembering your past and accessing your senses)

Allow yourself to drift into a place where you have easy access to your personal memory banks... Flick through a few memories of times in your life, however brief, where you felt especially good because you took care of someone or someone took care of you. Pick one scene to focus on and begin to recall it more fully. Where were you? What were you doing? Who was around you? Allow yourself to experience as fully as you can what you were feeling then. What did you feel in your stomach and in your heart? What was it like to be so in tune with someone that they knew what you needed, or you knew what they needed? See if you can now sense what enabled this experience of Nurturer. What part of you stepped forward and did you draw on?

When you are ready, come out of the memory and either take notes (if you are alone) or get feedback from your colleague. How did you feel and/or show up differently when you were accessing this memory?

b.   **Active Imagination 1 – imagining a real-life application**
(A Dreamer/Strategist approach – imagination with a practical focus)

Imagine yourself in a scene of your choice connected to your current life, where you feel that accessing the Nurturer would be helpful. See yourself inhabiting this scene with full access to the Nurturer and to all the gifts that come with this Archetype. Observe yourself in your mind's eye as you engage with others being responsive, emotionally intelligent and caring. Allow yourself to feel and sense the qualities that the Nurturer offers. Try to feel this in your body as an actual sensation and as an emotional response. How is this different from how you generally feel?

When you are ready, come out of the imagined scene and write down anything you want to remember. If you have a colleague with you, tell the story of your journey. You may wish to ask for feedback or to integrate the experience by yourself.

c.   **Active Imagination 2 – imagining an inner figure**
(A Dreamer/Storyteller approach – imagination to create a story)

Imagine yourself leaving the place where you are now and travelling through the air over varied landscapes until you land in a far-off comfortable setting that evokes caring Nurturer energy for you. (You can use the location prompts in 2a above if helpful.) Now imagine yourself preparing to meet a figure who will represent your Inner Nurturer. Know that you will be able to ask your Inner Nurturer an important question and that they will offer their caring wisdom in return. This may be a direct spoken answer to your question, or a symbolic gift that has some bearing on it, or both. When you are ready, imagine yourself entering the space where the Nurturer dwells. Allow the scene to unfold in front of you as you pay close attention to it: How does your Inner Nurturer look? What are they wearing? How do they hold themselves? How do they speak and what do they say? If a dialogue or some exchange of touch with them is appropriate, please imagine it unfolding. When the scene is nearing completion, allow this figure to offer you a hug, their gift and perhaps some closing words of comfort. Thank them for their time. With the knowledge that you can return here at other times, gradually exit this scene and imagine yourself travelling back through the air, over landscapes, and gently into the room you are physically in. Open your eyes slowly.

When you are ready, write down everything you can remember that may contain actual or symbolic clues about your Inner Nurturer, including any exchanges. If you received a gift, what was it? You might want to draw it or let your mind wander with free associations. What might this gift mean for you and your journey towards the Nurturer?

Any or all of these exercises can be repeated as often as you like. Then, when you are ready to try this out in a real-life situation where you wish to embody the Nurturer, take a minute to prepare. Remember the essence of your Sense Memory and/or Active Imagination journeys and the parts that felt most useful. What clues did they provide as to how you can confidently embody Nurturer energy? See if you can summon these into yourself and allow them to fill your being. Then, when you enter the actual scene, keep drawing on these to the extent that they are useful.

When you exit that scene, take a moment to notice if anything was different from how you might normally show up. If so, what was it? Did the preparation help you and, if so, how?

4. Outside-In: Rehearsal Cues

(A Sovereign approach – rehearsal and performance)

These are practical cues that you can use in real life, when you feel ready. You will probably want to rehearse them first – in private or with a trusted coach/colleague, and then in public, when you feel ready.

How to communicate as a Nurturer

These real-life attitudes, body language and voice cues, sample words and phrases are all resonant with the Nurturer. Please read through them and notice which might be useful for you to step into and rehearse for future use.

a. **Mood, attitude and mindset**

Friendly, welcoming, receptive, reflective, warm, positive, encouraging, caring, open to wide-ranging conversations, offering the personal touch, available, tuning into the collective emotional field

b. **Body language and physical cues**

Open posture, open palms, welcoming, easy eye contact, smiling, informal, responsive, mirroring, leaning forward, inclusive, full-body listening, relaxed

c. **Voice**

Soft, warm, positive, friendly, compassionate, heartfelt, inviting, caring, reassuring

d. **Typical words of a Nurturer**

Welcome, together, trust, listen, honesty, care, feel, sense, comfortable, consider, invite, support, reflect

e. **Typical phrases of a Nurturer**

"What can I do for you?"; "How are you getting on?"; "Is there anything you would like to talk about?"; "What do you need?"; "What I hear you say is…."; "How can I help?"; "What's your perspective on…?"; "How do you feel about?"; "I'm open to…"; "Tell us more about that"; "What matters to you?"; "I'll always make time for you"

If the Nurturer is in your Archetypal Development Plan, please take a moment to reflect on the suggestions above. Which do you feel drawn to try first? You may need to experiment with different ways until you find what suits you best. The first few attempts may feel odd or "not like me", so we invite you to keep at it until they feel familiar enough. You might want to find a simple shift in body and voice that feels relatively comfortable as a first step and then extend it from there. The more you practise, the easier it will become to embody the Nurturer.

When you are ready, we invite you to bring what you have learned into a real-life situation, preferably one where you have a trusted ally present to give you feedback afterwards. When you are in that situation, draw on the spirit and actions of the Nurturer that you have Acted-In through your rehearsals. Notice if you think, feel and/or act differently from usual. When you exit that situation, either get feedback from your ally or reflect by yourself. What worked? What if anything would you do differently next time? Then, wait until the next opportunity presents itself – and repeat the process.

5. Development Stories

(A Storyteller/Transformer approach – narrative to describe effective change)

We complete our journey through rehearsal options with an example of Acting-In an Archetype taken from our own consulting practice. This mini case study describes how an individual successfully activated their desired outcome. This will also serve as an invitation and model for you to write your own future-focused story, one that describes the successful outcome of your own development plan.

a. Our coaching story

Frank was managing director of a large nursing home conglomerate and his presenting issue was a 35% annual staff turnover rate. In his first coaching session, he identified his Leading Actors as Transformer and Warrior and the Nurturer as his More Offstage Actor. When prompted, he revealed that he had grown up with a single-parent mother he called cold and distant. "But it was OK. It taught me to get on with things and not expect anything in return."

He was interested in why he had ended up running a company whose purpose was caring for others. "I want to make sure that everyone has what they need but I prefer to do it from a distance. If I don't sweat the small stuff constantly, the patients' families complain immediately." With further prompting, he realized that what he really meant by this was, "If I let my guard down, the low-paid staff will take advantage and slack off". He soon recognized that his matter-of-fact way of managing his employees was deeply connected to his own past, specifically to the way his mother had organized his life without visible or tactile caring. He was never shown how to internalize his Nurturer because his mother, and later others, did not model this for him. "I didn't even know what to look for," he said.

When we turned to the reasons why staff were leaving, he was quite candid: "Can you blame them? Who wants to change soiled sheets for minimum wage?" As the coaching probed deeper into his underlying motivation, he recognized that underneath the Warrior shield he did care for his staff and that, if he could learn to show this more effectively, he could potentially create a more co-operative organizational culture for everyone's benefit.

Frank decided to initiate a free stress-management programme across all his operations. This included optional yoga classes for frontline staff. He also asked the larger retirement homes to put aside a suitable room for a day-care area. This enabled workers to bring their small children to work while professionals cared for them. A year after he entered coaching, his staff turnover rate was down to less than 10% and he reported hugely increased personal job satisfaction.

b. Storying your future

A creative writing exercise to activate the power of intention, by creating a story to guide you into your desired future. We invite you to write from the perspective of that desired future – as if you were looking back on your development having successfully

completed it. This will take 30–50 minutes of quiet, uninterrupted time with writing materials or computer.

Guideline

Using the loose framework of our coaching story above, you will craft your own story as if it were your own real-life case study set at a realistic time in the future. From that future time, you look back and "reflect on your success", i.e. you create a narrative that describes *how* you activated the Nurturer, from this point forward.

Story prompts (a loose guide to follow if helpful):

i)   *Presenting issue: What was it that motivated the desire to Act-In the Nurturer?*

ii) *Personal insights: What did you learn about yourself, your formative years, your primary care-givers' Archetypes that might have played a part in the presenting issue? (This part could be aided by an actual or imaginary coach or trusted confidant or be created from personal reflection or inner dialogue.)*

iii) *First steps and their results: What simple first steps did you take on your development journey? How did they help? What impact did they have?*
     What did you learn – about yourself and/or the Nurturer?

iv) *Next steps leading to integration: What else did you choose to do and over what time frame? How did these activations help? What was the felt difference in your life? What was the visible difference to others around you?*

So, that is the full collection of Rehearsal Method Options currently in our repertoire. In our experience, within this wide range of possibilities you will be able to find at least one way to effectively build a relationship with this Archetype. Then, with commitment and practice, and in a time frame that works for you, you will Act-In the Nurturer.

Developing the Lover

1. **Archetypal Gesture:** *"I relish the beauty of the world… and I delight in others"*

    (A Sovereign/Lover approach – visible and sensory)

    An Archetypal Gesture is a simple way to remind yourself of the Lover Gifts (also available as a video and download from www.archetypesatwork.com/gestures). It is a symbolic gesture to practise in private, using Archetype-appropriate words as a quick memory tool for embodiment.

    Stand in an open and soft stance. Imagine a beautiful vista in front of you, in which several different individuals from your intimate social circle are sitting or walking around. Touch your fingertips to your heart, then bring them out from your body to describe a small circle in front of you – as you say: ***"I relish the beauty of the world…"*** *Then close your fingertips together so they touch and then gently flick your fingertips out in two or three different directions to indicate specific friends close to you, as you say:* ***"…and I delight in others."***

    Using this Archetypal Gesture is a simple way to evoke Lover energy in yourself before any engagement where an appreciative consciousness and/or easy relatability would serve. You can learn these simple gestures and phrases and practise them as often as useful.

2. **Activities and Practices**

    Below is a selection of ideas we have gathered over the years that have helped people gain more access to the Lover in life and work. It is by no means a full list and we encourage you to find your own variations if none of these feel quite right for you. We hope the following will give you ideas and inspiration for your own personalized Lover Development Plan.

a. Locations and environments that are likely to evoke the Lover

(An Explorer approach – going somewhere new and different)

Social gatherings, friendly cafés, designer showrooms, fashion boutiques, art galleries, jewellery shops, fabric and furniture museums, busy street markets, artists' studios, dance classes, fabric stores, elegant banks, beauty and nail salons, massage spas, drawing rooms, the Taj Mahal

b. Activities to rehearse the Lover

(A Strategist/Warrior approach – planning and doing)

- *Smile more often*
- *Relieve tense situations with kindness or grace*
- *Say "yes" to social invitations*
- *Introduce yourself to new people and learn to listen to them*
- *Visit an art gallery and seek out objects of beauty that inspire you*
- *Surround yourself with beauty and style*
- *Pay attention to how flowers smell*
- *Treat yourself to relaxing spa treatments*
- *Compliment people at work and thank them*
- *Pay attention to your personal style and grooming*
- *Become smart about your money and only splurge on high quality*
- *Learn to sing*

c. Creative Research

(A Transformer/Nurturer approach – research and conversations)

Who do you admire that you assign Lover energy to? These can be people you know, people you admire from a distance (living or dead) or even fictional characters.

If they are available in your network, you could find time to be with them and notice how they interact socially. Ask them about their sense of style and what they find attractive.

If they are well-known, look at photos and videos of them. Look for articles, biographies, documentaries or films about them that you can absorb as you integrate what it means to embody Lover energy.

3. Inside-Out: Sense Memory and Active Imagination

These exercises are designed to give you inner access to the Lover. Please read through them and decide if you want to try one. If so, when you have time, we recommend that you find a private and comfortable space to work in, where you are not going to be disturbed. Have a notebook (or pen and paper) nearby. These exercises can be done alone or with a trusted colleague, friend or coach in attendance. If you prefer, they are also available as an audio download from www.archetypesatwork.com/guidedjourneys.

If you are alone, please read the relevant instructions for **a**, **b** or **c** below until they are familiar enough to start. Then close your eyes for anywhere from five to 15 minutes and allow yourself to enter the process as fully as possible. Be aware that you may feel as if you are moving in and out of the process at first. it may take a few attempts (perhaps three to five) for these exercises to feel comfortable – but you are stretching out of your previous comfort zone so this is to be expected. When you are finished, make a few notes about your experience.

If you have a companion, they can read the instructions below out loud in real time. For the Sense Memory exercise **a**, you can choose to remember in silence or speak the story of your memory as you relive it. For the Active Imagination exercises **b** and **c**, the instructions can be spoken to you but your journey is best imagined in silence.

If you are using the downloads, play them and pause them as helpful as you go through the journey they describe. Repeat whenever useful.

a. Sense Memory

(A Nurturer/Lover approach – remembering your past and accessing your senses)

Allow yourself to drift into a place where you have easy access to your personal memory banks... Flick through a few memories of times in your life, however brief, where you were in beautiful surroundings and felt loved in an easy social setting. Pick one scene to focus on and begin to recall it more fully. Where were you? What were you doing? Who was around you? How did you feel? Allow yourself to experience as fully as you can what you were feeling then. How did it feel when "love was in the air" and undivided attention was given to you as you gave it back? What was it like to have people respond to you just because of your elegance and charm? See if you can now sense what enabled this entry into the Lover's territory. What part of you stepped forward and allowed you to draw on this Archetype?

When you are ready, come out of the memory and either take notes (if you are alone) or get feedback from your colleague. How did you feel and/or show up differently when you were accessing this memory?

b. **Active Imagination 1 – imagining a real-life application**
(A Dreamer/Strategist approach – imagination with a practical focus)

Imagine yourself in a scene of your choice connected to your current life, where access to the Lover would be helpful. See yourself inhabiting this scene with full access to the Lover Gifts. Observe yourself in your mind's eye as you engage with others being charming, sociable and alluring. Allow yourself to feel and sense the qualities that the Lover offers. Try to feel it in your body as an actual sensation and as an emotional response. How is this different from how you generally feel?

When you are ready, come out of the imagined scene and write down anything you want to remember. If you have a colleague with you, tell the story of your journey. You may wish to ask for feedback or to integrate the experience by yourself.

c.   Active Imagination 2 – imagining an inner figure
(A Dreamer/Storyteller approach – imagination to create a story)

Imagine yourself leaving the place where you are now and travelling through the air over varied landscapes until you land in a distant, beautifully designed space or environment that evokes Lover energy for you. (You can use the location prompts in 2a above if helpful.) Now imagine yourself preparing to greet a figure who will represent your Inner Lover. Know that you will be able to ask your Inner Lover an important question and that they will offer their wisdom in return. This may be a direct spoken answer to your question, or a symbolic gift that has some bearing on it, or both. When you are ready, imagine yourself entering the space where the Lover awaits. Allow the scene to unfold in front of you as you pay close attention to it: How does your Inner Lover look? What are they wearing? How do they hold themselves? How do they speak and what do they say? If a dialogue with them is appropriate, please imagine it unfolding. When the scene is nearing completion, allow this figure to offer you a piece of art, another gift or closing words of wisdom. Thank them for their time. With the knowledge that you can return here at other times, gradually exit this scene and imagine yourself travelling back through the air, over landscapes, and gently into the room you are physically in. Open your eyes slowly.

When you are ready, write down everything you can remember that may contain actual or symbolic clues about your Inner Lover, including any exchanges. If you received a gift, what was it? You might want to draw it or let your mind wander with free associations. What might this gift mean for you and your journey towards the Lover?

4.   Outside-In: Rehearsal Cues
(A Sovereign approach – rehearsal and performance)
These are practical cues that you can use in real life, when you feel ready. You will probably want to rehearse them first – in private or

with a trusted coach/colleague, and then in public, when you feel ready.

How to communicate as a Lover

These real-life attitudes, body language and voice cues, sample words and phrases are all resonant with the Lover. Read through them and notice which might be useful for you to step into and rehearse for future use.

a. **Mood, attitude and mindset**

   Aesthetic sense, an eye for beauty, available, curious, communicative, receptive, generous, kind, open to connect, appreciative, yearning to make others feel good, lust for life

b. **Body language and physical cues**

   Light, upright, open, inviting, free and flowing, smiling, meaningful eye contact

c. **Voice**

   Easy and responsive, passionate, gentle tones, intimate, kind, intriguing, animated, alluring

d. **Typical words of a Lover**

   Stylish, fancy, buy-in, win-win, gorgeous, fabulous, beautiful, stylish, rich, perfect, sweet, attract, eye-catching, sexy, hot, cool, relationship

e. **Typical phrases of a Lover**

   "We love it…"; "An attractive proposition…"; "Our competitors will be so jealous…"; "This relationship is going to last"; "Let's shake hands on it"; "This looks spectacular"; "I can sell this"; "This is worth spending on"; "We have to look the part…"; "This is going to pay off"; "You will love what you get"; "We need a makeover!"

If the Lover is in your Archetypal Development Plan, please take a moment to reflect on the suggestions above. Which do you feel drawn to try first? You may need to experiment with different ways until you find what suits you best. The first few attempts may feel odd or "not like me", so we invite you to keep at it until they feel familiar enough. You might want to find a simple shift in body and voice that feels relatively comfortable as a first step and then extend it from there. The more you practise, the easier it will become to embody the Lover.

When you are ready, we invite you to bring what you have learned into a real-life situation, preferably one where you have a trusted ally present to give you feedback afterwards. When you are in that situation, draw on the spirit and actions of the Lover that you have Acted-In through your rehearsals. Notice if you think, feel and/or act differently from usual. When you exit that situation, either get feedback from your ally or reflect by yourself. What worked? What if anything would you do differently next time? Then, wait until the next opportunity presents itself – and repeat the process.

5. Development Stories

(A Storyteller/Transformer approach – narrative to describe effective change)

We complete our journey through rehearsal options with an example of Acting-In an Archetype taken from our own consulting practice. This mini case study describes how an individual successfully activated their desired outcome. This will also serve as an invitation and model for you to write your own future-focused story, one that describes the successful outcome of your own development plan.

a. Our coaching story

Candace was CEO of a rapidly growing mid-sized technology company that now faced significant competition from newer start-ups. She was aware that the story that had made them successful, "We're the first", now had to change to "We're the preferred supplier" in order to survive. She was "looking to upgrade her leadership skills to match the challenge". She identified Explorer and Renegade as her key strengths and the Lover as her furthest Offstage Actor.

Relevant history included that she was the youngest child with three older brothers. In her early years, her mother frequently told her how much she had wanted "a little princess" and had "waited for her". She rejected this notion, hung out with her brothers and other older boys rather than girls her own age, refused to wear dresses and preferred sports to dolls. As an adult she was driven and smart and quickly rose up the corporate ranks.

As coaching progressed, she realized how she had internalized what she had been told in business school – that women had to act like men to be successful – and how this had reinforced her earlier "tomboy" nature. She found it difficult to truly engage with people at work in a friendly manner and realized that her interpersonal relationship skills could use some fine-tuning. She also recognized that beyond all the stereotypical and sexist ideas about what it meant to be more feminine, there was more to be explored: she saw something in archetypal thinking that allowed for an expansion of her mind without the limitations of cultural pressures.

She was willing to try out a few simple ways to Act-In the Lover archetype at work. She practised smiling more and making more eye contact, and when she related to her senior team, she consciously gave more time for interesting but non work-related conversations. She shared more of herself and gave people feedback on what she had heard. She reported back that her relationships had improved. Encouraged by the fact that she soon felt both different and better at work she started expanding her wardrobe, changing from sensible to more carefully considered clothes, and redecorated her office using artworks and living plants to enhance the atmosphere.

A few months later she got together with her senior team and they collectively decided that customer service and relationships would be the prime focus of training over the coming 18 months. She later reported that this was the new "secret sauce" that maintained their competitiveness for the next stage of business development – but that she had had to bring her own inner Lover onto the stage before she could recognize the potential value for her business.

b. Storying your future

A creative writing exercise to activate the power of intention, by creating a story to guide you into your desired future. We invite you to write from the perspective of that desired future – as if you were looking back on your development having successfully completed it. This will take 30–50 minutes of quiet, uninterrupted time with writing materials or computer.

Guideline

Using the loose framework of our coaching story above, you will craft your own story as if it were your own real-life case study set at a realistic time in the future. From that future time, you look back and "reflect on your success", i.e. you create a narrative that describes *how* you activated the Lover, from this point forward.

Story prompts (a loose guide to follow if helpful):

i) *Presenting issue: What was it that motivated the desire to Act-In the Lover?*

ii) *Personal insights: What did you learn about yourself, your formative years, your primary care-givers' Archetypes that might have played a part in the presenting issue? (This part could be aided by an actual or imaginary coach or trusted confidant or be created from personal reflection or inner dialogue.)*

iii) *First steps and their results: What simple first steps did you take on your development journey? How did they help? What impact did they have? What did you learn – about yourself and/or the Lover?*

iv) *Next steps leading to integration: What else did you choose to do and over what time frame? How did these activations help? What was the felt difference in your life? What was the visible difference to others around you?*

So, that is the full collection of Rehearsal Method Options currently in our repertoire. In our experience, within this wide range of possibilities you will be able to find at least one way to effectively build a relationship with this Archetype. Then, with commitment and practice – and in a time frame that works for you – you will Act-In the Lover.

And that completes Developing the Realm of Relationship.

CHAPTER 12

DEVELOPING THE REALM OF

Creativity

1. Archetypal Gesture
2. Activities and Practices
3. Inside-Out: Sense Memory and Active Imagination
4. Outside-In: Rehearsal Cues
5. Development Stories

If you already know that you wish to develop the Dreamer or the Storyteller, please notice which of the following you could imagine committing to as you read. Otherwise you can revisit the relevant Archetypes for you at any later time.

Developing the Dreamer

1. **Archetypal Gesture:** *"Imagine what's possible…!"*
   (A Sovereign/Lover approach – visible and sensory)
   An Archetypal Gesture is a simple way to remind yourself of the Dreamer Gifts (also available as a video and download from www.archetypesatwork.com/gestures). It is a symbolic gesture to practise in private, using Archetype-appropriate words as a quick memory tool for embodiment.

   Stand upright, happy and light on your feet. Imagine an invisible energy lifting your body, spirits and imagination upwards. Let your hands be drawn up in front of your torso and head as they reach for the sky. Let them move slowly outwards to embrace the full breadth of possibilities as you take a small step back with one foot, look up and say with excitement: ***"Imagine what's possible…!"***

   Using this Archetypal Gesture is a simple way to evoke Dreamer energy in yourself, before an important meeting or presentation or anywhere else where you seek access to possibility and intuition. You can learn these simple gestures and phrases and practise them as often as useful.

2. **Activities and Practices**
   Below is a selection of ideas we have gathered over the years that have helped people gain more access to the Dreamer in life and work. It is by no means a full list and we encourage you to find your own variations if none of these feel quite right for you. We hope the following will give you ideas and inspiration for your own personalized Dreamer Development Plan.

a. **Locations and environments that are likely to evoke the Dreamer**
    (An Explorer approach – going somewhere new and different)
    Misty landscapes, clouds in the sky, fog over the ocean, seascapes, meditation sanctuaries, spiritually orientated art galleries, sculpture gardens, sacred places (without tourists), creative studios (quiet ones), small out-of-the-way churches and temples

b. **Activities to rehearse the Dreamer**
    (A Strategist/Warrior approach – planning and doing)
    * *Create a space at work for imagination and dreams*
    * *Develop a meditation practice*
    * *Read about other worlds and different belief systems*
    * *Develop your intuition – take a class or find a teacher*
    * *Write a dreamy poem about a difficult situation*
    * *Unplug your phone and day-dream once a day*
    * *Keep a dream journal and find a dream analyst*
    * *Engage in Active Imagination*
    * *Take photographs of strange objects, clouds, mist and fog*
    * *Read or write some fantasy fiction*
    * *Learn about spiritual practices that interest you*
    * *Paint with watercolours*

c. **Creative Research**
    (A Transformer/Nurturer approach – research and conversations)

    Who do you admire that you assign Dreamer energy to? These can be people you know, people you admire from a distance (living or dead) or even fictional characters.

    If they are available in your network, you could find time to be with them and notice how they might move through life differently from you. Ask them about what inspires them and how they draw on their imagination.

    If they are well-known, seek out their artwork or other products of their imagination. You can also look at articles, biographies, documentaries or films about them. Any or all of this can help you get closer to Dreamer energy.

3. **Inside-Out: Sense Memory and Active Imagination**

These exercises are designed to give you inner access to the Dreamer. Please read through them and decide if you want to try one. If so, when you have time, we recommend that you find a private and comfortable space to work in, where you are not going to be disturbed. Have a notebook (or pen and paper) to hand. These exercises can be done alone or with a trusted colleague, friend or coach in attendance. If you prefer, they are also available as an audio download from www. archetypesatwork.com/guidedjourneys.

If you are alone, please read the relevant instructions for **a**, **b** or **c** below until they are familiar enough to start. Then close your eyes for anywhere from five to 15 minutes and allow yourself to enter the process as fully as possible. Be aware that you may feel as if you are moving in and out of the process at first. it may take a few attempts (perhaps three to five) for these exercises to feel comfortable – but you are stretching out of your previous comfort zone so this is to be expected. When you are finished, make a few notes in a notebook about your experience.

If you have a companion, they can read the instructions below out loud in real time. For the Sense Memory exercise **a**, you can choose to remember in silence or speak the story of your memory as you relive it. For the Active Imagination exercises **b** and **c**, the instructions can be spoken to you but your journey is best imagined in silence.

If you are using the downloads, play them and pause them as helpful as you go through the journey they describe. Repeat whenever useful.

a. **Sense Memory**

(A Nurturer/Lover approach – remembering your past and accessing your senses)

Allow yourself to drift into a place where you have easy access to your personal memory banks... Flow through a few memories of times in your life, however brief they may have been, where you enjoyed being dreamy or imaginative or spiritually alive. Pick one scene to focus on and begin to recall it more fully. Where were you? What were you doing? Who was around you? How did you feel? Allow yourself to experience as fully as you can what you were feeling then. See if you can now sense what enabled this brief entry into Dreamer territory. What less familiar part of you emerged in this experience? What was moving you? How did it feel to be in a creative mode without any concern about outcomes? What was it like to feel images and sensations arising from within you?

When you are ready, come out of the memory and either take notes (if you are alone) or get feedback from your colleague. How did you feel and/or show up differently when you were accessing this memory?

b. **Active Imagination 1 – imagining a real-life application**
    (A Dreamer/Strategist approach – imagination with a practical focus)

    Imagine yourself in a scene of your choice connected to your current life, where having access to the Dreamer would be helpful. See yourself inhabiting this scene with full access to Dreamer gifts. Observe yourself in your mind's eye as you engage with others being sensitive, compassionate, idealistic and imaginative. Allow yourself to feel and sense the qualities that the Dreamer offers. Try to feel it in your body as an actual sensation and as an emotional response. How is this different from how you generally feel?

    When you are ready, come out of the imagined scene and write down anything you want to remember. If you have a colleague with you, tell the story of your journey. You may wish to ask for feedback or to integrate the experience by yourself.

c. **Active Imagination 2 – imagining an inner figure**
    (A Dreamer/Storyteller approach – imagination to create a story)

    Imagine yourself leaving the place where you are now and travelling through the air over varied landscapes until you choose to descend in a distant land or seascape that evokes Dreamer energy for you. (You can use the location prompts in 2a above if helpful.) Now imagine yourself preparing to meet a figure who will represent your Inner Dreamer. Wait until you are ready to be met by this figure. Know that you will be able to ask your Inner Dreamer an important question and that they will offer images, inspirations and wisdom in return. This may be a direct spoken answer to your question, or more symbolic responses or images that could have meaning for you. When you are ready, imagine the Dreamer appearing to you in whatever form they assume. Allow the scene to unfold in front of you as you pay close attention to it: How does your Inner Dreamer look? What are they wearing? How do they hold themselves? How do they speak and what do they say? What images and inspirations are guiding them? If a dialogue with them is appropriate, please imagine it unfolding. When the scene is nearing completion, allow this figure to offer you a final symbol or vision. Thank them for their time. With the knowledge that you can return here at other times, gradually exit this scene and imagine yourself travelling back through the air, over landscapes, and gently into the room you are physically in. Open your eyes slowly.

When you are ready, write down everything you can remember that may contain actual or symbolic clues about your Inner Dreamer, including any exchanges. If you saw any images or symbols, what were they? You might want to draw them or let your mind wander with free associations they inspire. What might all of this mean for you and your journey towards the Dreamer?

Any or all of these exercises can be repeated as often as you like. Then, when you are ready to try this out in a real-life situation where you wish to embody the Dreamer, take a minute to prepare. Remember the essence of your Sense Memory and/or Active Imagination journeys and the parts that felt most useful. What clues did they provide as to how you can confidently invoke Dreamer energy? See if you can summon these into yourself and allow them to fill your being. Then, when you enter the actual scene, keep drawing on these to the extent that they are useful.

When you exit that scene, take a moment to notice if anything was different from how you might normally show up. If so, what was it? Did the preparation help you and, if so, how?

4. **Outside-In: Rehearsal Cues**

(A Sovereign approach – rehearsal and performance)

These are practical cues that you can use in real life, when you feel ready. You will probably want to rehearse them first – in private or with a trusted coach/colleague, and then in public, when you feel ready.

How to communicate as a Dreamer

These real-life attitudes, body language and voice cues, sample words and phrases are all resonant with the Dreamer. Please read through them and notice which might be useful for you to step into and rehearse for future use.

a. **Mood, attitude and mindset**

Relaxed, gentle, diffused focus, open-minded, intuitive, welcoming the imaginal and the unknown, open to possibility, idealistic, otherworldly, artistic

b. **Body language and physical cues**

Light, varied, informal, non-linear, unpredictable, flowing, flexible, dancing, looking up for inspiration

c. **Voice**

Melodious, variable, light, evocative, inspired, unpredictable, soft, serene

d. **Typical words of a Dreamer**

Imagine, create, experiment, suppose, picture, future, belief, emerging, ideally, possible, symbol, fantasy, metaphor

e. **Typical phrases of a Dreamer**

"What if..."; "Let me paint you a picture..."; "Suppose we..."; "What might be a symbol or metaphor for this..."; "What are we not seeing here?"; "Let's all tune into this for a moment..."; "What is the image we are conveying?"; "What's waiting in our future...?"; "Maybe we need to sit with not knowing for a while..."; "What is emerging?"; "Nothing is off the table"; "Let's think outside of the box"

If the Dreamer is in your Archetypal Development Plan, please take a moment to reflect on the suggestions above. Which do you feel drawn to try first? You may need to experiment with different ways until you find what suits you best. The first few attempts may feel odd or "not like me", so we invite you to keep at it until they feel familiar enough. You might want to find a simple shift in body and voice that feels relatively comfortable as a first step and then extend it from there. The more you practise, the easier it will become to embody the Dreamer.

When you are ready, we invite you to bring what you have learned into a real-life situation, preferably one where you have a trusted ally present to give you feedback afterwards. When you are in that situation, draw on the spirit and actions of the Dreamer that you have Acted-In through your rehearsals. Notice if you think, feel and/or act differently from usual. When you exit that situation, either get feedback from your ally or reflect by yourself. What worked? What if anything would you do differently next time? Then, wait until the next opportunity presents itself – and repeat the process.

5. Development Stories

(A Storyteller/Transformer approach – narrative to describe effective change)

We complete our journey through rehearsal options with an example of Acting-In an Archetype taken from our own consulting practice. This mini case study describes how an individual successfully activated their desired outcome. This will also serve as an invitation and model for you to write your own future-focused story, one that describes the successful outcome of your own development plan.

a. Our coaching story

Charlie was a senior Navy submarine safety officer who had spent over two decades on active duty on a sub. He came to coaching in his mid-40s, due to a sense that his career was stalling and that "something was missing". He identified strongly with Nurturer, Warrior and Strategist – all well suited to the day job – and noticed the Dreamer was his More Offstage Actor. He said that when he was deep at sea and around highly dangerous machinery there was no time for "day-dreaming and goofing off". He spent his waking hours driving implementation of processes and looking out for the safety of others.

At the time, he was not aware that the ocean is a classic symbol of the Dreamer energy – a mysterious, fathomless, and sometimes murky world. Symbolically, the Navy can be seen as the guardian of these mysterious places, a metaphorical embodiment of the old sea god, Neptune, holding his trident to stave off predators. Charlie was fascinated by this coincidence and began remembering times in childhood when he had enjoyed day-dreaming, walking meditations around a nearby lake, and writing poems at school. He also remembered that as a teenager he had "put these aside in order to get a sensible degree".

Archetypal coaching allowed Charlie to make a far more personal connection to the Dreamer and through this to the watery world which he had been moving in most of his life. Within a few weeks he was reading and writing poetry, and when work permitted, going scuba-diving to immerse himself in the watery world. He realized that he had treated this magnificent element of the natural world simply as a "strategic location to be navigated through safely", rather than as a mystery to be experienced with wonder. As he allowed himself to let go of his normal "day job" priorities on a dive, he began to find access to images and ideas in a way that reminded him of his early childhood reveries.

Over the next few months he began to get new ideas for improving safety functions, often while he was diving, and started a careful process of innovation on his own submarine. The positive feedback from these initiatives reached the ears of his superiors and within a year he was being asked to attend interviews for more senior posts. He is not yet sure if he wants to leave the ocean for a desk job but he has found at least part of what he was looking for. He is still scuba-diving...

b. Storying your future

A creative writing exercise to activate the power of intention, by creating a story to guide you into your desired future. We invite you to write from the perspective of that desired future – as if you were looking back on your development having successfully completed it. This will take 30–50 minutes of quiet, uninterrupted time with writing materials or computer.

Guideline

Using the loose framework of our coaching story above, you will craft your own story as if it were your own real-life case study set at a realistic time in the future. From that future time, you look back and "reflect on your success", i.e. you create a narrative that describes *how* you activated the Dreamer, from this point forward.

Story prompts (a loose guide to follow if helpful):

i) *Presenting issue: What was it that motivated the desire to Act-In the Dreamer?*

ii) *Personal insights: What did you learn about yourself, your formative years, your primary care-givers' Archetypes that might have played a part in the presenting issue? (This part could be aided by an actual or imaginary coach or trusted confidant or be created from personal reflection or inner dialogue.)*

iii) *First steps and their results: What simple first steps did you take on your development journey? How did they help? What impact did they have? What did you learn – about yourself and/or the Dreamer?*

iv) *Next steps leading to integration: What else did you choose to do and over what time frame? How did these activations help? What was the felt difference in your life? What was the visible difference to others around you?*

So, that is the full collection of Rehearsal Method Options currently in our repertoire. In our experience, within this wide range of possibilities you will be able to find at least one way to effectively build a relationship with this Archetype. Then, with commitment and practice, and in a time frame that works for you, you will Act-In the Dreamer.

Developing the Storyteller

1. **Archetypal Gesture: *"You are NOT going to believe THIS!"***

   (A Sovereign/Lover approach – visible and sensory)

   An Archetypal Gesture is a simple way to remind yourself of the Storyteller Gifts (also available as a video and download from www. archetypesatwork.com/gestures). It is a symbolic gesture to practise in private, using Archetype-appropriate words as a quick memory tool for embodiment.

   *Imagine that you are about to tell a great story to a bunch of kids around a campfire at a birthday party. Stand up and crouch slightly forward to lower your centre of gravity. Your body is light, your heart open and your mind alert. Rub your hands rapidly together a few times from palm to tip, in eager anticipation. Then clap your hands together once – loudly – to gain everyone's attention. Now, with each hand separately, place the tips of your thumbs and forefingers together and bring both hands a few inches from you face, bringing the fingers forward for emphasis as you say: **"You are NOT going to believe THIS!"***

   Using this Archetypal Gesture is a simple way to evoke Storyteller energy in you, before an important meeting or presentation – or anywhere else where you need to be a quick-thinking, versatile communicator. You can learn these simple gestures and phrases and practise them as often as useful.

2. **Activities and Practices**

   Below is a selection of ideas we have gathered over the years that have helped people gain more access to the Storyteller in life and work. It is by no means a full list and we encourage you to find your own variations if none of these feel quite right for you. We hope the following will give you ideas and inspiration for your own personalized Storyteller Development Plan.

a.   Locations and environments that are likely to evoke the Storyteller

(An Explorer approach – going somewhere new and different)

Buzzy work spaces and hubs, newspaper and other open-plan offices, creative brainstorm spaces, fast-moving and culturally rich cities, storytelling events, interactive theatre happenings, speed-dating evenings, improvisation classes, close-up magic shows

b.   Exercises and activities to rehearse the Storyteller

(A Strategist/Warrior approach – planning and doing)

- *Create a space at work to synthesize different projects, products, ideas, methods etc*
- *Attend gatherings where ideas are vigorously debated – and join in*
- *Join a debating society and practise quick communication*
- *Make more time in meetings to tell the story of where you/we are and where you/we are going*
- *Practise writing – emails, letters, short stories, essays, blogs etc*
- *Join a book club, read different books and discuss them*
- *Take an improvisation class*
- *Practise multi-tasking – more than you normally find comfortable*
- *Play word games, for instance charades, Scrabble, crosswords*
- *Go to a trivia or quiz night nearby*
- *Learn to juggle and/or other circus games*
- *Play practical jokes, learn magic tricks to surprise children*
- *Learn a new language and/or practise speaking in a different accent*

c. **Creative Research**

(A Transformer/Nurturer approach – research and conversations)

Who do you admire that you assign Storyteller energy to? These can be people you know, people you admire from a distance (living or dead) or even fictional characters.

If they are available in your network, you could find time to be with them and notice their pace and ability to connect ideas when with others. Ask them about meaning-making, narrative and/or how they multi-task.

If they are well-known, look for articles, biographies, documentaries or films about them that you can absorb as you integrate what it means to embody Storyteller energy.

3. **Inside-Out: Sense Memory and Active Imagination**

These exercises are designed to give you inner access to the Storyteller. Please read through them and decide if you want to try one. If so, when you have time, we recommend that you find a private and comfortable space to work in, where you are not going to be disturbed. Have a notebook (or pen and paper) handy. These exercises can be done alone or with a trusted colleague, friend or coach in attendance. If you prefer, they are also available as an audio download from www.archetypesatwork.com/guidedjourneys.

If you are alone, please read the relevant instructions for **a**, **b** or **c** below until they are familiar enough to start. Then close your eyes for anywhere from five to 15 minutes and allow yourself to enter the process as fully as possible. Be aware that you may feel as if you are moving in and out of the process at first. It may take a few attempts (perhaps three to five) for these exercises to feel comfortable – but you are stretching out of your previous comfort zone so this is to be expected. When you are finished, make a few notes about your experience.

If you have a companion, they can read the instructions below out loud in real time. For the Sense Memory exercise **a**, you can choose to remember in silence or speak the story of your memory as you relive it. For the Active Imagination exercises **b** and **c**, the instructions can be spoken to you but your journey is best imagined in silence.

If you are using the downloads, play them and pause them as helpful as you go through the journey they describe. Repeat whenever useful.

a. Sense Memory

(A Nurturer/Lover approach – remembering your past and accessing your senses)

Allow yourself to drift into a place where you have easy access to your personal memory banks... Flick through a few memories of times in your life, however brief, where you enjoyed being versatile and thinking quickly on your feet or being a mediator in a creative network. Pick one scene to focus on and begin to recall it more fully. Where were you? What were you doing? Who was around you? How did you feel? Allow yourself to experience as fully as you can what you were feeling then. See if you can now sense what enabled this brief entry into Storyteller territory. What part of you stepped forward and did you draw on? How did it feel to be agile and/or making connections? What was it like to have people respond to you as an effective synthesizer or communicator of ideas?

When you are ready, come out of the memory and either take notes (if you are alone) or get feedback from your colleague. How did you feel and/or show up differently when you were accessing this memory?

b. Active Imagination 1 – imagining a real-life application

(A Dreamer/Strategist approach – imagination with a practical focus)

Imagine yourself in a scene of your choice connected to your current life, where having access to the Storyteller would be helpful. See yourself inhabiting this scene with full access to the Storyteller and their gifts. Observe yourself in your mind's eye as you engage with others being versatile, thinking quickly, making connections, and/or mediating between different perspectives.

Allow yourself to feel and sense the qualities that the Storyteller offers. Try to feel it in your body as an actual sensation and as a mental response. How is this different from how you generally feel and think?

When you are ready, come out of the imagined scene and write down anything you want to remember. If you have a colleague with you, tell the story of your journey. You may wish to ask for feedback or to integrate the experience by yourself.

c. **Active Imagination 2 – imagining an inner figure**
(A Dreamer/Storyteller approach – imagination to create a story)

Imagine yourself leaving the place where you are now and travelling through the air over varied landscapes until you land in a distant place that evokes Storyteller energy for you. (You can use the location prompts in 2a above if helpful.) Now imagine yourself preparing to meet a figure who will represent your Inner Storyteller. Wait until you are ready to be given audience by this figure. Know that you will be able to ask your Inner Storyteller important questions and that they will offer their sharp intelligence and creative insights in return. This may be direct spoken answers to your questions, metaphors or tales that can help you make relevant connections. When you are ready, imagine yourself entering the space where the Storyteller is at work, doing their thing. Allow the scene to unfold in front of you as you pay close attention to it: How does your Inner Storyteller look? What are they wearing? How do they hold themselves? How do they speak and what do they say? If a dialogue with them is appropriate, please imagine it unfolding. When the scene is nearing completion, allow this figure to offer you any final ideas. Thank them for their time. With the knowledge that you can return here at other times, gradually exit this scene and imagine yourself travelling back through the air, over landscapes, and gently into the room you are physically in. Now open your eyes slowly.

When you are ready, write down everything you can remember that may contain actual or symbolic clues about your Inner Storyteller, including any exchanges, ideas or stories they shared. If any interesting metaphors or images were used, what were they? You might want to draw them or let your mind wander with free associations. What might this meeting mean for you and your journey towards the Storyteller?

Any or all of these exercises can be repeated as often as you like. Then, when you are ready to try this out in a real-life situation where you wish to embody the Storyteller, take a minute to prepare. Remember the essence of your Sense Memory and/or Active Imagination journeys and the parts that felt most useful. What clues did they provide as to how you can confidently engage Storyteller energy? See if you can summon these into yourself and allow them to fill your being. Then, when you enter the actual scene, keep drawing on these to the extent that they are useful.

When you exit that scene, take a moment to notice if anything was different from how you might normally show up. If so, what was it? Did the preparation help you and, if so, how?

4. Outside-In: Rehearsal Cues

(A Sovereign approach – rehearsal and performance)

These are practical cues that you can use in real life, when you feel ready. You will probably want to rehearse them first – in private or with a trusted coach/colleague, and then in public, when you feel ready.

How to communicate as a Storyteller

These real-life attitudes, body language and voice cues, sample words and phrases are all resonant with the Storyteller. Please read through them and notice which might be useful for you to step into and rehearse for future use.

a. Mood, attitude and mindset

Alert, intelligent, inquiring, scanning the horizon, gathering information, interweaving, looking for insights, multi-tasking, quick-thinking, flexible

b. Body language and physical cues

Light-footed, bright, mercurial, fast-paced, varied gestures, expressive, talking with your hands, animated, spontaneous

c. Voice

Bright, brisk, cheeky-cheerful, lilting, bubbly, easy, slick, lively, animated, polished, eloquent

d. Typical words of a Storyteller

Connect, communicate, inform, reach out, investigate, solve, quiz, interview, shuffle, juggle, synthesize, mix and match, advertise

e. Typical phrases of a Storyteller

"On the other hand…"; "How do we story that?"; "There are several facets that you are missing"; "Are you ready for this…?"; "Did you hear about?"; "What about this option…?"; "There's another way to think about this…"; "You'll never believe what I just heard…"; "How do we get their attention?"; "Here's a great story…"; "That reminds me of…"; "Let me add this to the mix…"; "Here's another idea"; "Let me offer a criticism here…"; "I don't want to be sceptical, but…"

If the Storyteller is in your Archetypal Development Plan, please take a moment to reflect on the suggestions above. Which do you feel drawn to try first? You may need to experiment with different ways until you find what suits you best. The first few attempts may feel odd or "not like me", so we invite you to keep at it until they feel familiar enough. You might want to find a simple shift in body and voice that feels relatively comfortable as a first step and then extend it from there. The more you practise, the easier it will become to embody the Storyteller.

When you are ready, we invite you to bring what you have learned into a real-life situation, preferably one where you have a trusted ally present to give you feedback afterwards. When you are in that situation, draw on the spirit and actions of the Storyteller that you have Acted-In through your rehearsals. Notice if you think, feel and/or act differently from usual. When you exit that situation, either get feedback from your ally or reflect by yourself. What worked? What if anything would you do differently next time? Then, wait until the next opportunity presents itself – and repeat the process.

5. Development Stories

(A Storyteller/Transformer approach – narrative to describe effective change)

We complete our journey through rehearsal options with an example of Acting-In an Archetype taken from our own consulting practice. This mini case study describes how an individual successfully activated their desired outcome. This will also serve as an invitation and model for you to write your own future-focused story, one that describes the successful outcome of your own development plan.

a. Our coaching story

Sarah had recently been promoted to a high-profile role as CFO of a global cement and aggregate business. However, she had been told that while her technical performance was outstanding, the board needed her to develop Storytelling skills. They needed her to communicate the financial data so that others with less financial expertise could easily understand it.

In her archetypal diagnosis, she cast the Storyteller as a Minor Supporting Actor. She recognized that she could access critical thinking easily and that she had the ability to synthesize different pieces of data into a comprehensive pattern. However, using images and being a confident communicator capable of selling a story felt way out of her comfort zone. Her coach was curious as to what might have caused this distinction and gently probed further...

Sarah came from a very bright family; her father was a confident and well-respected political journalist and her mother a rather over-anxious documentary researcher/writer. Both had social circles full of other intelligent cultural creatives. She was the youngest of four talkative siblings, but she had not spoken properly until she was five. A favourite family tale told how, when her mother had taken her to the paediatrician for yet another check-up, the doctor had delivered his professional opinion: "Your daughter suffers from Neurotic Mother Syndrome."

In an early coaching session, Sarah realized why she had never wanted to articulate her thoughts: "How could I compete with all that?" From early on she chose numbers over words as a learning focus. "With numbers," she said, "I found a place to be me." She soon had a reputation for being a numbers geek and at work had habitually delegated the narrative parts of her financial reports to other staff.

Her coach suggested that the task at hand was to gently encourage the Storyteller to step more centre stage – and so the development plan began. Sarah agreed to start reading short stories and to find interesting links between different tales. She learned to group them into themes as a synthesizing practice. She enrolled in an online creative writing class to develop her own voice in the written word. She also engaged in a more therapeutic constellation session where a small group of people in a room embodied parts of her and responded intuitively to the created "field" in the space between all of them. Here she was able to first honour her parents for the intelligence and conceptual gifts they had passed on to her. Secondly, she claimed back the right to have a worthy voice for herself, which she had given away in childhood.

As this process unfolded, Sarah began to get more involved in the language around her financial reporting and found she actually enjoyed using metaphors and images to describe trends and patterns. The board reported that they now genuinely looked forward to her presentations and praised her for accomplishing her development goal so effectively. Sarah was now proud that she had internalized an Archetype that had been around her all her life but which she had previously sought to reject: "I feel I can now honour both my family and myself."

b. Storying your future

A creative writing exercise to activate the power of intention, by creating a story to guide you into your desired future. We invite you to write from the perspective of that desired future – as if you were looking back on your development having successfully completed it. This will take 30–50 minutes of quiet, uninterrupted time with writing materials or computer.

Guideline

Using the loose framework of our coaching story above, you will craft your own story as if it were your own real-life case study set at a realistic time in the future. From that future time, you look back and "reflect on your success", i.e. you create a narrative that describes *how* you activated the Storyteller, from this point forward.

Story prompts (a loose guide to follow if helpful):

i)   *Presenting issue: What was it that motivated the desire to Act-In the Storyteller?*

ii) *Personal insights: What did you learn about yourself, your formative years, your primary care-givers' Archetypes that might have played a part in the presenting issue? (This part could be aided by an actual or imaginary coach or trusted confidant or be created from personal reflection or inner dialogue.)*

iii) *First steps and their results: What simple first steps did you take on your development journey? How did they help? What impact did they have? What did you learn – about yourself and/or the Storyteller?*

iv) *Next steps leading to integration: What else did you choose to do and over what time frame? How did these activations help? What was the felt difference in your life? What was the visible difference to others around you?*

So, that is the full collection of Rehearsal Method Options currently in our repertoire. In our experience, within this wide range of possibilities you will be able to find at least one way to effectively build a relationship with this Archetype. Then, with commitment and practice, and in a time frame that works for you, you will Act-In the Storyteller.

And that completes our journey through Developing the Realm of Creativity.

CHAPTER 13

DEVELOPING THE REALM OF

Rehearsal Method Options

1. **Archetypal Gesture**
2. **Activities and Practices**
3. **Inside-Out: Sense Memory and Active Imagination**
4. **Outside-In: Rehearsal Cues**
5. **Development Stories**

If you already know that you wish to develop the Renegade or the Transformer, please notice which of the following you could imagine committing to as you read. Otherwise you can revisit the relevant Archetypes for you at any later time.

Developing the Renegade

1. **Archetypal Gesture: *"I break the old rules... for the right reasons!"***
    (A Sovereign/Lover approach – visible and sensory)
    An Archetypal Gesture is a simple way to remind yourself of the Renegade Gifts (also available as a video and download from www. archetypesatwork.com/gestures). It is a symbolic gesture to practise in private, using Archetype-appropriate words as a quick memory tool for embodiment.

    *As you might imagine by now, the Renegade does things differently. The invitation here is to use the phrase **"I break the old rules... for the right reasons!"**, but to make up your own gesture/s to suit these words. Don't think about it too much, allow your body to express itself spontaneously and invent a unique gesture that you have not knowingly done before...*

    (For those for whom the Renegade is way offstage, this move may prove a step too far. In which case there is a simple way to get you started below. Once you get the idea please do stretch yourself and make up your own...

    *Stand in a loose informal way and swing your arms a couple of times to loosen up. Then face in any direction you wish and put your hands out, one in front of the other, as if grasping two sides of a big instruction booklet of rules and regulations. As you begin to speak the words **"I break the old rules..."**, tense your hands into fists and make a ripping action, imagining you are tearing up the rule book. Then as you say the words **"...for the right reasons!"**, imagine you are throwing the two ripped halves of the books down in a strong, dramatic way.)*

Using an Archetypal Gesture like this is a simple way to evoke Renegade energy in yourself before an important gathering or anywhere else you want access to a creatively disruptive energy. You can use this exercise as often as you wish or need.

2. Activities and Practices

Below is a selection of ideas we have gathered over the years that have helped people gain more access to the Renegade in life and work. It is by no means a full list and we encourage you to find your own variations if none of these feel quite right for you. We hope the following will give you ideas and inspiration for your own personalized Renegade Development Plan.

a. Locations and environments that are likely to evoke the Renegade

(An Explorer approach – going somewhere new and different)
Activist communities/gatherings/protests, innovation hubs, Museums of Invention, hi-spec, hi-tech spaces, Virtual Reality experiences, innovative or outlandish architecture (Gaudi, Gehry, Le Corbusier etc), funky art galleries and installations, World Wide Web, Area 51, block-chain communities and gatherings, Cape Canaveral, Burning Man festival

b. Activities to rehearse the Renegade

(A Strategist/Warrior approach – planning and doing)
- *Hold a work meeting in an unexpected way and/or place*
- *Create spaces for brainstorming more regularly*
- *Open a problem you have to a network of colleagues to contribute to*
- *Find someone very different from you at work to learn from or with*
- *Listen to and/or play innovative, offbeat music*
- *Get connected to a new piece of technology you have been avoiding*
- *Devote more time to your unusual or eccentric talents*
- *Research something that is at the "cutting edge" of science*
- *Do something unfamiliar that feels like a risk*

- *Find a cause that raises your heartbeat and join it*
- *Seek out a gathering of Renegades and attend a meeting (see locations above for ideas)*

c. **Creative Research**

(A Transformer/Nurturer approach – research and conversations)

Who do you admire that you assign Renegade energy to? These can be people you know, people you admire from a distance (living or dead) or even fictional characters.

If they are available in your network, you could find time to be with them and notice how they invoke freedom or provoke disruption around them. Ask them how they see the world and the future.

If they are well-known, research their innovations and radical ideas – and experience these for yourself if you can. Look for articles, biographies, documentaries or films about them that you can absorb as you integrate what it means to embody Renegade energy.

3. **Inside-Out: Sense Memory and Active Imagination**

These exercises are designed to give you inner access to the Renegade. Please read through them and decide if you want to try one. If so, when you have time, we recommend that you find a private and comfortable space to work in, where you are not going to be disturbed. Have a notebook (or pen and paper) nearby. These exercises can be done alone or with a trusted colleague, friend or coach in attendance. If you prefer, they are also available as an audio download from www.archetypesatwork.com/guidedjourneys.

If you are alone, please read the relevant instructions for **a**, **b** or **c** below until they are familiar enough to start. Then close your eyes for anywhere from five to 15 minutes and allow yourself to enter the process as fully as possible. Be aware that you may feel as if you are moving in and out of the process at first. It may take a few attempts (perhaps three to five) for these exercises to feel comfortable – but you are stretching out of your previous comfort zone so this is to be expected. When you are finished, make a few notes in a notebook about your experience.

If you have a companion, they can read the instructions below out loud in real time. For the Sense Memory exercise **a**, you can choose to remember in silence or speak the story of your memory as you relive it. For the Active Imagination exercises **b** and **c**, the instructions can be spoken to you but your journey is best imagined in silence.

If you are using the downloads, play them and pause them as helpful as you go through the journey they describe. Repeat whenever useful.

a. Sense Memory

(A Nurturer/Lover approach – remembering your past and accessing your senses)

Allow yourself to drift into a place where you have easy access to your personal memory banks... Flick through a few memories of times in your life, however brief, where you enjoyed doing something no one expected you to do. Perhaps you broke free from confining rules or you dared others to catch up with your forward-thinking. Pick one scene to focus on and begin to recall it more fully. Where were you? What were you doing? Was anyone else around – who? Allow yourself to experience as fully as you can what you were feeling then. How did it feel to be on the edge? What positive outcomes did you achieve by breaking out of old patterns? What did you draw on to achieve this? See if you can now sense what enabled this brief entry into Renegade territory. What part of you stepped forward and did you draw on?

When you are ready, come out of the memory and either take notes (if you are alone) or get feedback from your colleague. How did you feel and/or show up differently when you were accessing this memory?

b. Active Imagination 1 – imagining a real-life application

(A Dreamer/Strategist approach – imagination with a practical focus)

Imagine yourself in a scene of your choice connected to your current life, where access to the Renegade would be helpful. See yourself inhabiting this scene with full access to Renegade gifts. Imagine yourself as a maverick: independent, unfettered and tuned into the future. Observe yourself in your mind's eye as you embody innovative energy, whether by yourself or with others. Allow yourself to feel and sense the qualities that the Renegade offers. Try to feel it in your body as an actual sensation and as an emotional response. How is this different from how you generally feel?

When you are ready, come out of the imagined scene and write down anything you want to remember. If you have a colleague with you, tell the story of your journey. You may wish to ask for feedback or to integrate the experience by yourself.

c. **Active Imagination 2 – imagining an inner figure**
    (A Dreamer/Storyteller approach – imagination to create a story)

Imagine yourself leaving the place where you are now and travelling through the air over varied landscapes until you land in a distant space that evokes Renegade energy for you. (You can use the location prompts in 2a above if helpful.) Now imagine yourself preparing to meet a figure who will represent your Inner Renegade. Know that you will be able to observe your Inner Renegade as they follow their intuitions. You can ask an important question and they will offer a unique response in return. When you are ready, enter their space and allow yourself to be surprised by how or where they appear in it. Now allow the scene to unfold in front of you as you pay close attention to it: How does your Inner Renegade look? What are they wearing? How do they hold themselves? How do they speak and what do they say? If a dialogue with them is appropriate, imagine it unfolding. When the scene is nearing completion, allow this figure to offer you a gift, an invention or a closing insight. Thank them for their time. With the knowledge that you can return here at other times, gradually exit this scene and imagine yourself travelling back through the air, over landscapes, and gently into the room you are physically in. Open your eyes slowly.

When you are ready, write down everything you can remember that may contain actual or symbolic clues about your Inner Renegade, including any exchanges. If you received a gift, what was it? You might want to draw it or let your mind wander with free associations. What might this gift mean for you and your journey towards the Renegade?

Any or all of these exercises can be repeated as often as you like. Then, when you are ready to try this out in a real-life situation where you wish to embody the Renegade, take a minute to prepare. Remember the essence of your Sense Memory and/or Active Imagination journeys and the parts that felt most useful. What clues did they provide as to how you can confidently invoke Renegade energy? See if you can summon these into yourself and allow them to fill your being. Then, when you enter the actual scene, keep drawing on these to the extent that they are useful.

When you exit that scene, take a moment to notice if anything was different from how you might normally show up. If so, what was it? Did the preparation help you and, if so, how?

4. Outside-In: Rehearsal Cues

(A Sovereign approach – rehearsal and performance)

These are practical cues that you can use in real life, when you feel ready. You will probably want to rehearse them first – in private or with a trusted coach/colleague, and then in public, when you feel ready.

How to communicate as a Renegade

These real-life attitudes, body language and voice cues, sample words and phrases are all resonant with the Renegade. Please read through them and notice which might be useful for you to step into and rehearse for future use.

a. Mood, attitude and mindset

Questioning, creatively disrupting, challenging, different, making big leaps, inventive, non-conformist, embracing radical alternatives, reaching for the future, oppositional

b. **Body language and physical cues**
Unpredictable, informal, energized, irreverent, sparky, sudden, spontaneous, unique, restless

c. **Voice**
Cool, unemotional, surprising, atonal, quick, making non-verbal noises, questioning, unstructured

d. **Typical words of a Renegade**
New, invent, reinvent, future, challenge, change, disrupt, electrify, leap, technology, machines, science, cutting edge

e. **Typical phrases of a Renegade**
"We are creating the future here"; "This will be a breakthrough..."; "We are going to disrupt the status quo"; "It's not evolution, it's revolution!"; "What rules do we need to break around here?"; "We have to take a radical leap"; "Change or die!"; "These norms are stifling"; "Structures only protect those in power"; "Let's not limit ourselves to what we know"; "Let's create an app for that"; "There has to be a techno-fix for that"

If the Renegade is in your Archetypal Development Plan, please take a moment to reflect on the suggestions above. Which do you feel drawn to try first? You may need to experiment with different ways until you find what suits you best. The first few attempts may feel odd or "not like me", so we invite you to keep at it until they feel familiar enough. You might want to find a simple shift in body and voice that feels relatively comfortable as a first step and then extend it from there. The more you practise, the easier it will become to embody the Renegade.

When you are ready, we invite you to bring what you have learned into a real-life situation, preferably one where you have a trusted ally present to give you feedback afterwards. When you are in that situation, draw on the spirit and actions of the Renegade that you have Acted-In through your rehearsals. Notice if you think, feel and/or act differently from usual. When you exit that situation, either get feedback from your ally or reflect by yourself. What worked? What if anything would you do differently next time? Then, wait until the next opportunity presents itself – and repeat the process.

5. Development Stories

(A Storyteller/Transformer approach – narrative to describe effective change)

We complete our journey through rehearsal options with an example of Acting-In an Archetype taken from our own consulting practice. This mini case study describes how an individual successfully activated their desired outcome. This will also serve as an invitation and model for you to write your own future-focused story, one that describes the successful outcome of your own development plan.

a. Our coaching story

Sanjay worked as a successful engineer in a multinational infrastructure construction company. He now led a large team but was struggling to get his younger, Millennial recruits to follow his rules. He confessed he had no idea how to relate to them: "They just don't understand procedure; they think a rule is only a suggestion. These young Millennials are like aliens to me."

Unsurprisingly, as an accomplished engineer, Sanjay had a natural aptitude for the Strategist and the Explorer and felt comfortable in the Nurturer, carefully developing those who responded well to the boundaries he imposed. The Renegade was way offstage and when he saw it in others it made him feel uneasy and somewhat threatened. In coaching, he reported that his family had taught him to follow strict rules, traditions and expectations. Now in his 50s, these values were deeply engrained.

When prompted, Sanjay recalled a time as a young teenager when he had freed himself of rules. He was obsessed with objects that could fly and one holiday decided to invent his own home-made rocket. He spent weeks on this; first drawing possible new shapes, then slowly assembling the parts. His zest for pursuing his invention led to him "liberating" some necessary parts from nearby junk yards at night. When he ran out of money towards the end, he even snuck out one night to siphon gasoline from the big cars parked outside in the nearby richer neighbourhood.

When he was ready, he got his friends together to witness the big launch, which went well – until the rocket exploded 50 feet off the ground, to the great amusement and enthusiasm of the witnesses present. As he recalled this event, a mischievous grin spread over his face. His eyes lit up as he described in great detail how he had imagined himself soaring through the sky in his unique invention.

His coach then suggested that Sanjay begin to see the young engineers as "fellow rocketeers", wanting to soar freely in the air, willing to break the old rules in search of innovation and a "big bang". He got it. He had found a personal way to relate to his newer recruits' need for freedom. Now he started figuring out how to utilize the gift of their wild imaginations for the benefit of all.

He set up an outing so he and his staff could attend an innovation conference – and then set up a debrief of what they had learned in a nearby museum of modern art. He found a lesser used meeting room at work that he asked the younger staff to design and decorate – on a limited budget – as their innovation hub. Tables and chairs duly disappeared. Beanbags, a table football game, Lego, plasticine and other creative materials took their place. In coaching, he referred to this proudly as "the Rocket Room". He started holding informal drop-in brainstorm meetings there for two hours a week. He asked for feedback on the current rules and guidelines and agreed to remove the ones that limited his staff's freedom to innovate appropriately. Several months later Sanjay reported huge progress. Having met his Millennials in their own Renegade archetypal preference, he had earned their respect for the more Strategic structures and processes that he deemed essential to their collective tasks. He could now harness the innovative potential of his younger staff rather than feel threatened by it.

b. Storying your future

A creative writing exercise to activate the power of intention, by creating a story to guide you into your desired future. We invite you to write from the perspective of that desired future – as if you were looking back on your development having successfully

completed it. This will take 30–50 minutes of quiet, uninterrupted time with writing materials or computer.

Guideline

Using the loose framework of our coaching story above, you will craft your own story as if it were your own real-life case study set at a realistic time in the future. From that future time, you look back and "reflect on your success", i.e. you create a narrative that describes how you activated the Renegade, from this point forward.

Story prompts (a loose guide to follow if helpful):

i)   *Presenting issue: What was it that motivated the desire to Act-In the Renegade?*

ii)   *Personal insights: What did you learn about yourself, your formative years, your primary care-givers' Archetypes that might have played a part in the presenting issue? (This part could be aided by an actual or imaginary coach or trusted confidant or be created from personal reflection or inner dialogue.)*

iii) *First steps and their results: What simple first steps did you take on your development journey? How did they help? What impact did they have? What did you learn – about yourself and/or the Renegade?*

iv)   *Next steps leading to integration: What else did you choose to do and over what time frame? How did these activations help? What was the felt difference in your life? What was the visible difference to others around you?*

So, that is the full collection of Rehearsal Method Options currently in our repertoire. In our experience, within this wide range of possibilities you will be able to find at least one way to effectively build a relationship with this Archetype. Then, with commitment and practice – and in a time frame that works for you – you will Act-In the Renegade.

Developing the Transformer

1. **Archetypal Gesture: *"I dig in the depths... and bring back a gift"***
    (A Sovereign/Lover approach – visible and sensory)
    An Archetypal Gesture is a simple way to remind yourself of the Transformer Gifts (also available as a video and download from www.archetypesatwork.com/gestures). It is a symbolic gesture to practise in private, using Archetype-appropriate words as a quick memory tool for embodiment.

    *Stand and feel your feet deeply rooted to the ground. Relax your knees so you have a low centre of gravity. Allow yourself to feel heavy and serious. Look down and then allow your arms and torso to slowly drop down as you release your spine towards the floor. Now allow your hands to do some imaginary digging into moist earth at your feet, as you say: "**I dig in the depths...**" Then imagine finding a jewel or a nugget of precious metal down there. Grasp it in one or both hands and then raise yourself back up to standing, extend your hands in front of you with an offering to others, as you say: "**...and bring back a gift.**"*

    Using this Archetypal Gesture is a simple way to evoke Transformer energy in yourself, before an important gathering, meeting or anywhere else where depth and/or a psychological perspective would be of service. You can learn these simple gestures and phrases and practise them as often as useful.

2. **Activities and Practices**
    Below is a selection of ideas we have gathered over the years that have helped people gain more access to the Transformer in life and work. It is by no means a full list and we encourage you to find your own variations if none of these feel quite right for you. We hope the

following will give you ideas and inspiration for your own personalized Transformer Development Plan.

a. Locations and environments that are likely to evoke the Transformer

(An Explorer approach – going somewhere new and different)
Cave systems, regenerative earth projects, dark woods in moonlight, therapeutic communities, quiet and dim coaching and therapy rooms, anywhere underground, ritual sites, graveyards and burial sites, stone circles, labyrinths, memorials for the dead, ruins

b. Activities to rehearse the Transformer

(A Strategist/Warrior approach – planning and doing)
- *Work with a life coach or a therapist to understand your past, present and future*
- *Read psychology and books about transformation*
- *Journal about times of "death and rebirth" in your life*
- *Find a project at work or in your local community that is intending a big transition that you resonate with*
- *Take recycling on as a lifestyle choice – find small projects to start with, perhaps at home*
- *Go through old stuff and give away old clutter*
- *Be a detective and discover how your family, community or organization survived times of necessary change*
- *Research your family roots – or the roots of your organization – and identify the origins with its particular DNA. What has made us what we are today?*
- *Go antique-hunting – look for treasures others do not see*
- *Restore an old car or an old piece of furniture*
- *Identify an old behavioural pattern that is now in your way and create a ritual where you symbolically burn or bury it*
- *Do some extended research into a subject that has depth and meaning for you*

c. Creative Research

(A Transformer/Nurturer approach – research and conversations)

Who do you admire that you assign Transformer energy to? These can be people you know, people you admire from a distance (living or dead) or even fictional characters.

If they are available in your network, you could find time to be with them and notice how they engage with life and work. You might ask their advice about issues that are troubling you. You could ask them about their experiences of regeneration: death and rebirth.

If they created a transformational practice within their work, research and experience it, if possible. If they are well-known, look for articles, biographies, documentaries or films about them that you can absorb as you integrate what it means to embody Transformer energy.

3. Inside-Out: Sense Memory and Active Imagination

These exercises are designed to give you inner access to the Transformer. Please read through them and decide if you want to try one. If so, when you have time, we recommend that you find a private and comfortable space to work in, where you are not going to be disturbed. Have a notebook (or pen and paper) nearby. These exercises can be done alone or with a trusted colleague, friend or coach in attendance. If you prefer, they are also available as an audio download from www.archetypesatwork.com/guidedjourneys.

If you are alone, please read the relevant instructions for **a**, **b** or **c** below until they are familiar enough to start. Then close your eyes for anywhere from five to 15 minutes and allow yourself to enter the process as fully as possible. Be aware that you may feel as if you are moving in and out of the process at first. Indeed, it may take a few attempts (perhaps three to five) for these exercises to feel comfortable – but you are stretching out of your previous comfort zone so this is to be expected. When you are finished, make a few notes about your experience.

If you have a companion, they can read the instructions below out loud in real time. For the Sense Memory exercise **a**, you can choose to remember in silence or speak the story of your memory as you relive it. For the Active Imagination exercises **b** and **c**, the instructions can be spoken to you but your journey is best imagined in silence.

If you are using the downloads, play them and pause them as helpful as you go through the journey they describe. Repeat whenever useful.

a. Sense Memory

(A Nurturer/Lover approach – remembering your past and accessing your senses)

Settle yourself and start breathing deeply to get in touch with the deeper parts of yourself... Drift into a place where you have easy access to your personal memory banks... Delve into a few memories of times in your life where you either voluntarily or involuntarily were taken to the edge of your capacities – and came out wiser afterwards. Times when you were asked to tap into your deepest reserves and face an inner or outer truth that had been hidden. Now choose one experience to focus on and slowly allow yourself to recall it more fully. What was the situation and the context? Where were you? What were you doing? Who was around you? How did you feel? Allow yourself to experience as fully as you can what you were feeling then. See if you can uncover what got you through this experience. What enabled you to stick with the discomfort, even if it was not an experience you would have willingly chosen? What rituals did you engage in or create to help with the transformation process? How did you feel when you realized you were going to make it through, even though you may have doubted this at times? What was the hidden gold that you brought back from the Underworld?

When you are ready, come out of the memory and either take notes (if you are alone) or get feedback from your colleague. How did you feel and/or show up differently when you were accessing this memory?

b. **Active Imagination 1 – imagining a real-life application**

(A Dreamer/Strategist approach – imagination with a practical focus)

Imagine yourself in a situation of your choice connected to your current life, where access to the Transformer would be helpful. See yourself inhabiting this scene with full access to Transformer gifts. Imagine yourself as a depth-seeking agent of change, never letting up on finding the deep truth behind the trivial. Observe yourself in your mind's eye as you engage with others with powerful intensity to enable transition. Allow yourself to feel and sense the qualities that the Transformer offers. Try to feel it in your body as an actual sensation and as an emotional response. How is this different from how you generally feel?

When you are ready, come out of the imagined scene and write down anything you want to remember. If you have a colleague with you, tell the story of your journey. You may wish to ask for feedback or to integrate the experience by yourself.

c. **Active Imagination 2 – imagining an inner figure**

(A Dreamer/Storyteller approach – imagination to create a story)

Imagine yourself leaving the place where you are now and travelling through the air over varied landscapes until you land in a distant place in nature that evokes Transformer energy for you. (You can use the location prompts in 2a above if helpful.) Now imagine yourself preparing to meet a figure who will represent your Inner Transformer. Wait until you are ready to be given audience by this figure. Know that you will be able to ask your Inner Transformer an important question and that they will offer their wisdom in return. This may be a direct spoken answer to your question, or a symbolic gift that has some bearing on it, or both. When you are ready, imagine yourself entering the space where the Transformer awaits. Allow the scene to unfold in front of you as you pay close attention to it: How does your Inner Transformer look? What are they wearing? How do they hold themselves? How do they speak and what do they say? If a dialogue with them is appropriate, please imagine it unfolding. When the scene is nearing completion, allow this figure to offer you their gift or closing words of wisdom. Thank them for their time. With the knowledge that you can return here at other times, gradually exit this scene and imagine yourself travelling back through the air, over landscapes, and gently into the room you are physically in. Open your eyes slowly.

When you are ready, write down everything you can remember that may contain actual or symbolic clues about your Inner Transformer, including any exchanges. If you received a gift, what was it? You might want to draw it, or let your mind wander with free associations. What might this gift mean for you and your journey towards the Transformer?

Any or all of these exercises can be repeated as often as you like. Then, when you are ready to try this out in a real-life situation where you wish to embody the Transformer, take a minute to prepare. Remember the essence of your Sense Memory and/or Active Imagination journeys and the parts that felt most useful. What clues did they provide as to how you can confidently embody Transformer energy? See if you can summon these into yourself and allow them to fill your being. Then, when you enter the actual scene, keep drawing on these to the extent that they are useful.

When you exit that scene, take a moment to notice if anything was different from how you might normally show up. If so, what was it? Did the preparation help you and, if so, how?

4. Outside-In: Rehearsal Cues

(A Sovereign approach – rehearsal and performance)
These are practical cues that you can use in real life, when you feel ready. You will probably want to rehearse them first – in private or with a trusted coach/colleague, and then in public, when you feel ready.

How to communicate as a Transformer

These real-life attitudes, body language and voice cues, sample words and phrases are all resonant with the Transformer. Read through them carefully and notice which might be useful for you to step into and rehearse for future use.

a. **Mood, attitude and mindset**

Profound, honouring mystery, trusting descent, doggedly determined, quest to uncover what is hidden, speaking to that which is repressed, understanding the need for rituals during transition

b. **Body language and physical cues**

Undemonstrative, methodical, slow, measured, deliberate, unhurried, holding space

c. **Voice**

Slow, powerful, deep, intense, sincere, wise, deliberate, truthful, magnetic

d. **Typical words of a Transformer**

Depth, research, discover, investigate, dig, roots, source, death and rebirth, ritual, regeneration, transition, letting go, penetrating, unearthing

e. **Typical phrases of a Transformer**

"We have to break down to break through"; "We are not going deep enough"; "What (or who) is really behind this?"; "We need to get back to our roots"; "Let's look for the healing potential in this crisis"; "Can we make this into a symbolic event?"; "Let's not rush to a solution"; "It's OK to stay with the not knowing"; "There is more potential we can tap into here"; "This needs more research, more time and more resources"

If the Transformer is in your Archetypal Development Plan, please take a moment to reflect on the suggestions above. Which do you feel drawn to try first? You may need to experiment with different ways until you find what suits you best. The first few attempts may feel odd or "not like me", so we invite you to keep at it until they feel familiar enough. You might want to find a simple shift in body and voice that feels relatively comfortable as a first step and then extend it from there. The more you practise, the easier it will become to embody the Transformer.

When you are ready, we invite you to bring what you have learned into a real-life situation, preferably one where you have a trusted ally present to give you feedback afterwards. When you are in that situation, draw on the spirit and actions of the Transformer that you have Acted-In through your rehearsals. Notice if you think, feel and/or act differently from usual. When you exit that situation, either get feedback from your ally or reflect by yourself. What worked? What if anything would you do differently next time? Then, wait until the next opportunity presents itself – and repeat the process.

5. Development Stories

(A Storyteller/Transformer approach – narrative to describe effective change)

We complete our journey through rehearsal options with an example of Acting-In an Archetype taken from our own consulting practice. This mini case study describes how an individual successfully activated their desired outcome. This will also serve as an invitation and model for you to write your own future-focused story, one that describes the successful outcome of your own development plan.

a. Our coaching story

Rachel was running several departments in a major hospital. Due to reduced funding she had recently managed the closure of a maternity department. She was aware that she and other key figures were feeling low or depressed, demotivated, and unable to let go of a deep sense of loss.

She identified as a Storyteller, Nurturer and Sovereign who normally thrived on being the bright spark at the centre of her organizational stage. But now, "It's like the lights have gone out and I can't see my way forward." The Transformer showed up as one of her More Offstage Actors. The key words reminded her of horror movies which she habitually avoided. She had never related much to the mysterious or, as she said, "the dark side of life".

As far as Rachel could tell there were no buried family traumas that might have put her off this Archetype but more of a general sense of "not wanting to go digging in the dark". So, the coach proceeded gently to look for where the archetypal expression of the Transformer might show up. Rachel was fascinated to recognize that the department that had just closed was one designed to look deeper into the mysteries of pre-birth – and to transform potential threats into opportunities for timely healing. Hidden treasures were revealed and sometimes unspeakable tragedies as well.

She needed to find new ways to connect to this part of her, a part that had been externalized into a department that was now no more. Rachel's coach reconnected her with other Transformer experiences she had experienced in her past. Asked to relate the key words of the Transformer to her childhood, Rachel revealed with a sparkle in her eyes that she once had an ant farm with a glass wall where she could watch the secret life of the colony. She also liked to solve puzzles and had several books of butterflies – whose journey from the caterpillar is a classic symbol of transformation and rebirth.

She saw that she had been and could be fascinated with things that lie below the surface and committed to exploring the Transformer in life and work. Rachel took conscious time out to read books about great mysteries and healing practices. She began to study Reiki. Over several months she did some grief work to release the buried trauma of closing one of her favourite departments. She brought a Process Coach into her leadership team to let them all understand and move through their loss – and then started thinking about how the now empty space could be transformed. The team eventually settled on a quiet room with soft music, where staff and visitors alike could go to de-stress from busy or painful times. When everything was ready, Rachel held a celebration to open the new space, inviting some doctors and mothers who had experienced the old department to come. This honoured both what had been let go and what was now being reborn from it. Rachel says that the whole experience has given more depth to her leadership – and even though she is no longer the compulsive shiny storyteller she used to be, her team and staff seem more mature, re-motivated and are working well together again.

b. Storying your future

A creative writing exercise to activate the power of intention, by creating a story to guide you into your desired future. We invite you to write from the perspective of that desired future – as if you were looking back on your development having successfully completed it. This will take 30–50 minutes of quiet, uninterrupted time with writing materials or computer.

Guideline

Using the loose framework of our coaching story above, you will craft your own story as if it were your own real-life case study set at a realistic time in the future. From that future time, you look back and "reflect on your success", i.e. you create a narrative that describes *how* you activated the Transformer, from this point forward.

Story prompts (a loose guide to follow if helpful):

i) *Presenting issue: What was it that motivated the desire to Act-In the Transformer?*

ii) *Personal insights: What did you learn about yourself, your formative years, your primary care-givers' Archetypes that might have played a part in the presenting issue? (This part could be aided by an actual or imaginary coach or trusted confidant or be created from personal reflection or inner dialogue.)*

iii) *First steps and their results: What simple first steps did you take on your development journey? How did they help? What impact did they have? What did you learn – about yourself and/or the Transformer?*

iv) *Next steps leading to integration: What else did you choose to do and over what time frame? How did these activations help? What was the felt difference in your life? What was the visible difference to others around you?*

So, that is the full collection of Rehearsal Method Options currently in our repertoire. In our experience, within this wide range of possibilities you will be able to find at least one way to effectively build a relationship with this Archetype. Then, with commitment and practice, and in a time frame that works for you, you will Act-In the Transformer.

And that completes our journey through Developing the Realm of Change.

CHAPTER 14

DEVELOPING THE REALM OF

Action

1. **Archetypal Gesture**
2. **Activities and Practices**
3. **Inside-Out: Sense Memory and Active Imagination**
4. **Outside-In: Rehearsal Cues**
5. **Development Stories**

If you already know that you wish to develop the Warrior or the Explorer, please notice which of the following you could imagine committing to as you read. Otherwise you can revisit the relevant Archetypes for you at any later time.

Developing the Warrior

1. **Archetypal Gesture:** *"Ready, aim, FIRE!"*
   (A Sovereign/Lover approach – visible and sensory)
   An Archetypal Gesture is a simple way to remind yourself of the Warrior Gifts (also available as a video and download from www.archetypesatwork.com/gestures). It is a symbolic gesture to practise in private, using Archetype-appropriate words as a quick memory tool for embodiment.

   The gestures follow three actions that imitate firing an arrow from a bow to hit a target. Stand upright and allow yourself to be filled with steely determination. Put your feet together, reach your non-dominant hand and arm forward, bend your fingers as if they were holding a firm, heavy bow. Reach your dominant hand and arm forward until it is nearly touching the first and bend the fingers as if they were grasping the bowstring. Say the word **"Ready"***. Take a small step back (with the foot on the bowstring side) as you pull the bowstring back (until your elbow is as far back as it can go). Focus your eyes on the chosen target in front of you, as you say* **"Aim"***. The firing action will involve moving your back foot and back arm simultaneously; the back foot moves forward to end up in front of your other foot. Your "bowstring hand" comes forward as you open the "bow hand" so that the back hand slaps the front hand on the way towards the target. Make it all one single, fluid and explosive movement as you assertively say* **"FIRE!"** *Freeze for a second in the final posture with your front hand pointing at the desired target.*

   Using this Archetypal Gesture is a simple way to evoke Warrior energy in yourself, before any situation where you need to be assertive and/or motivate others to make things happen. You can learn these simple gestures and phrases and practise them as often as useful.

2. Activities and Practices

Below is a selection of ideas we have gathered over the years that have helped people gain more access to the Warrior in life and work. It is by no means a full list and we encourage you to find your own variations if none of these feel quite right for you. We hope the following will give you ideas and inspiration for your own personalized Warrior Development Plan.

a. Locations and environments that are likely to evoke the Warrior

(An Explorer approach – going somewhere new and different)
Martial arts studios, target ranges, long-term rival teams competing in sports stadia, castle battlements, war museums, intense drumming concerts, workout areas in gyms, racetracks

b. Activities to rehearse the Warrior

(A Strategist/Warrior approach – planning and doing)
- *Engage in competitive or extreme sports*
- *Exercise fiercely in a gym, particularly aerobics*
- *Practise martial arts – karate, Aikido, Judo, Taekwando, Tai Chi*
- *Set yourself challenging physical tasks*
- *Hit a punch bag, learn archery, fencing or spear-fishing*
- *Set yourself goals and targets and discipline yourself to hit them*
- *Get a personal trainer*
- *Take up running – set yourself times to make and break*
- *Drive a fast car around a racetrack, ride a motorcycle or race a bike*
- *Try paint-balling or go-kart racing*
- *Learn how to debate without destroying your opponent*
- *Strive to be the best and first at something*
- *Learn to defend your personal space and time: practise saying "no" when people ask too much from you*

c. **Creative Research**

(A Transformer/Nurturer approach – research and conversations)

Who do you admire that you assign Warrior energy to? These can be people you know, people you admire from a distance (living or dead) or even fictional characters.

If they are available in your network, you could find time to be with them and watch how and when they compete. Ask them about their drive and attitude towards fear.

If they are well-known, look for examples of them defending the weak, being brave and/or winning. Look for video clips, articles, biographies, documentaries or films about them that you can absorb as you integrate what it means to embody Warrior energy.

3. **Inside-Out: Sense Memory and Active Imagination**

These exercises are designed to give you inner access to the Warrior. Please read through them and decide if you want to try one. If so, when you have time, we recommend that you find a private and comfortable space to work in, where you are not going to be disturbed. Have a notebook (or pen and paper) nearby. These exercises can be done alone or with a trusted colleague, friend or coach in attendance. If you prefer, they are also available as an audio download from www.archetypesatwork.com/guidedjourneys.

If you are alone, please read the relevant instructions for **a**, **b** or **c** below until they are familiar enough to start. Then close your eyes for anywhere from five to 15 minutes and allow yourself to enter the process as fully as possible. Be aware that you may feel as if you are moving in and out of the process at first. It may take a few attempts (perhaps three to five) for these exercises to feel comfortable – but you are stretching out of your previous comfort zone so this is to be expected. When you are finished, make a few notes about your experience.

If you have a companion, they can read the instructions below out loud in real time. For the Sense Memory exercise **a**, you can choose to remember in silence or speak the story of your memory as you relive it. For the Active Imagination exercises **b** and **c**, the instructions can be spoken to you but your journey is best imagined in silence.

If you are using the downloads, play them and pause them as helpful as you go through the journey they describe. Repeat whenever useful.

a. Sense Memory

(A Nurturer/Lover approach – remembering your past and accessing your senses)

Allow yourself to drift into a place where you have easy access to your personal memory banks… Flick through a few memories of times in your life, however brief, when you achieved something out of the ordinary. Something that took effort, passion and/or discipline where you met a tough challenge and stood up for yourself or others. Now select one memory to focus on and begin to recall it more fully. Where were you? What were you doing? Who was around you? Allow yourself to experience as fully as you can what you were feeling then. What unusual and positive outcome did it lead to? What did you draw on to meet your goal? What enabled you to do this? How did you feel when you achieved your aim? If others you trusted were around, how did they respond? What was different about this time from your more usual way of being?

When you are ready, come out of the memory and either take notes (if you are alone) or get feedback from your colleague. How did you feel and/or show up differently when you were accessing this memory?

b. Active Imagination 1 – imagining a real-life application

(A Dreamer/Strategist approach – imagination with a practical focus)

Imagine yourself in a scene of your choice connected to your current life, where access to the Warrior would help you or others around you. See yourself inhabiting this scene with full access to Warrior gifts. Observe yourself in your mind's eye as you engage with this situation as a champion or a defender: brave, forceful and decisive. Allow yourself to feel and sense the qualities that the Warrior offers. Try to feel it in your body as an actual sensation and as an emotional response. How is this different from how you generally feel?

When you are ready, come out of the imagined scene and write down anything you want to remember. If you have a colleague with you, tell the story of your journey. You may wish to ask for feedback or to integrate the experience by yourself.

c.   Active Imagination 2 – imagining an inner figure
(A Dreamer/Storyteller approach – imagination to create a story)

Imagine yourself leaving the place where you are now and travelling through the air over varied landscapes until you land in a distant place that evokes Warrior energy for you. (You can use the location prompts in 2a above if helpful.) Now imagine yourself preparing to meet a figure who will represent your Inner Warrior. Wait until you are ready to be given audience by this figure. Know that you will be able to ask your Inner Warrior an important question and that they will offer their wisdom in return. This may be a direct spoken answer to your question, or a symbolic gift or weapon that has some bearing on it, or both. When you are ready, imagine yourself entering the space where the Warrior is standing. Allow the scene to unfold in front of you as you pay close attention to it: How does your Inner Warrior look and move? What are they wearing? How do they hold themselves? How do they speak and what do they say? If a dialogue with them is appropriate, please imagine it unfolding. When the scene is nearing completion, allow this figure to offer you their gift or closing words of wisdom. Thank them for their time. With the knowledge that you can return here at other times, gradually exit this scene and imagine yourself travelling back through the air, over landscapes, and gently into the room you are physically in. Open your eyes slowly.

When you are ready, write down everything you can remember that may contain actual or symbolic clues about your Inner Warrior, including any exchanges. If you received a gift, what was it? You might want to draw it or let your mind wander with free associations. What might this gift mean for you and your journey towards the Warrior?

Any or all of these exercises can be repeated as often as you like. Then, when you are ready to try this out in a real-life situation where you wish to embody the Warrior, take a minute to prepare. Remember the essence of your Sense Memory and/or Active Imagination journeys and the parts that felt most useful. What clues did they provide as to how you can confidently embody Warrior energy? See if you can summon these into yourself and allow them to fill your being. Then, when you enter the actual scene, keep drawing on these to the extent that they are useful.

When you exit that scene, take a moment to notice if anything was different from how you might normally show up. If so, what was it? Did the preparation help you and, if so, how?

4. Outside-In: Rehearsal Cues

(A Sovereign approach – rehearsal and performance)

These are practical cues that you can use in real life, when you feel ready. You will probably want to rehearse them first – in private or with a trusted coach/colleague, and then in public, when you feel ready.

How to communicate as a Warrior

These real-life attitudes, body language and voice cues, sample words and phrases are all resonant with the Warrior. Please read through them and notice which might be useful for you to step into and rehearse for future use.

a. Mood, attitude and mindset

Ready to act, task-focused, to the point, wanting to be first, exhibiting the will to win, effective, effortlessly assertive, disciplined and passionate

b. Body language and physical cues

Upright, positive, forceful, direct, strong eye contact, energized, firm, urgent, animated, rousing, challenging

c. Voice

Forceful, loud, positive, strong, swift rhythm, persuasive, committed, fierce, fast, confident, motivating

d. Typical words of a Warrior

Win, goal, can, will, must, risk, commit, confront, action, discipline, delivery, ruthless, unstoppable, outstanding

e. Example phrases of a Warrior

"I know we can do this"; "We are going out there to win"; "This goal is vital!"; "Let's make this happen!"; "Failure is not an option"; "Our target is clear…"; "What I need you to do is this…"; "Ready? Then let's go"; "The time for action is Now"; "Don't just sit there, do something!"; "This is going to be a team game"; "We need to watch our backs"; "No one gets left behind!"; "I need to see more from you"; "We're going to train hard for this one…"; "We cannot afford any doubts…"; "Our time is now…"

If the Warrior is in your Archetypal Development Plan, please take a moment to reflect on the suggestions above. Which do you feel drawn to try first? You may need to experiment with different ways until you find what suits you best. The first few attempts may feel odd or "not like me", so we invite you to keep at it until they feel familiar enough. You might want to find a simple shift in body and voice that feels relatively comfortable as a first step and then extend it from there. The more you practise, the easier it will become to embody the Warrior.

When you are ready, we invite you to bring what you have learned into a real-life situation, preferably one where you have a trusted ally present to give you feedback afterwards. When you are in that situation, draw on the spirit and actions of the Warrior that you have Acted-In through your rehearsals. Notice if you think, feel and/or act differently from usual. When you exit that situation, either get feedback from your ally or reflect by yourself. What worked? What if anything would you do differently next time? Then, wait until the next opportunity presents itself – and repeat the process.

5. Development Stories

(A Storyteller/Transformer approach – narrative to describe effective change)

We complete our journey through rehearsal options with an example of Acting-In an Archetype taken from our own consulting practice. This mini case study describes how an individual successfully activated their desired outcome. This will also serve as an invitation and model for you to write your own future-focused story, one that describes the successful outcome of your own development plan.

a. Our coaching story

Roberto was HR director of an insurance company attempting to reposition itself for the digital world – a strategy which included a large number of layoffs. It was a stressful time and a number of senior heads of department (HOD) would give him a hard time if he suggested layoffs from their areas. One day, when anxiety in the organization was running high, a full-on Warrior HOD attacked Roberto in front of a full table of senior colleagues, accusing him of being weak and biased in his decision-making. Roberto suddenly and unusually exploded, using a flurry of foul language that further disrupted the meeting. He came to coaching to find out the cause and the solution to this "out of character" outburst.

He identified as Nurturer, Lover and Sovereign with Warrior and Renegade being most offstage. When his coach asked him about his past experience of Warrior energy, he reported having a father who was often angry, a period of bullying at school due to being "crap at sports", and an overtly aggressive first boss who yelled at staff. The coaching identified that Roberto had learned early on that being a "sociable peacemaker" was much safer than standing up to aggression. However, Roberto had not found a healthy way to express his own anger and had repeatedly buried it, thinking it served no purpose. He had effectively externalized his Warrior and rejected it from his inner stage, often judging those around him with ready access to its energies as "bullies". But it was pointed out to him that he could not avoid the Warrior, and if he did not find his own way to inhabit it, he might continually find it mirrored back to him in unhelpful ways. He now saw that this is what had happened with the over-assertive HOD in the meeting room.

His coach proposed martial arts to Roberto who laughed at the idea, but he eventually tried two things, hot yoga and Qigong. He stuck with the former and his coach showed him how to ritualize the practice, honouring the Warrior with an assertive mantra every time he entered the hot yoga classroom. Roberto created his own Archetypal Gesture and words. He began to use these before meetings where he was likely to be in disagreement with other senior staff.

He practised the Warrior Active Imagination exercises in which he saw himself as the defender of those who did not have a voice in the organization. He gradually reinvented himself from "sociable peacemaker" to "protector of fair play", a new role that combined his old favourite Archetypes with a more integrated Warrior. He also reports that his meetings are shorter now, as he is able to cut to the chase and be more decisive.

b.   Storying your future

A creative writing exercise to activate the power of intention, by creating a story to guide you into your desired future. We invite you to write from the perspective of that desired future – as if you were looking back on your development having successfully completed it. This will take 30–50 minutes of quiet, uninterrupted time with writing materials or computer.

Guideline

Using the loose framework of our coaching story above, you will craft your own story as if it were your own real-life case study set at a realistic time in the future. From that future time, you look back and "reflect on your success", i.e. you create a narrative that describes *how* you activated the Warrior, from this point forward.

Story prompts (a loose guide to follow if helpful):

i)   *Presenting issue: What was it that motivated the desire to Act-In the Warrior?*

ii) *Personal insights: What did you learn about yourself, your formative years, your primary care-givers' Archetypes that might have played a part in the presenting issue? (This part could be aided by an actual or imaginary coach or trusted confidant or be created from personal reflection or inner dialogue.)*

iii) *First steps and their results: What simple first steps did you take on your development journey? How did they help? What impact did they have? What did you learn – about yourself and/or the Warrior?*

iv) *Next steps leading to integration: What else did you choose to do and over what time frame? How did these activations help? What was the felt difference in your life? What was the visible difference to others around you?*

So, that is the full collection of Rehearsal Method Options currently in our repertoire. In our experience, within this wide range of possibilities you will be able to find at least one way to effectively build a relationship with this Archetype. Then, with commitment and practice, and in a time frame that works for you, you will Act-In the Warrior.

Developing the Explorer

1. **Archetypal Gesture: *"There it is... follow me!"***
   (A Sovereign/Lover approach – visible and sensory)
   An Archetypal Gesture is a simple way to remind yourself of the Explorer Gifts (also available as a video and download from www.archetypesatwork.com/gestures). It is a symbolic gesture to practise in private, using Archetype-appropriate words as a quick memory tool for embodiment.

Stand tall, now lean forward with your arms out in front of you, as if gently sweeping aside vines and branches hanging down from a forest canopy. You are the adventurous head of an expedition looking for the mountain lodge that will be your safe haven for the night. You see a light up ahead, stop and point to it, stating, "There it is..." Then keep your front hand pointing at the destination, while your back hand signals back to your team and waves them forward, as you say: "Follow me!"

Using this Archetypal Gesture is a simple way to evoke Explorer energy in you, before an important meeting or presentation or anywhere else where you need to be visible. You can learn these simple gestures and phrases and practise them as often as useful.

2. Activities and Practices

Below is a selection of ideas we have gathered over the years that have helped people gain more access to the Explorer in life and work. It is by no means a full list and we encourage you to find your own variations if none of these feel quite right for you. We hope the following will give you ideas and inspiration for your own personalized Explorer Development Plan.

a. Locations and environments that are likely to evoke the Explorer

(An Explorer approach – going somewhere new and different)
Outward-bound adventures, philosophy departments and lectures, social justice meetings and groups, multicultural cities, comedy shows, comic improv classes, jungles, safaris, the Himalayas, Patagonia, and exotic faraway places

b. Activities to rehearse the Explorer

(A Strategist/Warrior approach – planning and doing)
- *Walk and spend time in nature – hiking, camping, mountaineering*
- *Read a philosophy book*
- *Think and talk about the meaning of life*
- *Find something new to learn – take a class*
- *Teach something you know to others*

- *Get involved in a social justice project*
- *Create a project or form a team to increase fairness in your workplace or community*
- *Write a passionate letter to support a hopeful project*
- *Consciously experiment with being more optimistic and enthusiastic in conversations*
- *Travel to an exotic place*
- *Make time and space to have some fun!*
- *Learn some good jokes and find an appropriate place to share them*

c. **Creative Research**

(A Transformer/Nurturer approach – research and conversations)

Who do you admire that you assign Explorer energy to? These can be people you know, people you admire from a distance (living or dead) or even fictional characters.

If they are available in your network, you could find time to be with them and notice how they operate around others. Ask them about their philosophy and outlook on life.

If they are well-known, look for articles, biographies, documentaries or films about them and their ideas that you can learn from as you integrate what it means to embody Explorer energy.

3. **Inside-Out: Sense Memory and Active Imagination**

These exercises are designed to give you inner access to the Explorer. Please read through them and decide if you want to try one. If so, when you have time, we recommend that you find a private and comfortable space to work in, where you are not going to be disturbed. Have a notebook (or pen and paper) to hand. These exercises can be done alone or with a trusted colleague, friend or coach in attendance. If you prefer, they are also available as an audio download from www.archetypesatwork.com/guidedjourneys.

If you are alone, please read the relevant instructions for **a**, **b** or **c** below until they are familiar enough to start. Then close your eyes for anywhere from five to 15 minutes and allow yourself to enter the process as fully as possible. Be aware that you may feel as if you are moving in and out of the process at first. Also bear in mind that it may take a few attempts (perhaps three to five) for these exercises to feel comfortable – but you are stretching out of your previous comfort zone so this is to be expected. When you are finished, make a few notes in a notebook about your experience.

If you have a companion, they can read the instructions below out loud in real time. For the Sense Memory exercise **a**, you can choose to remember in silence or speak the story of your memory as you relive it. For the Active Imagination exercises **b** and **c**, the instructions can be spoken to you but your journey is best imagined in silence.

If you are using the downloads, play them and pause them as helpful as you go through the journey they describe. Repeat whenever useful.

a. Sense Memory

(A Nurturer/Lover approach – remembering your past and accessing your senses)

Allow yourself to drift into a place where you have easy access to your personal memory banks... Flick through a few memories of times in your life, however brief, when you enjoyed a new and different journey, adventure or philosophical approach. Pick one scene to focus on and begin to recall it more fully. Where were you? What were you doing? Who was around you? How did it feel to be on an inner or outer quest? Allow yourself to experience as fully as you can what you were feeling then. See if you can now sense what enabled this entry into Explorer territory. What part of you stepped forward and did you draw on? What did you learn? How did this experience expand your sense of yourself?

When you are ready, come out of the memory and either take notes (if you are alone) or get feedback from your colleague. How did you feel and/or show up differently when you were accessing this memory?

b. Active Imagination 1 – imagining a real-life application

(A Dreamer/Strategist approach – imagination with a practical focus)

Imagine yourself in a scene of your choice connected to your current life, where access to the Explorer would be helpful. See yourself inhabiting this scene with full access to the Explorer and their gifts. Observe yourself in your mind's eye as you engage with this life situation as a quest, being a truth-seeker, and expansively joyful. Allow yourself to feel and sense the qualities that the Explorer offers. Try to feel it in your body as an actual sensation and as an emotional and mental response. How is this different from how you generally think and feel?

When you are ready, come out of the imagined scene and write down anything you want to remember. If you have a colleague with you, tell the story of your journey. You may wish to ask for feedback or to integrate the experience by yourself.

c. Active Imagination 2 – imagining an inner figure

(A Dreamer/Storyteller approach – imagination to create a story)

Imagine yourself leaving the place where you are now and travelling through the air over varied landscapes until you land in a natural environment that evokes Explorer energy for you. (You can use the location prompts in 2a above if helpful.) Now imagine yourself preparing to meet a figure who will represent your Inner Explorer. Know that you will be able to ask your Inner Explorer an important question and that they will offer their wisdom in return. This may be a direct spoken answer to your question, or a symbolic gift that has some bearing on it, or both. When you are ready, imagine yourself meeting the Explorer as they walk through the landscape and journeying with them for a while. Allow the scene to unfold in front of you as you pay close attention to it: How does your Inner Explorer look? What are they wearing? How do they hold themselves? How do they speak and what do they say? If a dialogue with them is appropriate, imagine it unfolding. When the scene is nearing completion, allow this figure to offer you their gift or closing words of wisdom. Thank them for their time. With the knowledge that you can return here at other times, gradually exit this scene and imagine yourself travelling back through the air, over landscapes, and gently into the room you are physically in. Open your eyes slowly.

When you are ready, write down everything you can remember that may contain actual or symbolic clues about your Inner Explorer, including any exchanges. If you received a gift, what was it? You might want to draw it, or let your mind wander with free associations. What might this gift mean for you and your journey towards the Explorer?

Any or all of these exercises can be repeated as often as you like. Then, when you are ready to try this out in a real-life situation where you wish to embody the Explorer, take a minute to prepare. Remember the essence of your Sense Memory and/or Active Imagination journeys and the parts that felt most useful. What clues did they provide as to how you can confidently embody Explorer energy? See if you can summon these into yourself and allow them to fill your being. Then, when you enter the actual scene, keep drawing on these to the extent that they are useful.

When you exit that scene, take a moment to notice if anything was different from how you might normally show up. If so, what was it? Did the preparation help you and, if so, how?

4. Outside-In: Rehearsal Cues

(A Sovereign approach – rehearsal and performance)

These are practical cues that you can use in real life, when you feel ready. You will probably want to rehearse them first – in private or with a trusted coach/colleague, and then in public, when you feel ready.

How to communicate as an Explorer

These real-life attitudes, body language and voice cues, sample words and phrases are all resonant with the Explorer. Please read through them and notice which might be useful for you to step into and rehearse for future use.

a. **Mood, attitude and mindset**
Questing, expansive, jovial, seeking the as-yet unexplored and unknown, always open to new experiences, unshackled, optimistic and 'can-do', open to teaching and being a teacher

b. **Body language and physical cues**
Taking up a large space, striding, effusive, demonstrative, grand, colourful, confident and unselfconscious, rounded, inclusive, pointing, sweeping, eyes wide, looking towards the horizon

c. **Voice**
Loud, jolly, full and rounded tones, hearty, personal, casual, excited, positive, upbeat

d. **Typical words of an Explorer**
Journey, distance, optimism, "we can", discovery, enjoy, gratitude, fun, far, seek, find, unknown, learning, lessons, philosophy, meaning, reward, just, fair, multicultural

e. **Typical phrases of an Explorer**
"Let's go!"; "What are we waiting for?"; "We can't stay where we are"; "There is always something new to learn"; "Let's go further"; "Teach me"; "Let's look on the bright side…"; "Let's make it to the top"; "I've got something to show you"; "There is so much more out there"; "We need to stretch ourselves"; "What's next?"; "This is what I have found"; "The journey is the destination"; "See the forest, not the tree"; "We need to move ahead…"

If the Explorer is in your Archetypal Development Plan, take a moment to reflect on the suggestions above. Which do you feel drawn to try first? You may need to experiment with different ways until you find what suits you best. The first few attempts may feel odd or "not like me", so we invite you to keep at it until they feel familiar enough. You might want to find a simple shift in body and voice that feels relatively comfortable as a first step and then extend it from there. The more you practise, the easier it will become to embody the Explorer.

When you are ready, we invite you to bring what you have learned into a real-life situation, preferably one where you have a trusted ally present to give you feedback afterwards. When you are in that situation, draw on the spirit and actions of the Explorer that you have Acted-In through your rehearsals. Notice if you think, feel and/or act differently from usual. When you exit that situation, either get feedback from your ally or reflect by yourself. What worked? What if anything would you do differently next time? Then, wait until the next opportunity presents itself – and repeat the process.

5. Development Stories

(A Storyteller/Transformer approach – narrative to describe effective change)

We complete our journey through rehearsal options with an example of Acting-In an Archetype taken from our own consulting practice. This mini case study describes how an individual successfully activated their desired outcome. This will also serve as an invitation and model for you to write your own future-focused story, one that describes the successful outcome of your own development plan.

a. Our coaching story

Ella was logistical support officer of a medium-sized training company whose senior team was engaged in a three-day Transformational Leadership programme. When introduced to the Archetype key words for an archetypal assessment session, Ella found herself feeling tearful and upset when she read the words for the Explorer. She approached a programme coach who recommended that she think about her history with this Archetype as preparation for the Breakthrough Coaching session she would engage in the next day with a small group.

In that session, Ella announced as her goal the wish to renew her relationship with the Explorer. As a child she had loved adventure. Her parents were both teachers and subscribed to the "National Geographic" magazine. She liked nature, took care of her pets and played games outdoors during long hot summers. Ella recalled many nights lying awake with a flashlight and reading stories while dreaming about visiting faraway lands and peoples. Her family was also relatively poor and she never got to actually travel as a child.

In college she finally got her wish and travelled to South America as an exchange student. Although she settled in well, she had the traumatic experience of being briefly kidnapped by a local guerrilla group. On her release she returned home deflated and disillusioned, finished her studies and settled into a comfortable role in a career that, as she said, "is safe and fine, but not a stretch for me".

The coach set up the scene as a constellation – with other members of the small group representing different characters or parts of Ella. There was a future Ella, with ready access to Explorer gifts, a representative for the negative impact of her kidnapping experience, and Ella as she was in the present. As the process moved forward, Ella was able to clearly see the impact that the kidnapping had had in her subsequent life choices, and then let it go. She was also able to forgive herself for allowing this to shut down her horizons for a while. She now saw that it was still not too late to live a more adventurous life. At the end of the session she made a moving statement to her group. She committed to a walking adventure in nature for her own benefit, one day a month in different, new locations. She also decided to create a project team to look at new ways for the training company to expand their horizons and their service lines.

She did some follow-up coaching and was thrilled to report six months later that a new training product had come out of her initiative, one that involved taking teams out into nature to learn about themselves and explore group dynamics. She was exploring new roles in her company, including a role that would allow her to be part of these expeditions. As she said to her coach, "Those dark moments were part of the journey as well, I entered the dark forest for a while but now I am back in the sunlight." She added, "It's all part of a much longer journey."

b. Storying your future

A creative writing exercise to activate the power of intention, by creating a story to guide you into your desired future. We invite you to write from the perspective of that desired future – as if you were looking back on your development having successfully

completed it. This will take 30–50 minutes of quiet, uninterrupted time with writing materials or computer.

Guideline

Using the loose framework of our coaching story above, you will craft your own story as if it were your own real-life case study set at a realistic time in the future. From that future time, you look back and "reflect on your success", i.e. you create a narrative that describes *how* you activated the Explorer from this point forward.

Story prompts (a loose guide to follow if helpful):

i)   *Presenting issue: What was it that motivated the desire to Act-In the Explorer?*

ii) *Personal insights: What did you learn about yourself, your formative years, your primary care-givers' Archetypes that might have played a part in the presenting issue? (This part could be aided by an actual or imaginary coach or trusted confidant or be created from personal reflection or inner dialogue.)*

iii) *First steps and their results: What simple first steps did you take on your development journey? How did they help? What impact did they have? What did you learn – about yourself and/or the Explorer?*

iv) *Next steps leading to integration: What else did you choose to do and over what time frame? How did these activations help? What was the felt difference in your life? What was the visible difference to others around you?*

So, that is the full collection of Rehearsal Method Options currently in our repertoire. In our experience, within this wide range of possibilities you will be able to find at least one way to effectively build a relationship with this Archetype. Then, with commitment and practice – and in a time frame that works for you – you will Act-In the Explorer.

And that completes our journey through Developing the Realm of Action.

CHAPTER 15

HYBRID ROLES:
COMBINING ARCHETYPES FOR
Development

We have found that realistic and effective Horizontal Development rarely involves pushing a Leading Actor away and then dragging a More Offstage Actor to the centre of your stage. Your intention is usually better served by bringing the less favoured Archetype further onstage to affect and moderate the behaviour of a favourite who still maintains a primary position. So, you create a new *hybrid role* that combines the old Leading Actor with the More Offstage Actor you desire to Act-In.

We introduced the notion of hybrid roles in Chapter 9, How to Use Part Two. You may remember the example of the Warrior wanting to embody more Nurturer but reverting quickly to habitual patterns (for example, buying croissants followed by cutting lunch breaks). A better way would have been to create the hybrid role of a Nurturing Warrior – and develop actionable practices that could support this.

The path to activate a hybrid role is simple enough, and here are the headlines. You identify the presenting issue and a development goal to help resolve it. You then select the Archetype whose gifts can best serve this process. Now you combine this with your current favourite

Leading Actor to name a new role. You may choose to do some "word-pairing", finding a key word from each Archetype and creating a positive affirmation with both of these words (see below). You then come up with a plan to activate the intention and new role.

If this feels like a good step for you, you can follow the process as you read through the rest of this chapter or come back to it later.

The following has become a popular "take away" exercise when we work with intact teams. At the end of a programme, each individual makes a public statement as to their new hybrid role development intention, and buddies up with a fellow team member on a temporary co-coaching contract (normally set as three follow-up conversations over six months). Both then put their plan into action to try out, and can then discuss progress (and regressions) with a co-coach who understands and supports their intention. Some teams also agree to a regular collective check-in, where everyone can state what they have been working on and how. Others can then give feedback and share what difference they have seen and what impact it has had.

Word-pairing

This simple exercise gives you numerous different ways to think about the hybrid role you wish to embody. It can offer motivation, behavioural guidelines, and even actions that the new role can aspire to. So, following our Warrior example from above, we would invite this Warrior to save money on croissants (for now) and instead look at the lists of Gift words for both Warrior and Nurturer.

Warrior

Champion, Spearhead, Amazon, Defender, Trouble-Shooter, Brave, Fierce, Passionate, Forceful, Decisive, Fearless, Surgical, Leads from the Front

Drives: Competition, Challenge, Action, Direction, Tactics, Risk-Taking, Seed-Planting, Making Things Happen, Adrenaline, Competitive Advantage

Nurturer
Supportive, Caring, Reassuring, Protective, Responsive, Instinctive, Parental, Trusting, Nourishing, Sensitive, Empathetic, Receptive, Cosy

Values: Relationships, Potential, Growth, Feedback, Togetherness, Time to Reflect, 'Keeping the Hearth', Legacy, Conservation, Emotional Intelligence, Natural Cycles, Tending Gardens, Feeling at Home, Full-Body Listening

Our Warrior client would then create a few different word pairings that sound good to them and that could lead to positive steps forward. They might choose: *Champion* and *Growth, Risk-Taking* and *Time to Reflect, Feedback* and *Direction*. The next step is to use these words to create strong statements of personal intention about future actions and behaviours. These include a clear "I" statement. For example:

> *I champion our people's right to grow*
> *I make time to reflect on our risk-taking*
> *I receive feedback about our direction*

They would then select one or more that they recognize to be a positive developmental step and find an action to support it that can be implemented to deliver a practical result, e.g. an action to *champion people's right to grow* could be for everyone to attend a workshop on emotional intelligence. *Time to reflect on risk-taking* could be activated by a quarterly review of risky initiatives. *Feedback on direction* could be implemented via an all-staff annual 360-degree assessment of current strategy and projects. Hopefully you get the idea...

Hybrid roles – creation and activation

So, the process in more detail (with examples) looks like this:

a) Identify the presenting issue: What do I want to improve or develop and why? (e.g. *"My Warrior is overpowering and people don't tell me what they really think"*).

b) Select a new Archetype and a capacity they have that can help with the issue (e.g. *"the Nurturer's ability to care for people could help me rebuild trust"*).

c) Place the newer Archetype (Nurturer) in front of the Leading Actor (Warrior) to create the new hybrid role (*"The Nurturer–Warrior"*) and/or a behavioural goal (*"I am a Nurturing Warrior"*).

d) Use word-pairing to create an active intention that brings the two Archetypes together
(*Risk-Taking* and *Time to Reflect*).

e) Brainstorm implementable actions that can both bring this intention to life *and* offer a way to resolve the presenting issue. Then select at least one to commit to. (*"I will initiate a quarterly review of risky initiatives, to encourage others to tell me what they really think".*) What can you initiate or do differently so that you will feel this role in action, and so that others around you can see or feel the difference?

This new combination of more and less familiar Archetypes can then, over time, reduce the impact of the presenting issue.

For those who wish to think about or do this now, we attach all 10 lists of key words in Appendix 2. What could be an interesting hybrid role and what mix of words could be a useful next step in bringing your favourite Leading Actor and a More Offstage Actor into partnership?

Integrating inner conflicts

Word-pairing is also a highly effective technique when your archetypal pattern contains contradicting drives. For instance, an architect client identified the Dreamer and the Strategist as her two Leading Actors. At first glance these appear as opposites: the Dreamer loves structureless reveries while the Strategist insists on organized containment. Our practice has shown that it is common for people to be pulled between such apparently oppositional poles. Her word pairings became a manageable way to merge her two Leading Actors more productively.

She created the following statements: "*I make my dreams a reality*", "*I organize and focus fantasies*", and "*I build compassionate structures*". By combining seemingly different Archetypes into a new third option – an affirmation that requires input from both – she was able to resolve her previous inner tension.

Resolving outer differences

This method can also be used for conflict resolution between two people. For example, an Explorer and a Lover co-created a clothing store business on a wave of optimistic excitement, only to realize later that they disagreed on how to lead their organization. The Explorer wanted lots of affordable clothes from all over the world while the Lover wanted fewer, more exclusive and high-quality items. In coaching, they co-created statements that could respect both their Leading Actors' gifts, and quickly settled on a new business motto they could both sign up to: "*An abundance of quality*".

HYBRID ROLE TEMPLATE

To reference the complete list of Gifts key words, see Appendix 2. Begin using this template by writing in your Leading Actor (either below or in a separate notebook). Then add the presenting issues or what difficulties you have with this Archetype. Next, write down the name of a More Offstage Actor and then create a hybrid name (for instance, a Nurturing Warrior). To complete the Template, fill out the rest as prompted.

Leading Actor: _____

Presenting issue:_____

_____

_____

More Offstage Actor: _____

Hybrid name: _____

Key words you respond to from both:_____

_____

_____

Sample word pairings: _____

_____

_____

_____

Statement/s of Intention: _____

_____

_____

_____

Action/s to deliver intention/s: _____

_____

_____

_____

CHAPTER 16

MEETING THE ARCHETYPES IN

"I suppose leadership at one time meant muscles; but today it means getting along with people."

MAHATMA GANDHI

In addition to providing clear insights into personal and leadership development, awareness of how these archetypal patterns operate in others can greatly enhance your interactive impact. If you can learn how to effectively meet other people where they are, rather than expect them to adjust to your preferred style, you are more likely to build rapport. This then increases the likelihood of a mutually beneficial outcome. A famous phrase in the influencing world says, "If you would seek to influence someone else, you must first understand how they influence themselves". Your own preferred or core archetypal pattern is a key way in which you guide, lead and/or influence yourself – and the same, of course, is true for everyone else.

Generally, we tend to get on best with people who share the same values and outlook as us, and at work we find it easiest to understand and motivate others who share at least one of our Leading Actors.

Those we usually find most difficult to understand and lead (or be led by) are those people whose Leading Actors coincide with one of our own More Offstage Actors. With this it can sometimes feel as if you are both speaking different languages. Before you were aware of the notion of archetypal patterns, it would have been natural to hold a negative projection about another. For example, if I push away the Warrior on my inner stage, I am likely to negatively judge assertive Warriors on the outer stage of my life as well.

In our experience, the majority of personality conflicts we see in organizations are actually archetypal in nature. Annie does not understand or value Bert's Dreamer; Bert does not value Annie's Strategist etc. So, the very process of understanding that *all* archetypal patterns have value is a key to enhancing mutual understanding. This in turn can enable respect for differences rather than resentment.

To do this effectively you will need to get a sense of the other's preferred pattern. If they are a colleague at work, you could invite them to do their own archetypal self-assessment, and then both of you share this with the other, as a way into a conversation about alignment and effective communication. If that is not practical, you can probably work out their likely Leading and Offstage Actors just by paying careful attention when you are in their company. Where are they coming from? What are their priorities? What do they place most and least value on at work? And so on.

Our practice often brokers courageous conversations between colleagues in conflict, using the Archetypes as an impersonal and impartial arbitrating tool: "Annie, do you notice that when your logical-analytical Strategist shows up, Bert's Dreamer gets shut down...?" When the archetypal difference can be understood, finding more effective ways to communicate is then relatively easy. Learning to feel, speak and inhabit our least favoured Archetypes is a great way of expanding our empathy for others generally. Understanding the archetypal priorities of another can enhance communication with that other specifically. Your own knowledge of how your less favoured Archetypes are likely to show up in others and be expressed by them is a great start. Sometimes the most effective route is for you to stretch out of your comfort zone and meet others where they are.

What follows is a series of cues and big picture tips that can help you prepare and act effectively around someone with an obviously different archetypal pattern from yours. Please remember that no one is ever just *one* of the Archetypes, and although some of us will change a Leading Actor occasionally, most of us have an obvious favourite, the one that most often takes the lead. That is usually the Archetype it will help you to tune into during future interactions, using some of the suggestions below. You are welcome to read them all, or simply skip to the Archetypes that you recognize as Minor Supporting and Offstage Actors for you – as the suggestions connected to your Leading Actors are likely to be familiar. Alternatively, if you have a specific colleague in mind for whom this concept could be useful, then go to the relevant suggestions for what you imagine their Leading Actor is – and see what might help improve future communications.

We have divided our suggestions into the following categories:

1. **How to meet an Archetype in others:**
   a. **In general – what to bear in mind**
   b. **What to emphasize – conversational priorities**
   c. **What to avoid**
   d. **Most effective environment to meet an Archetype – pay attention to the mood, style and "set dressing" of the meeting place, when you can**
   e. **Least effective environment to meet an Archetype**

2. **Effective Leadership and Followership**
   Some of us may work in egalitarian systems where hierarchies do not appear or need to be managed, but in our experience these environments are few and far between. The majority of us work in systems where an implicit or explicit hierarchy necessitates both leadership and followership. These cues can therefore help you maximize your effectiveness in either role:

   a. *How to be the most effective leader (or care-giver) to an Archetype*
   b. *How to be the most effective follower to an Archetype*

As always, when applying Archetypes at Work™ concepts, we invite you to take it easy, slowly and don't try too much at once. If you go into a weekly meeting tomorrow with too many new ideas to try out, you may feel fake and others may also perceive you differently. Both of these responses can undermine the intention to enable more effective communication. You might want to try some of the Acting-In suggestions for the relevant Archetype to establish some basic level of comfort before you "try it on for size" in an upcoming meeting.

Meeting the Sovereign
Vision and Purpose

1. **How to meet the Sovereign in others:**
   a. **In general**
      Be clear about purpose, be generous about their gifts, give them space to respond, thank them for their service

   b. **What to emphasize**
      The vision, the broad benefits for the realm, the generative effort, the ambition, the big picture, clarity, the bright future, getting perspective, the need for courage, visibility, being confident, the chance to shine

   c. **What to avoid**
      Interrupting them, disrespecting them, their efforts or their people, don't present ideas as a competing vision

      Phrases unlikely to work include: "Forget about a vision"; "Let's not show off"; "It's all about the money"; "Our people are not the priority"; "Let's play this really safe"; "I've got a hunch this is going to work"; "Let's limit our ambition for now"; "I need you to be more in the background on this"

   d. Most effective environment to meet a Sovereign
Classy, well furnished, opulent, well lit, happy

   e. Least effective environment to meet a Sovereign
Untidy, uncomfortable, run down, dark and dank, dour

2. Effective Leadership and Followership

   a. How to be the most effective leader (or care-giver) to a Sovereign
Give them space, give them appropriate power, praise their good deeds, see and bless them, show purpose, let them shine, encourage their ambition, give honest feedback, connect their efforts to a bigger purpose, let them be visible

   b. How to be the most effective follower to a Sovereign leader
Visibly and vocally support their vision, show them that you care, pay attention to what they say, be respectful, give them positive feedback, dress well, be confident

Meeting the Strategist
Structure and Mastery

1. How to meet the Strategist in others

   a. In general
Be logical, present ideas as low risk, give the opportunity to be analytical, provide details and/or examples of best practice, connect new ideas to established practices where possible

b. **What to emphasize**

The facts and sensible conclusions, the logical next step, risk management, achieving better balance, having a clear overview, balancing the budget, saving money, cutting unnecessary costs, assessing results, using demonstrable facts, delivering clear information

c. **What to avoid**

Uncertainty and unpredictability; don't rush or switch subjects quickly or jump to conclusions without evidence

Phrases unlikely to work include: "We just can't know"; "Let's take a chance"; "Time to shake things up"; "Trust me on this one"; "Let's get creative"; "You can't plan everything"; "I've got a hunch about this"; "The details can wait"; "The figures aren't relevant"; "A bit of chaos can be productive"; "A change is as good as a rest"

d. **Most effective environment to meet a Strategist**

Orderly, sparse, tidy, clean, uncluttered, grey, functional, practical

e. **Least effective environment to meet a Strategist**

Chaotic, random, highly emotional, frantic, over-busy, messy, unordered, cluttered

2. **Effective Leadership and Followership**

a. **How to be the most effective leader (or care-giver) to a Strategist**

Be organized, stay detail-orientated, be objective and consistent, be systematic, be fair

b. **How to be the most effective follower to a Strategist leader**

Be logical, be respectful, conform to the norms, stick to the facts, dress sensibly, stay focused

Meeting the Nurturer
Care and Empathy

1. How to meet the Nurturer in others

a. In general

Be personable, make it a two-way conversation, be open to feedback, allow ample time, present ideas as people-friendly, honour all relevant history

b. What to emphasize

How this will help people, growth, development opportunities, historical legacy and those that have gone before, relationship-building, people focus, increase quality time with others (including clients, patients, customers), enhance sustainability, improve communication

c. What to avoid

Creating fear and discomfort, being hasty and rushing, overlooking the human cost of decisions, raising stress levels, criticism and ridicule of them and others, competitive comparisons and aggressive tones

Phrases unlikely to work include: "It's going to be tough"; "It's survival of the fittest"; "We need to get rid of the deadwood"; "We're going out of our comfort zone"; "We can't let feelings get in our way"; "Cancel the holidays"; "No pain no gain"

d. Most effective environment to meet a Nurturer

Welcoming, comfortable furniture, cosy, warm, soft lighting, soft hues, reassuring, well catered

e. **Least effective environment to meet a Nurturer**
    Spartan, cold, grey, function over form, busy distractions, mechanical noises, aggressive and pushy settings

2. **Effective Leadership and Followership**
    a. **How to be the most effective leader (or care-giver) to a Nurturer**
        Give recognition, trust and appreciation, mutual goal-setting, be physically accessible and emotionally available/accessible, give consistent feedback and ongoing support, give time for personal conversations, bring food to share

    b. **How to be the most effective follower to a Nurturer leader**
        Be honest, be responsive, allow yourself to be supported, be willing to ask for help, be team-orientated, demonstrate loyalty, be open to personal conversation, be available to talk through their problems and concerns

Meeting the Lover
Desire and Beauty

1. **How to meet the Lover in others**
    a. **In general**
        Be sociable, dress well, show style, make eye contact, present ideas as attractive

    b. **What to emphasize**
        The aesthetic result, the look and feel of things, the sensual enjoyment, harmony and delight, the value of the exchange, the benefit of sociability

c. **What to avoid**
Relentless task focus, reducing social opportunities, a culture of secrecy, vulgar and demeaning talk and jokes, purely transactional relationships

Phrases unlikely to work include: "No more chit-chat around the water cooler"; "Let's cut the frills"; "Less talk, more action"; "This expense is overly indulgent"; "We can use the cheaper one"; "Don't wine and dine them, just close the deal"

d. **Most effective environment to meet a Lover**
Elegant, well designed, artful, tasteful, luxurious, high quality, relaxing, comfortable, classy

e. **Least effective environment to meet a Lover**
Ugly, functional, cheap, plastic, artificial, unkempt, hard, harsh lighting

2. **Effective Leadership and Followership**
   a. **How to be the most effective leader (or care-giver) to a Lover**
   Be appreciative, be sociable, be nice, be friendly, engage in social small talk, encourage quality

   b. **How to be the most effective follower to a Lover leader**
   Keep aesthetics in the forefront, be attentive to their wants, respond to their offers, be graceful around them, be an effective personal assistant, respond appropriately to their signals and mood

Meeting the Dreamer
Imagination and Inspiration

1. How to meet the Dreamer in others

   a. In general

   Be creative, encourage co-creation, be open to their ideas, allow for unstructured conversation and time, welcome the strange

   b. What to emphasize

   The creative possibilities, lateral thinking, receptive to what wants to emerge, imaginative thinking, going beyond the known, reimagining a problem, believing before seeing, reading the signs, symbolic thinking

   c. What to avoid

   Certainty, normality, predictability, limiting the conversation to facts and short-term measurable goals

   Phrases unlikely to work include: "Let's not reinvent the wheel"; "If it ain't broke, don't fix it"; "The obvious thing to do is..."; "It's the logical solution"; "You have to make a decision now..."; "Keep this simple"; "Where's the evidence?"; "That's unrealistic"; "Is this really going anywhere?"; "How can we be sure?"

   d. Most effective environment to meet a Dreamer

   Creative, artistic, easy lighting, water features, nice views, wide horizons, comfortable and informal seating, creative materials, libations, music

   e. Least effective environment to meet a Dreamer

   Over-ordered, tight, dry and information-heavy presentations, windowless, formal seating, rigid format

2. Effective Leadership and Followership

    a. How to be the most effective leader (or care-giver) to a Dreamer

        Encourage their dreams, give them creative space, extend deadlines, give them long lead times for desired outcomes, trust their imagination, be patient with non-linear thinking and conversation, believe in them, support their empathy for worthy causes

    b. How to be the most effective follower to a Dreamer leader

        Step into their dreams, be optimistic, engage with their half-formed ideas, develop empathy, engage in free-flowing conversation without looking for outcomes

Meeting the Storyteller
Communication and Synthesis

1. How to meet the Storyteller in others

    a. In general

        Meet their rapid pace, be broad-minded, accept multiple options, be witty and intelligent, value multiple modes of communication

    b. What to emphasize

        The quality of the ideas, the alternate possibilities, the synthesizing of ideas, integrating multiplicity, flexibility and adaptability, making connections, clever use of words

    c. What to avoid

        Single-minded thinking, limited options, sitting still, monotony, boredom, dry and boring language, business-speak, acronyms, limiting ideas

Phrases unlikely to work include: "I don't want to hear it"; "Stay focused"; "That's just a tall tale"; "Focus on a single option"; "Can we dumb it down a bit?"; "Can we just narrow it down?"

    d. Most effective environment to meet a Storyteller
Buzzing, speedy, high traffic, exciting, creative, informal, varied, fresh, bright, multiple seating options

    e. Least effective environment to meet a Storyteller
Staid, limiting, narrow, tradition-bound, dark, silent, reverent, dank, over-emotional

2. Effective Leadership and Followership

    a. How to be the most effective leader (or care-giver) to a Storyteller
Encourage their ideas, respect their intelligence, be open-minded, ask for more options, give them freedom to investigate, use them to bounce ideas back and forth, communicate fast and frequently

    b. How to be the most effective follower to a Storyteller leader
Be a good listener, take good notes, help them organize and summarize their ideas, enjoy the mental gymnastics, keep up to date with the news and trivia, stay sharp

Meeting the Renegade
Invention and Disruption

1. How to meet the Renegade in others

    a. In general
Meet them at their edge, give opportunities to be revolutionary, allow for rule-bending, encourage the unconventional

b. **What to emphasize**

The radically new, the innovative possibilities, freedom, breaking-the-box thinking, intuiting the yet unknown, edgy ideas, experimental thinking, prototyping, revitalizing, jump-starting, unique opportunities, paradigm-shifting ideas

c. **What to avoid**

Limitations, rules, boundaries, formal structures and traditions, hierarchical thinking

Phrases unlikely to work include: "Did you get permission for that?"; "Don't do anything without checking first"; "What's your rationale?"; "Let's take this slowly and sensibly"; "Show me where that has been done before"; "Have you thought this through properly?"; "Have you ever done this before?"; "Stay in your lane"

d. **Most effective environment to meet a Renegade**

Unique, modern, high-tech, informal, cool, trendy, mechanistic, funky, unconventional, mobile, pop-up, virtual

e. **Least effective environment to meet a Renegade**

Structured, ordered, formal, closed, cubicles, traditional opulence, old-fashioned, hierarchical

2. **Effective Leadership and Followership**

a. **How to be the most effective leader (or care-giver) to a Renegade**

Give them freedom, encourage them to ask forgiveness not permission, give them flexible hours, agree to expectations collaboratively, be flexible

b. **How to be the most effective follower to a Renegade leader**

Keep track of their radical ideas, expect the unexpected, relax into their rhythm, trust the unknown, be excited about the wild ride, be yourself, speak your mind, add your own ideas

Meeting the Transformer
Mystery and Regeneration

1. How to meet the Transformer in others

    a. In general

    Honour their depth, be patient while things unfold, trust their process, appreciate their holding capacity

    b. What to emphasize

    The transformative potential in any situation, that broken things can mend, the profound learning available, the deeper meaning, the long-term view, the benefit of personal development

    c. What to avoid

    Reactive, short-term thinking and decisions, being superficial, being inauthentic, lying, dishonesty, lack of integrity, impatience, impulsive demands, unnecessary surprises

    Phrases unlikely to work include: "Let's keep this simple"; "Let's not go there"; "Let sleeping dogs lie"; "We don't have time for navel-gazing"; "Don't think about it, just do it"; "The truth will only scare them"; "Let's just bury this quickly and move on"; "Forget about a background check"; "Don't open that can of worms"

    d. Most effective environment to meet a Transformer

    Contained, low lighting, quiet, mysterious, dark colours, natural things growing, decorated with symbolic objects, circular seating, candles

    e. Least effective environment to meet a Transformer

    Superficial, quick and busy, well lit, noisy, formal seating, open-plan offices, in public view and hearing

2. Effective Leadership and Followership

a. How to be the most effective leader (or care-giver) to a Transformer

Be prepared to go deep, allow time for meaningful conversation, give them time to come up with their own learning, offer them big challenges and time to research the causes and potential solutions, honour their need to create ritual and mark notable beginnings, endings and transitions

b. How to be the most effective follower to a Transformer leader

Understand their need to question and change things, keep them briefed with all relevant information and newly emerged facts, admit when you don't know something, be authentic, be willing to share your personal learning challenges, include them in your big life transitions but not in trivia

Meeting the Warrior
Challenge and Defence

1. How to meet the Warrior in others

a. In general

Present ideas as a good challenge, give them appropriate command, create an opportunity to compete, tie the result to courageous effort

b. What to emphasize

The ambitious goal, the reward for success, making us more competitive, being the best, an opportunity to show up and prove skill, a test of their mettle, fighting for a noble cause, protecting those under threat, defending tactically important boundaries, taking a risk for the right reason

c. **What to avoid**

Comfort zones, caution, complacency, routine and business as usual

Phrases unlikely to work include: "Anyone could do this"; "You can take it easy on this one"; "Just relax..."; "Let's cut our losses"; "Don't push the boundaries"; "Let's run this according to the old playbook"; "Let's give the others a chance to catch up..."; "Maybe it is someone else's turn to go in first..."; "It's a workable compromise..."; "It will be less effort to settle..."; "You can't win 'em all..."; "Probably not worth fighting for..."

d. **Most effective environment to meet a Warrior**

Fast-paced, well organized, bright lighting, clean, upright chairs with hard backs, functional furniture, direct eyeline to what is being presented, efficient, clear hierarchy, ambitious and competitive, urgent, driven, passionate

e. **Least effective environment to meet a Warrior**

Cosy, sociable, comfy, low sofa and armchairs, soft lighting and lampshades, random patterns, flowers and elaborate decoration, highly emotional, messy, unordered, fussy

2. **Effective Leadership and Followership**

a. **How to be the most effective leader (or care-giver) to a Warrior**

Be decisive and confident, provide autonomy and don't micro-manage, set firm boundaries but appreciate initiative, set clear expectation for performance goals, challenge them to be their best, agree stretch targets, give simple and clear directions, give direct and effective feedback, err on the side of challenge over support and give them credit when due, reward results

b. **How to be the most effective follower to a Warrior leader**

Be capable, independent, effective, and a quick learner, offer visible results whenever possible, stay alert, be ready to change tactics, give straight feedback, speak short, sharp and to the point, watch their back, be a good "scout", be willing to take appropriate risks and "take a hit for the team", push yourself to perform at high levels

Meeting the Explorer
Adventure and Truth

1. How to meet the Explorer in others

a. In general

Give them freedom, present big ideas, give opportunities for growth, appreciate their new impulses

b. What to emphasize

The quest for learning, the journey rather than the destination, the biggest growth potential, the big picture, the best possible outcome, exploring different cultures, the philosophical underpinnings, educational potential, having fun, being the first

c. What to avoid

Limitations, restrictions, insisting on follow-through for prior commitments, too many boring and repetitive tasks, making them stick to bread-and-butter work

Phrases unlikely to work include: "Get back in your box"; "Well, last year I thought we agreed that…"; "Time to tighten our belt and limit our reach"; "Let's stick to what we know"; "No time to explore"; "Stop it; it's too much"; "We don't need any more big ideas"; "But how are you going to get there?"; "There is no budget for travel"

   d. Most effective environment to meet an Explorer
   Open, big windows with big views, penthouse, nature, room to stretch, informal seating, comfortable, airy, light and bright, open fire, log cabin, on a walk

   e. Least effective environment to meet an Explorer
   Closed, dark, uncomfortable, formal, fluorescent lighting, confined, cramped, limited legroom, functional

2. **Effective Leadership and Followership**
    a. How to be the most effective leader (or care-giver) to an Explorer
    Give them space and freedom to explore, trust their instincts, unshackle them, give time for long and meaningful conversations, let them go, allow them to find other teachers and mentors, give them opportunities to teach and mentor others, allow them to travel when possible, let them be scouts

    b. How to be the most effective follower to an Explorer leader
    Be ready to move fast and far, put on your hiking boots, be prepared to change direction, learn how to multi-task and collect all their emerging big ideas into a whole, think ahead on their behalf, manage the details

These cues are for you to bear in mind, and you can revisit them at any time, so no worries if there are no obvious uses for them right now. In any case, it would be way too mechanical to decide in advance how you are going to speak to several different people in the same meeting. However, having a sense of which Archetypes are likely to be most present in any group will always be a useful guide for what to emphasize and what to avoid when you are communicating.

These cues bring to an end our exploration of Horizontal Development. The next chapter will offer you other developmental possibilities.

CHAPTER 17

EVOLVING YOUR CORE STRENGTHS

Horizontal Integration

There are many good reasons why you might choose to develop an existing Leading Actor, rather than a More Offstage Actor. You may realize that while you have ready access to some of a Leading Actor's gifts, there are others that could serve you that are not currently accessible. You may be in a phase where you choose – or work demands – that you hone and refine an existing strength: a need for depth rather than breadth. Or, you may just feel an inner calling to evolve and explore the leading edges of currently emerging archetypal gifts.

Here is a quick review of how we define different development approaches...

Horizontal Development is a move *across* the Archetype Circle from a Leading Actor to a lesser used one (explored in Chapters 10–16).

Horizontal Integration is a move *within* a Leading Actor that you want to inhabit more fully (Chapter 17).

Vertical Development is a move *upwards* to evolve a current Leading Actor in order to access more of its emerging potential (Chapter 18).

This chapter explores the uses of Horizontal Integration; why, when and how it might serve you. This involves a look at the past and delving into the origins of limited archetypal access.

Are there any of your Leading Actors or Major Supporting Actors that you notice you are ambivalent about? If you have easy access to some of an Archetype's gifts, but some sense of aversion to others, this could be an interesting inquiry and line of development for you (examples below). This will not be true for everyone, but for those for whom it is, it can lead to lasting benefits in life and work. For reference, the Gift Words for all Archetypes are in Appendix 2.

If there is no ambivalence about any of your Leading Actors or Major Supporting Actors, you may want to move on to the Vertical Development Chapter 18. Otherwise, please read on...

Our experience is that the ambivalence almost always arises due to an event or sequence of events from earlier in life where a lesson was learned – often the hard way – that some parts of a Leading Actor were not welcome or led to trouble. This then caused the maturing psyche to compartmentalize the different parts of an Archetype's Gifts, effectively creating an internal message: "These parts are OK, you can do these. But those other parts are not, they are off limits!"

This internalized inhibition is usually resistant to the simpler activation techniques outlined in the last chapter, until the original cause of the limitation has been recognized and then effectively neutralized. Once the deeper roots have been explored, understood and, to the extent that is possible, cleared, it is then relatively simple to activate the missing pieces of the Archetype, as it is one that you naturally respond to anyway.

While the initial identifying of such a pattern is something easy enough to do by yourself or with a trusted close confidant, the more permanent solution to the dilemma is often best enabled by a professional guide of some kind: a coach, counsellor or therapist.

Here are two recent examples from our coaching and consulting practice:

a) *Helena runs her own niche Purpose Consultancy, helping young entrepreneurs to find their "sweet spot" in the market. She identified as having a love/hate relationship with the Sovereign, feeling ideas of purpose and vision were "at her core", while notions of radiance and visibility were currently offstage.*

In a coaching session, she reported being a multi-talented "golden child" with bright ginger hair who was habitually elevated by peers and teachers into a Sovereign role model and natural leader. However, in her early teens her friendship circle suddenly turned against her and ostracized her (probably out of jealousy). At the same time an influential older man in the local community became obsessed with her and began making inappropriate advances. Horrified by the negative consequences of her natural ability to shine, she started deliberately dressing down and taking herself out of sports teams, school plays and generally away from the spotlight. Now, years later, she loved helping others to shine in purposeful work, but she was deeply unwilling to speak at conferences, or otherwise put herself forward.

By re-staging the impact of these formative incidents in a breakthrough coaching session she was able to accept that these circumstances were not her fault. When she had completed this resolution with the past, she was able to turn away from its negative impact without feeling held back. The final step was for her to symbolically "reclaim her full crown", including the parts of the Sovereign she had pushed away, and give herself renewed permission to shine in her own right. As she began embodying the Sovereign and practised relevant words and body language, a weight seemed to lift off her shoulders. As she spoke from the heart about the vision she wanted her work to serve in the world, her smile became broader as her voice stronger. At the end, the group spontaneously broke into inspired applause. She later reported that she now felt able to be centre stage in her own right.

b) *Ramparsad was a sharply intelligent and driven IT specialist, who would challenge himself to keep exceeding past best performance in high-pressure projects. However, he was now leading a large team and was very uncomfortable addressing the unacceptably low-performing members of his team. He identified his Leading Actors as Strategist, Nurturer and Warrior. But he noticed that while he felt close to the inner competitive nature, decisiveness and drive of the Warrior, the ability to be forceful, fearless and to publicly challenge others was "way offstage".*

In a coaching session, he revealed that he had grown up in a religious lower caste family in India. His father was a meek and compliant man who constantly warned his son of the danger of "stepping out of line" to challenge anything or anyone. In his local area there was a well-known in-group of youths from a higher caste. These boys routinely demanded that lower caste boys run errands for them, while directing verbal and sometimes physical abuse at them. To stand up to them would risk his father's disapproval and the vestiges of the caste system itself – a big risk for a young teenager trying to figure out his place in the world. Ramparsad had reluctantly surrendered his own sense of righteous anger and submitted to the group's will for years.

Now, long after this formative experience, when he wanted to draw on his Warrior's ability to challenge others at work, he was backing down rather than standing up. He found it especially hard to confront the underperformers whom he perceived to originate from a higher caste.

In his constellation coaching session, various representatives were set up on the stage: for Ramparsad himself, his father, the caste system, the current underperformers at work and Ramparsad's Inner Warrior. Ramparsad selected other members of the small group to represent these roles. In the course of the next hour Ramparsad was able to see how his loyalty to both his family and caste system had compromised his integrity then and was having even more impact on his leadership now.

At a certain point, he was invited to step into his own role and engaged in meaningful dialogues with each of the representatives in turn. Most significantly, he was able to honour his father's attitude but also separate himself from it: "I leave your compliance with you – it is not mine and I choose to live my own life in my own way."

Now he was ready to address the underperformers. With his Warrior representative standing by his side, and having found a strong Warrior stance to hold, Ramparsad was able to confront their behaviour appropriately with a determined force and clear logic that was undeniable. He was able to do this without slipping into anger or aggression. When he was finished, he was invited to internalize the memory of this Warrior communication and bring it to mind just before he went into his upcoming annual review meetings with the relevant staff.

Notice that in both cases what started in their external world at some point became internalized as part of their own story: "It is dangerous to shine/challenge others". This internalized voice then acts as a protection to shield them from further harm. This is one of the reasons that these voices are quite stubborn and hard to shift by themselves; they were actually created to help us. Except now they are getting in the way.

The inner work required to move through memories that have contributed to limited archetypal access can be insightful, illuminating and even liberating. It often brings awareness to a part of our story that has been unacknowledged for a long time. For some people, such inner work can also be disturbing, especially if the memories in question included a big shock and have been repressed or buried for years.

If you are aware from reading the above examples that the particular memories likely to surface could be painful or even traumatic for you, please seek a professional guide who can accompany you in a safe environment, as you identify the specific impacts of the past on your present.

If you are clear enough that the impact of these past events was closer to being a "lesson learned" rather than a traumatizing shock, you are welcome to engage in the exercise below whenever you choose. Many people have given feedback that they prefer to do this with someone else they trust present, a few have preferred to go solo. Please choose whichever route is likely to make you feel less self-conscious and more comfortable.

Horizontal Integration Reflection exercises

For your benefit the following guided journeys are available for download at www.archetypesatwork.com/guidedjourneys if you prefer. These downloadable audio files are linked and named Horizontal Integration Reflection Exercises 1 and 2. Find a place where you can be quiet and uninterrupted. If you are playing the download, please reflect along and pause it as helpful, and when you are finished, take notes in a notebook.

Otherwise you can read the following a few times and then go through the process by yourself, pausing to take notes when helpful, or work with a trusted colleague. If you are with a trusted companion, ask them to read the instructions below (with pauses between each activating question) and as you speak your thoughts in answer to these prompts invite them to take notes.

Reflection Exercise 1 – Memory Recall and Sense-Making
(Nurturer/Transformer – memory and personal research)

Relax and allow yourself to drift into a place where memories of your past become available. Hold the relevant Archetype in mind. Begin a memory scan to flick through different activities and events in your life where you might have learned that full access to this Archetype might not be OK, or safe, or good. You can work with one or more of these specific memories.

What was the context? Where were you, who was around you and what was happening? What were you expressing or wanting to achieve? How did circumstances and/or people interfere with that? What was your initial emotional response? Remember relevant details as fully as you can...

When you are ready to move on...

Can you now imagine that at that time or soon after you would have tried to make sense of this experience, to learn a useful lesson from it? What sense did you make of it? What message or lesson might you have internalized? Is any part of that original message still applicable and useful to you today? If not, can you imagine letting it go?

When you are ready, come back to the present, make some notes and/ or debrief. Notice that what started as an outside event or words from others at some point became an internal "truth". This may be enough, or you may want to engage in exercise 2 below. You may also realize that you would prefer to examine this further with a professional counsellor.

Reflection Exercise 2 – Active Imagination Resolution
(Dreamer and Transformer – imagination in service of healing)

You can do this exercise immediately after exercise 1 or at any later time that you prefer. The suggested words below are drawn from Systemic Constellation theory and practice and designed to help an individual step away from an old protective pattern that has outlived its usefulness. You can use the following as a guide to make up your own words if you prefer. As above, you can download this to guide you, read and guide yourself through it, or have a trusted ally read it to you.

> On an inner landscape of your choice, conjure up an image of the internalized message from exercise 1. This may be an abstract shape, a known object or even a figure of some kind. Say (out loud or in your head) some version of the following: "You have been with me a long time. You served a purpose for a while." Name the purpose in your own words as you express gratitude for the earlier necessary protection: "Thank you for... (keeping me safe/helping me adapt to others/ keeping me focused enough to get a well-paid job... etc). I am grateful for what you have done but you are now getting in the way. I am ready to move on without you. I am now letting you go." Imagine the image moving away from you until it arrives at a safe distance or disappears altogether. Notice how you feel. What, if anything, has changed?

Come back into the actual present and make any notes that you choose and share them with your colleague. Notice how complete you feel towards the presenting issue. Has this inner awareness work shifted it sufficiently? Or would further work on it be useful?

This process can go surprisingly deep and we recommend that you take your time and do not rush the steps towards resolution. It can take a few attempts to make a meaningful difference to an internalized attitude you have lived with for years. However, once you feel that the old voice has been muted or neutralized you will be more ready and able to step into previously unloved parts of a favoured Archetype. Further activation of this can then be greatly enabled by any or all of the suggestions in the previous chapter that speak to the particular qualities you are seeking to release in your chosen Archetype.

Symbolic actions

(Transformer/Sovereign – regeneration through purposeful play)

A final practice that can help this horizontal integration is to find or create a symbolic action. This is something that you can repeat as often as necessary to remind you that you are moving away from an old pattern of behaviour. It can be as simple or as complex as you choose and should be symbolic to you, in that it evokes the presenting issue and reminds you of your desired resolution. It can include statements or affirmations, as many as are helpful. It could be putting a few symbolic objects in a particular place in an office, home, garden or in nature where you will notice them regularly.

Coaching example

Gemma had been brought up by two driven parents to believe that winning was everything but that showing you cared and expressing passion was "not done". She identified an inner figure she called "the Warrior without a heart" that she wanted to distance herself from. After engaging in the reflection exercises above, she went out and chose a particularly prickly tree in a nearby park where she would walk regularly to represent this figure. Once a week she would visit this tree and remember her intention, sometimes speaking her affirmation out loud: "I am a passionate Warrior". She reported that this simple mini ritual was extremely helpful for the integration of her inner work.

That concludes our exploration of Horizontal Integration. If you are engaging with this practice, we would advise you to allow it to take its own time. First ensure that the new learning sticks before you think about embracing a Vertical Development practice for the Archetype in question. The next chapter may offer some clues as to potential further development of this Archetype for you in the future.

CHAPTER 18

EVOLVING YOUR CORE STRENGTHS

Vertical Development

This final development option can help you refine a current Leading Actor's gifts further, to tap into an as-yet unknown future potential. It is a long-term inquiry and is likely to appeal most to those who have already experienced various developmental practices and who now seek a new route to evolve.

The premise of this approach is that *Conscious Evolution* is possible. Barbara Marx Hubbard describes the term as "an effort to respond to the immense challenges and opportunities of our age […] and [Conscious Evolution] seeks to discover the designs of evolution inherent in all nature with which we can consciously co-operate to guide our actions."[1] Whereas the study of evolution has largely focused on biology, Jean Houston describes how "patterns of possibility never before available to the Earth's people as a whole"[2] now suggest an evolutionary way of thinking about consciousness itself. She joins Hubbard, Fritjof Capra, Ervin Laszlo, Larry Dossey, Jonas Salk, Teilhard de Chardin and other scholars who explore the possibility of Conscious Evolution. As the complexities facing us increase exponentially, Conscious Evolution suggests that we are co-creators in the grand process of redefining how we think, live and work together.

We hold the 10 Archetypes to be foundational principles of human nature and culture that deeply affect how we think, live and work together, and how we address issues. We are therefore committed to a lifelong inquiry into how we can effectively imagine and activate more evolved versions of these Archetypes for our collective future.

Evolutionary biologist Elisabet Sahtouris offers a couple of key learnings from her life's work:

1) Evolution only happens under stress.
2) Evolution involves an increase in both complexity and compassion.

The so-called "VUCA" world (Volatile, Uncertain, Complex and Ambiguous) that for many at both extremes of society seems to be the new normal – whether for CEOs of global corporations or refugees fleeing famine and warzones – indicates that we are on track to qualify for a new wave of evolution. Humanity as a whole is already entering a time of high stress and high complexity – and all available evidence points to both of these increasing rather than decreasing. We therefore need to prepare ourselves to manage both more complexity – which includes an enhanced way of thinking – and more compassion – an enhanced way of feeling. Early evidence from our *Evolving Archetypal Wisdom Labs* suggests that the Archetypes are available and willing to be "consciously evolved", if this is done with the right attitude and intention.

This development path is the beginning of a potentially continuous journey of creative exploration. It is a questing for the future, actively seeking the most evolved potential that is emerging in each Archetype. What we propose, in essence, is that as humanity evolves to a greater level of consciousness and awareness, another veil is stripped away from an Archetype. We can then begin to access attitudes and capacities that were previously unavailable.

Example: The Evolving Warrior

As we mentioned in Warrior Gifts in Chapter 6, while the essence of an Archetype does not go away, it can be re-purposed and reimagined to meet an emerging need in a new time.

Two thousand years ago a good Warrior could be a violent and murderous berserker. Warriors would be applauded and rewarded for raiding neighbouring settlements, killing all the men, stealing all the gold, kidnapping the women and children, and coming home to great acclaim. In those days that was a "good Warrior".

A thousand years ago there was generally less encouragement to raid a neighbouring village. But if another country had a different religion from yours, Warriors could enlist as "Defenders of the Faith". Then they would invade that territory and go about business as before: killing all the men, stealing all the gold and kidnapping the women and children, and they again would be applauded and rewarded upon their return.

By 2000, invading countries on the grounds of differing faiths was no longer condoned. However, if another country threatened the world order or was led by a tyrant, it was still deemed permissible, even though by now most Warriors were on basic pay rather than claiming a share of the loot.

At the same time in history, the NGO Greenpeace had a ship called *Rainbow Warrior* which the crew used to place themselves between harpoon-firing whaling vessels and whales. In these instances, humans put their own lives at risk, not for reward but on a point of principle: to protect defenceless members of another species. This is a markedly different notion of being a protector compared to most previous epochs.

More recently, the #MeToo movement has created the opportunity for victims of sexual predators to name and shame the perpetrators, at least temporarily "turning the predators into the prey": putting them in the spotlight and speaking their previously repressed or suppressed truths.

The Extinction Rebellion (XR) protests and the school strikes initiated by Swedish teenager-activist Greta Thunberg are further examples of the emerging Warrior Archetype for our times. It takes courage, determination and fearlessness to superglue your own body parts to large structures and to risk arrest, fines and imprisonment on behalf of sustainable eco-systems for future generations.

The point is, all epochs find and access the level of Warrior consciousness that feels right for them. It is reasonable to believe that all Archetypes have this evolutionary potential within them. Though in periods of intense innovation and stress there seems to be greater possibilities for this potential to emerge.

An invitation to co-explore
(Storyteller/Renegade – synthesizing different ideas to create future insights)

Activating this evolving potential will require imagination, will and courage. We believe that in our times humanity is being invited, perhaps required, to leave previous comfort zones to enter the experimental unknown. There we may learn to listen to the whispers of the future that are waiting for us. In his bestselling book, *Theory U: Leading from the future as it emerges*, MIT professor Otto Scharmer refers to this as "Presencing the Future by Pre-sensing the future",[3] which, it seems to us, is exactly what inspired humans in all disciplines have done throughout history: they have been ahead of their time, tapping into the future zeitgeist before others. In our times this now seems to be a collective rather than an individual calling. This inquiry inevitably starts with questions, the two most compelling ones for us are:

> *What else could we be that we are not being yet?*

> *How could our Leading Actors become "future-fit" for the benefit of the many?*

We do not know yet what the future holds in terms of emerging archetypal wisdom and access, although the Labs we have held over the last three years have given us some clues and early intimations of what they might be (our report on these follows below).

If this concept appeals to you, we invite you to consider initiating your own inquiry into the emerging evolved practice of your favourite Archetype. You can do this research inquiry by yourself, with a partner or with a group. You are also welcome to join our mailing list for future Labs (see www.archetypesatwork.com).

Some sample initiating questions to consider:

Where in the world are people accessing this archetypal energy in a way you intuit is more evolved than the norm?

What are they doing? How are they doing it? How are they operating as they engage in the new?

What are the increased benefits (potential or actual) of accessing this higher level of archetypal wisdom and insight?

Active Imagination to seek the Evolving Archetypes
(Dreamer/Renegade – imagination to serve the future)

Another way into the evolving Archetypes is to create and engage your own Active Imagination journeys. You can use the templates of these from the earlier chapters on Developing the Realms, simply changing the figure you meet to be an evolving aspect of an Archetype (rather than one holding the already known Gifts). Recorded guided journeys to meet the evolving Archetypes are also available for download at www. archetypesatwork.com/guidedjourneys if you prefer this to a self-guided experience. These downloadable audio files are linked and named Vertical Development Active Imagination Journeys.

If you are familiar enough with this practice, the simple guidelines are: find time to be alone; imagine yourself travelling to a distant landscape; meet a figure representing the most evolved aspect of the Archetype you are researching; have an imaginary interaction with them. Then take notes and reflect as helpful about what learning this journey offered or could be pointing to.

Early Intimations of the Evolving Archetypes
We have noticed, perhaps not surprisingly, that as the Archetypes evolve, they seem to learn more from each other and have more access to one another. For example, a more evolved Strategist is willing and able to "go with the flow" as they create future-fit structures, a gift usually associated with the Dreamer. The more evolved Archetypes also seem to take responsibility for doing good in increasingly wider circles of influence. The example above of the Warrior evolving over 2,000 years shows how each

step forwards is also an expansion to include a wider circle of compassion, i.e. there is a broader group that the Warrior chooses to defend or assert themselves to serve. That sense of felt responsibility grew over time from My Gang, to My Village, to My Tribe, to My Nation, then to all Nations, and in our age is beginning to embrace the shift to All Living Creatures (and perhaps all life forms). There is a broader group (or ecosystem) involved with each evolutionary shift and the direction is, as Elisabet Sahtouris posits, towards both greater complexity and greater compassion; from "me" to "us" to "all of us" (however we currently define "all" and "us"!).

We invite you to take the following intimations of the evolving Archetypes as potential prompts and cues. They are cast as first-person statements using the "I" form, as our Labs have found this the most effective and direct way of receiving them. They are not currently provable in the traditional sense, but they feel intuitively in the right arena. Some are fairly logical extensions of what we know to be true of an Archetype's already visible gifts, others are more like leaps of faith. We offer them to stimulate your own intuitions and intimations of how a Leading Actor could become even more fit for the future. You are welcome to browse through them all or go to your Leading Actors first, as these are likely to be the ones you will be most drawn to evolve. Do you already have a sense of which of your Leading Actors you might want to evolve in this way?

Evolving Archetype affirmation

(Renegade/Sovereign: embracing a brilliant future vision for the self)

A group of us from our Labs are already exploring how to develop more evolved access to Leading Actors. Many of us have taken a key phrase or sentence from the relevant Archetype sections below and used it as an affirmation for a desired future intention.

The practice is simple. Choose the words that most appeal to your future-fit ideal self (or create your own words). Either read the chosen words or say them out loud, once a day, and then notice if and how that day presents you with an opportunity to practise the intention. We invite you to keep a journal to record your findings, so you can track your progress over time, perhaps sharing it with a trusted friend, colleague or coach to get feedback when you are ready.

We complete our development journey with some early intimations of what these evolving aspects of each Archetype can offer us and our collective future. These are drawn from the Labs we have been running over the last three years as well as many inspired conversations with friends and colleagues. We look forward to building a more complete repertoire of what the evolving Archetypes can offer as our research continues, and to share these in further Labs, podcasts and writings.

Intimations of the Evolving Sovereign

"The real guide is the one who makes you see your inner beauty, not the one who wants to be admired and followed."

SHAMS TABRIZI

I work in service of a better future for the many. I know my purpose and work to become a selfless instrument through which this can be realized. I track how that purpose might evolve to suit the changing world around me. I seek the places where I am uniquely qualified to serve. My decisions are weighed by how much they will contribute to or damage the higher purpose of the project.

I help others develop their own sense of purpose within a common cause. I hold the space for collective vision to be birthed and held. I share any limelight, rewards and praise fairly. I welcome feedback and seek out wise critics to hear diverse views. I question practices and paradigms to check current relevance. I look for and develop potential successors. I watch out for when the time is right to step back or down and bless others into position.

I create interconnected networks and look to eliminate pyramids of power, top-down command and control. I am willing to be central to the network as long as it serves the collective intention. I can also co-create projects and then step back, trusting empowered others to exhibit collective Sovereignty.

I seek the new essentials that need to be included in the big picture. I allow myself to think big and generate ambitious visions. I open myself to guidance from many quarters. I am connected to the wider world. I have compassion and concern for the suffering I witness in the collective, without getting entangled in this in a debilitating way.

I am in a continuous co-creative dance with the energies around me and see how these are shaping me as much as I am shaping them. There is no "I" in the way there has been at other levels of access to the Sovereign. Rather, I have become an instrument for visionary leadership and purposeful action at a crucial time in human history.

Intimations of the Evolving Strategist

"Failure is nothing more than a chance to revise your strategy."
ANONYMOUS

I get to the essence of things, projects and life. I assess what is required here and now, rather than imposing a set of pre-constructed rules. I select what to focus on, respecting the limits of my own capacity and energy. I work with the minimum required and never waste anything. Less is more. The older I get the less stuff I need.

When I plan, I work backwards from the goal to assess if the journey is worthwhile. When the goal changes, I don't mind as I understand that nothing is predictable. I distinguish which borders are necessary and what kind of separation between things and people is genuinely helpful to the common good. I work towards appropriate distribution of resources. I manage waste and look to recycle everything in appropriate ways.

I acknowledge the limits to growth on the planet. I propose growth that is manageable within natural limits. I understand that in a balanced ecosystem, growth and decay will be in equilibrium. I offer appropriate constraints on those who seek to exceed these limits.

I believe in equal opportunity and a properly structured education to achieve this. I create maps for new kinds of exchange, including financial exchange, fair trade and experiments in a "gift economy".

I value traditions for the time and culture they arose within and discern what value they still hold. I respect a natural hierarchy of wisdom and expertise. I do not suffer fools and do not pander to the undeserving high and mighty.

I embrace elderhood, when the time is right. I mentor the young to help them focus and set appropriate limits. I ask the questions that narrow a conversation to its essential focus.

Intimations of the Evolving Nurturer

"Any fool can break something, criticise someone and tear things apart. It takes a far more skilled, wise and kind soul to build something, nurture someone, fix things and help others thrive over time."

RASHEED OGUNLARU

I create the conditions for others to flourish and evolve. I know the will to love is greater than the will to power – and I model this in my own life. I do not judge. I accept and expand into a larger circle of compassion.

I share precious resources to benefit the many. I empower myself and others to make circumstance better for as many as possible. I give refuge to the needy. I care for those who cannot (yet) care for themselves, whether abandoned children, the differently abled or refugees.

I give voice to and support the feminine that is arising all over the world. I nurture all living things in my sphere of influence. I have a deep connection to Mother Earth and seek to be in reciprocal maintenance with her. I feel the pain of the increasing amplification of natural disasters. I know this is related to the separation so many experience, both from their own hearts and from the miracle of nature.

I know which nutrients feed us and avoid food that destroys our immune systems. I cultivate the application of plant and food science. I know we are what we eat, and therefore also what we eat ate, and seek healthy food from nutrient-rich sources. If I choose to eat animal protein, I do so with respect and reverence.

I create space for collective memory to be honoured and for collective tragedy to be appropriately mourned and gradually healed. I help others reminisce without getting lost in the past. I support the earth-wisdom traditions that can help us through the painful process of rebirthing our world.

I honour and appreciate the emerging different styles of family and relationships. I recognize that many new forms of family and relationships have their place as we transition into a new phase, slowly but surely becoming one global family.

I believe in "inter-being" and feel deeply on a cellular level that we are all connected. I feel the current divisions as instinctive, defensive reactions to the evolutionary pressure of our time; in the same way that a dying caterpillar eats the first imaginal cells of the butterfly. I help to hold the divisions in my community with healing energy. Our species' rebirthing will take longer than my lifetime to complete but I commit to it for the sake of our grandchildren and their grandchildren.

Intimations of the Evolving Lover

"A man should hear a little music, read a little poetry, and see a fine picture every day of his life, in order that worldly cares may not obliterate the sense of the beautiful which God has implanted in the human soul."

JOHANN WOLFGANG VON GOETHE

I use the power of love unselfishly. I love and value myself and my life force. I recognize that if I do not love myself then I will be needy in relationships. I do inner work to ensure I do not project unmet past needs onto others. I deepen my relationship with my soul's path. I let go of all selfish motivation and follow my heart's desires prompted by forces beyond me.

I practise the attitude of gratitude every day, starting with those around me and expanding to include all living things and Mother Earth herself. I embrace joy and grief as twins. I consciously grieve for the damage done to countless species by insensitive, outdated practices driven by an over-materialistic world view. I am passionate about helping others reconnect to the glory and artful genius of the natural world.

I trust in an abundance mentality; that the world will provide what we need. I enjoy having resources but not hoarding them. I have a felt sense of what is enough. I care about delightful exchange. I buy ethically and invest wisely in future-focused products; clothes made from recycled materials; great tasting, nutritious meals with low environmental impact. I treat my body as a temple and look after it with love and wonder. I design beautiful spaces that can entice and heal others. I joyfully create random acts of beauty in unusual places.

I seek a beautiful future I can fall in love with and passionately commit to. I act as a Muse to others, sparking them into passionate life. I have a capacity for intimate honesty and speak truth to power gracefully. I relish

347

shaping attractive language and music. I enjoy connecting networks of diverse groups. I can create new social networks and be a central attractor while they germinate.

On my best days, I am filled with universal love that connects me with everyone and everything. I raise Eros energy above the old uses of procreation and creation to focus on evolving the desired future. I share my heart freely with others and inspire them to find the light in their own hearts.

Intimations of the Evolving Dreamer

"Yes: I am a dreamer. For a dreamer is one who can only find his way by moonlight, and his punishment is that he sees the dawn before the rest of the world."

OSCAR WILDE

I live creatively and function coherently in the world. I embrace the power of images and dreams without getting lost in them. I think non-literally and sense what is waiting to be created. I listen for the whispers of the future.

I keep the doors of perception open to other realities, knowing they are ever-present with normal states. I can choose to visit other realms of creative imagining and spiritual insight. I hold a space for waking dreams and out-of-body experiences.

I have a profound sense that everything is interwoven so there is little that "throws me". What others see as negative I see as a natural unfolding of things. It is all energy, and this, too, will pass. I maintain this sense of unity without losing agency to act with spirited purpose in the world.

I compassionately connect with others. I sense what others feel without words or intellectual exchange. I look for the synchronistic connection with things, people and events, trusting the flow. I feel life as a numinous experience that enables the natural unfolding that "wants to happen" through me and around me. The right people and resources show up at the right time. I offer myself freely and with gratitude to what life wants from me in return.

My dreams are now not only creative but "prophetic". I can surface images and themes from the collective unconscious and what is emerging at or beyond the leading edges of human consciousness. I intuitively collect and activate the dreams that can best serve the future.

I understand quantum reality. I connect the leading edges of science and spirituality. I see "life is a dream" and believe it will become as we imagine it, what Bruce Lipton calls "the biology of belief". I can choose to step into a possible future and see it, in my mind's eye.

If it is a desirable future, I choose to activate it, knowing that putting energy into it starts to bring it to life, making what was invisible, visible. The more I and others put energy into it, the more form it gathers until it becomes visible to the many. I am a Dream-Maker for a more imaginative and compassionate world.

Intimations of the Evolving Storyteller

"There are no facts, only interpretations."

FRIEDRICH NIETZSCHE

I look for the emerging edges of a new and more sustainable story that can serve the whole. I question the given narratives generally accepted in current culture. I see through and show up the old stories that have outlived their usefulness. I use my advanced communication skills to hold a mirror up to human nature. I help free myself and others from stuck perspectives that no longer serve. I am able to help you recast your story quickly as the world around you changes.

I find an appropriate balance between head and heart in my life and in my words. I embrace a multi-dimensional approach that stimulates intellectual inquiry as well as relational and emotional responses. On a good day, I can "move the furniture around" in others' heads. As I have fingers in many pies, I can feel as if I am in many places at the same time. I can shape-shift and co-ordinate how I show up to suit the situation in the room.

I am always curious about different people and how they communicate. I see how information is used and shared and can cross-fertilize different ways and styles to improve my reach. The poet Rumi holds that "Silence is the Language of God", so while I am a master communicator, I listen deeply – to the person in front of me and to the voices at the edge of cultures. I am interesting because I am interested.

I understand alluring, magnetic language. I gather universal expressions of the soul, of what connects us beyond culture and locality. I speak in many tongues and create understanding through translation.

I can absorb and digest information from multiple perspectives and know how to find the story in the noise. On a personal level, I help others find meaning in their stories, joining the dots of distinct life experiences to help them find their unique pattern and gift. For the collective, I re-story tragedies in ways that help healing and connect others to a larger order of things. I tell stories so others can find meaning in chaos.

Intimations of the Evolving Renegade

"If you're not living on the edge, you're taking up too much space."

STEPHEN HUNT

I create and co-create the reality I want, so the felt need to rebel against something else diminishes. I don't push back but allow myself to be pulled forward – more by evolutionary impulses than revolutionary ones.

I distinguish between what is new and shiny and what is emerging and essential. I tune into the deeper moral consequences of unfeeling technological advancement. I seek to marry the best of the new with the best of the old.

My individuality is what connects me to my core networks, and is no longer a cause of separation. These networks have their own unique field to them, each inhabiting a part of the emerging zeitgeist that I respond to and help accelerate into being. I regularly find synchronicities between what my peer groups and I are intuiting.

I often feel as if I am living in two realities at once. One is fast and the other slow; one abstract, one real; one visible and one invisible, one human and one non-human. It is like living in an altered state, feet on the ground and head in the clouds. Being in the system but not of it I no longer get caught in my own process but can be there for others in an objective way, without being cold. I am present but non-reactive.

My networks include those who experiment with what role artificial intelligence can have to benefit humankind. I keep an open mind to adding AI into human systems over the long term as humans evolve.

I constantly seek where I have the most to learn right now and allow life to guide me towards those places, things and people. "Otherness" no longer exists in the ways it did before, and radical learning edges are part of the new normal. I see and feel deeply how everything is in constant flux and interaction. I intuit what connects micro and macro systems and use these to stimulate innovative ideas.

My capacity for spontaneous self-reinvention liberates me from attachment and fear. I feel as if I am in a near continuous state of breakthrough. I am truly willing to let go all I have and all that I know in order to be synched with this new moment, ready to step into the next opportunity that life offers at the edge...

Intimations of the Evolving Transformer

"A thousand times we die in one life. We crumble, break and tear apart until the layers of illusion are burned away and all that is left, is the truth of who and what we really are."

TEAL SCOTT

I specialize in transformational learning as student and teacher. I investigate magical, shamanic and initiatory traditions of the past to learn which pieces can best serve the present needs. I ask deep questions more than I give answers. I have developed what the poet John Keats called "Negative capability, that is, when (one) is capable of being in uncertainties, mysteries and doubts, without any irritable reaching after fact and reason".

My life and my wounds are my teachers. I live by the Inuit myth that tells of the last initiation into shamanic consciousness. Here the Shamans-to-be are ritually killed, chopped up and dropped into the Underworld where Demons gnaw on the bones. After three days the bones are recovered and the Shamans brought back to life, ready to heal others; their gift being to cure those afflicted by the specific demons that gnawed on their bones. I come back from the Underworld with a gift to offer to the world.

I have learned to hold apparent opposites and dilemmas as tensions to be witnessed and held rather than problems to be solved. I manifest what poet David Whyte calls a *robust vulnerability*, a willingness to be with or express my own weakness or wounding to serve a process or a conversation. I maintain my power as I do this and do not slip into victim mode.

I operate at a meta-level, seeing all systems as fields of energy and all symptoms as hidden messages. I do not judge individuals but seek to see which other systems of belief and behaviour they have been nested in which may now be restricting their growth and potential. I create meaningful rituals and rites of passage that allow individuals and groups, when they are ready, to go through a profound death and rebirth experience, often over years.

I help organizations and institutions transform from being part of the problem to being part of the solution. I find effective ways for them to face up to their responsibilities, both for what they have been and what they could be. I guide the process as they assume the dignity of rightful weight, taking responsibility for past blind spots, mistakes, manipulations and/or damaging decisions. I can then hold the space for the healing vision of the future to arrive.

I see the collective systemic breakdowns around us not as signs of an inevitable Armageddon but rather as cracks in a collective story that is already dying. I appreciate these symptoms of decline that need to be held, before they yield up the splinters of light that shine through the cracks. I know that what is breaking in and breaking down has a message that needs to be listened to and deciphered before the new can be born. I am a patient mid-wife of the future, ready and able to incubate the seeds and tend them over time.

Carl Jung said: "Every victory for the soul is a necessary defeat for the ego." I can face my own shadow and help others do the same. I have a profound capacity to hold and eventually change energy. I know and teach how to live through despair to get to hope, to live through failure to get to success, and to endure the death that must precede rebirth.

Intimations of the Evolving Warrior

"One by one she slew her fears, and then planted a flower garden over their graves."

JOHN MARK GREEN

I operate from a powerful combination of strength, intention and humility as to outcome. I choose my causes carefully and commit to them fully. I am willing to spend my life force to make a positive difference. I do not seek or take credit for extraordinary acts of courage.

I stand up for all living systems. I challenge those who continue to destroy the environment and risk eco-system collapse. I defend my beliefs assertively without violence. As a Master Martial Artist, I have a quietly commanding presence that others respect and pay attention to. I do what needs to be done to make the right things happen. I know that "Today is a good day to die", meaning today is simultaneously a good day to live passionately with no regrets.

I am less attached to striking the target and more focused on how I move towards it. Rather than acting from impulse, I ask questions: "Am I doing the right thing and am I approaching in the right way?" I will not be drawn into conscious or unconscious competition and am willing to walk away if the situation demands it.

Fitness is a way of life that hones my energy for precision. I use my power and drive to raise others up. I actively seek equal partnerships in projects and enterprises, particularly those that maximize impact on the common good.

I look beyond the socially sanctioned testosterone release of organized sports to wonder: What really constitutes victory? Where traditional Warriors were rewarded for coming up with quick solutions to solve problems, I am just as comfortable with playing the long game; holding big questions patiently. What does winning mean in the world today, with its multiple challenges and radical inequalities?

I am a Warrior of the Human Spirit and a champion for an equitable human future. Beyond notions of fighting the other and survival of the fittest, I envision everyone as part of a vast collective team of shared interests. I am committed to seeding a better future.

Intimations of the Evolving Explorer

"It takes a lot of courage to release the familiar and seemingly secure, to embrace the new. But there is no real security in what is no longer meaningful."

ALAN COHEN

My questing in the outside world is a conscious mirror for inner exploration. Nature is my teacher and my guide. I bring the freedom I find in the wild into every other part of life. I know in my core that the journey *is* the destination and experience the journey through time as a continuous sequence of meaningful interaction.

The wisdom I offer emerges naturally from a continuous loop of living, learning, experiencing and teaching. I author my own story without being bound by any past, personal or cultural expectations of what that story should be. As a natural teacher, I am able to seed a multitude of ideas and am not worried if or how they get implemented. I trust that ideas germinate in their own time and place.

I can reach out and make an offer, without needy grasping or greedy expectation of return. I put out ideas that allow people to think about themselves. I understand how to present myself to the world as both a humble teacher and a leader by example.

Ego games of the past are a source of humour. My humour has become a compassionate way of holding the troubles of the world, no longer fueled by a need to make others laugh or be the "life of the party".

I hold onto a radical optimism, especially in the face of increasing tragedy. The darkest hour is before the dawn. I believe that the human species is working towards a greater truth of purpose, which we will not be able to see until we find ourselves living it.

I expand my sense of self without imposing on others or taking up space that they could otherwise usefully occupy. I can accommodate opposite points of view and learn to hold increasingly complex paradoxes. I recognize that there are many different shades of truth – and that no one can ever hold "The Truth". I enjoy exploring each space I enter to find the thread of truth it has to offer.

Although I can thrive in worldly leadership, I recognize that I have to lead myself first. I seek to live an exemplary life true to the future self I am questing, the one who I could become. I accept the responsibility that comes with knowing that we are the ones we have been waiting for...

Notes

1   Barbara Marx Hubbard, *Conscious Evolution: Awakening the power of our social potential* (Novato, CA: New World Library, 1998)
2   Jean Houston, *Jump Time: Shaping your future in a world of radical change* (Boulder, CO: Sentient Publications, 2004)
3   Otto Scharmer, *Theory U: Leading from the future as it emerges* (San Francisco, CA: Berrett-Koehler Publishers, 2009)

INTERMISSION:
Archetypal Development Plan

This intermission comprises a brief summary of the options laid out in Part Two and a final exercise to help you integrate the learnings from this book. You can either complete the exercise within the pages of this book, or in a separate notebook.

You may have already decided what you are going to do to activate a personalized Archetypal Development Plan, in which case we wish you all the best with it. If not, what follows can be a useful shorthand reminder of the options available.

Development approaches
a) **Horizontal Development** is a move *across* the Archetype Circle from a Leading Actor to a lesser used one.
b) **Horizontal Integration** is a move *within* a Leading Actor that you are ambivalent about.
c) **Vertical Development** is a move *upwards* to evolve a current Leading Actor in order to access its emerging potential.

Time frames
1. **Short Term – quick win – 1 day to 1 month.** Identify an upcoming event or task in life or work that would benefit from a different archetypal approach from one you habitually use. Identify which lesser used Archetype would help. Decide on a new approach that you feel comfortable enough to apply quickly. Plan a simple commitment or strategy to help implement the intention and try it out.

2. **Medium term – professional and task improvement – 1 month to 6 months.** Identify a current work/life challenge or big goal and work

on creating a new archetypal pattern to improve your performance. Here it is often productive to include a hybrid role (where you combine a favourite Archetype with a less favoured one to give a new "flavour").

3. **Long term – enhancing greater life fulfilment – 6 months to 5 years.** Identify an underused Archetype that you realize is causing an unnecessary and undesirable cost to your quality of life. Commit to a long-term personal inquiry into how to best liberate that potential in yourself.

We start with some simple questions:

    What are the presenting issues you wish to address?
    What time frame will they require?
    What is your intended remedy and new archetypal pattern?
    What activities and practices will initiate your rehearsal process?

Short term

Archetype to develop:

_____

Presenting issue:

_____

_____

_____

Intended remedy:

_____

_____

_____

Activities and practices:

_____

_____

_____

Medium term

Archetype to develop:

_____

Presenting issue:

_____
_____
_____

Intended remedy:

_____
_____
_____

Activities and practices:

_____
_____
_____

Long term

Archetype to develop:

_____

Presenting issue:

_____
_____
_____

Intended remedy:

_____
_____
_____

Activities and practices:

_____
_____
_____

Feedback Loops

For all of the above, getting effective feedback on your progress will help. In theatre, this is the role of the director, who will offer reflections and advice as useful during the rehearsal process. We invite you to find a mentor, work with a coach or create a co-coaching contract with someone you trust (who is also interested in applying this approach). This person can also operate as an accountability coach, reminding you of your intentions and helping you stick to them, even when they might feel uncomfortable. Having a resource to back you up as you activate your development plan for a new archetypal pattern is invaluable.

Below, our simple model of applied learning follows four simple steps. Raising awareness, creating intention (based on the new awareness), practising the intention (rehearsal and Acting-It-In) and getting feedback (on the practice: what worked and what needs more work?). The feedback then enhances awareness and the cycle starts again, creating a virtuous feedback loop of improved performance.

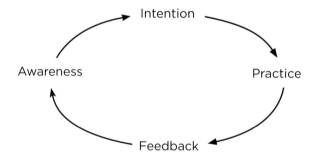

Who could you approach to be your guide or co-coach? Personal growth is often best practised with a witness who also gives you honest feedback and support. It is well worth spending time and energy finding such a person.

CODA

DEVELOPING AN ARCHETYPAL EYE

Part One gave you a way to identify your current story, by finding your Leading Actors and assessing how they are currently "running your show". Part Two offered different ways you can choose to "Evolve your Story, One Character at a Time", by selecting Archetypes to develop and rehearsal methods to Act-Them-In. The two parts together provide a powerful and proven tool for personal and professional development.

If you have enjoyed these ideas, our final invitation is that you allow the 10 Archetypes to begin to infuse the way you look at the world. This is what James Hillman called "developing an archetypal eye". It is a simple practice to observe events and situations in the world around you while applying an archetypal lens. You notice and reflect on the archetypal patterns that show up in daily life, in other people you meet, in the news and entertainment. The more you do this, the more the Archetypes become a shorthand that helps you make sense of what is going on around you.

In essence, developing this "eye" is a practice that unites those who work in the varied dimensions of archetypal research. Archetypal psychology and mythology, archetypal coaching and consulting, archetypal astrology and the recently emerged archetypal cosmology, all use Archetypes in distinct ways. What links them is a passionate belief that archetypal wisdom profoundly helps make sense of a fast-moving and at times chaotic world.

Many ancient cultures had their ways of "reading the signs of the times", many of them based on the visible planets in the solar system (see Appendix 1 for more details) – and the 10 Archetypes are a way to re-vision this ancient wisdom for today. The 10 archetypal lenses described in Part One can help you see through the rational limitations of the prevailing scientific–materialistic world view we inhabit much of the time. They help us penetrate the literal to the more imaginal worlds beneath where more primary forms dwell. When you extend your ability to read the archetypal signs around you, you can begin to tune into the spirit of the time itself, the zeitgeist.

What you have been experimenting with throughout this book is *seeing through*, and you have thereby developed the first steps towards an archetypal eye. James Hillman coined the term "seeing through" with which he meant shifting one's perspective from the literal to the imaginal.[1] Hillman makes an important distinction between a picture and an image. The picture is the literal, measurable and optical, whereas the image is evoked in our imagination. The image is far more complex than the light waves detected by the retina. It is a soulful response to the world as the soul speaks in images. When we 'see through' the literal level of a conversation, the physical way people show up, the measurable environment we live and work in, then we are shifting our perspective from picture to image. Another way of saying this is, "It's not what you are saying, it's what you are telling me". There are more layers to what we usually consider to be reality. An archetypal eye enables you to see through to the depth of what is informing the conversations, people and environments.

If you want to continue your exploration and further develop your archetypal eye, we suggest several different avenues.

First, find others who speak and write in this language. There are an increasing number of books, websites and articles that address various aspects of an archetypal world view. There are Jung societies around the world and they, for instance, speak an archetypal language and often have well-known guest lecturers.

Secondly, find yourself a mentor or coach who understands this language. There are archetypally trained therapists, coaches, astrologers, clergy and constellations experts, to name just a few specialists. Alternatively, pair up with someone else who has experienced an archetypal development programme or who has read this book. Engage in conversations as regularly as you can using archetypally informed language and questions. Is the government getting too Strategist–Warrior with their cost-cutting? Is your organization failing to change quickly enough because no one really embodies the Renegade or the Transformer? Is your teenager's addiction to video games dangerous escapism or a nascent Dreamer finding themselves through imaginal worlds?

Thirdly, as you develop your archetypal eye, see how you can apply your skills as you watch people on TV and in movies, eat certain foods and use certain products. What Archetypes are at play in these moments? What is emerging from these scenes? What characters are on the stage that you are observing or engaging with?

Finally, join our community of archetypally informed researchers. This book was written to reveal the underlying archetypal patterns that exist just beneath the surface of things and people. The work continues to develop, and we find out more about how the Archetypes help us evolve our personal and collective stories at every event we run. If you are interested in connecting with this growing community, you can find us at www.archetypesatwork.com.

Parts One and Two of this book provide practical tools to help you manage transitions, changes and upgrades in your personal and professional skillset. Developing an archetypal eye can further lead you towards a more imaginal way of looking at your world.

Notes

1   James Hillman, *Re-visioning Psychology* (New York, NY: Harper & Row, 1975)

APPENDIX 1
THE PLANETARY ROOTS OF THE 10 ARCHETYPES

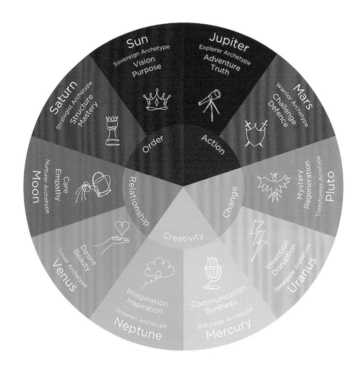

Planetary Roots Wheel

In our Archetypes at Work™ assessment method, the 10 Archetypes correspond to the 10 planets in our solar system. The Sovereign corresponds to the Sun, the Strategist to Saturn, the Nurturer to the Moon, the Lover to Venus, the Dreamer to Neptune, the Storyteller to Mercury, the Renegade to Uranus, the Transformer to Pluto, the Warrior to Mars and, finally, the Explorer to Jupiter. In this Appendix we explain why this is so and how we came to use this method. It is a purely optional read for those interested in the deeper roots of the work. No knowledge of these roots is necessary for you to fully apply all the learnings so far, but over the years many individuals and groups have expressed interest, and some have followed this up with their own study.

We named the 10 by carefully selecting key words that summarize the complex nature of each planetary Archetype. Combined, the 10 Archetypes make up a full set of characters that describe our inner life. They can also describe the inner workings of an organization or any other system. If one – or several – of these Archetypes remains unexpressed in a person or a culture (organizational or otherwise), difficulties arise that can be pinpointed through our method. The language of our Archetypes at Work™ assessment method is rooted in archetypal astrology and adapted to be fit for purpose in the more rational, left-brained business world many of our clients inhabit.

Shakespeare and Astrology

The first time we worked together was at the Globe Theatre in London in 1998, co-leading an event with the actor (and Artistic Director of the Globe) Mark Rylance and James Hillman, the founding voice within archetypal psychology. The workshop was called "Shakespeare and Astrology – Star Cross'd Lovers". Alongside Laurence's career as an archetypal coach, he is also an expert in archetypal astrology, with a practice extending over four decades. He was bringing his deep knowledge of the 10 planets into a rich mix that included his father's psychological insights, Richard's expertise in rehearsal techniques and experiential learning, and Mark's brilliance with Shakespeare text. It is a fact that the most famous author in the English language, writing in the late 16th century, refers in his plays to astronomy, astrology and to the seven planets that were visible in his age over 100 times. This is far more than Shakespeare uses more orthodox Christian images and saints. He also uses them "archetypally" in that he assigns planets to people's characters to describe them, much as we have been doing in this book. As, for example, the famous opening lines of *Henry V* make clear:

Chorus

> *O for a muse of fire, that would ascend*
> *The brightest heaven of invention:*
> *A kingdom for a stage, princes to act,*
> *And monarchs to behold the swelling scene.*
> *Then should the warlike Harry, like himself,*
> *Assume the port of Mars, and at his heels,*
> *Leashed in like hounds, should famine, sword, and fire*
> *Crouch for employment. But pardon, gentles all,*
> *The flat unraised spirits that hath dared*
> *On this unworthy scaffold to bring forth*
> *So great an object...*

The Chorus is effectively apologizing to the audience in advance that the actors do not have the power of imagination (the Muse of Fire) sufficient enough to make Henry appear as the great Warrior he truly is, as if he were the embodiment of the planet Mars, known as the god of war.

As we researched and developed this workshop, we all became fascinated with the correlation that Shakespeare was making between the planets in the sky above and the characters that men and women presented on the Earth below. (The Earth is not represented in the systems used by Shakespeare and western astrologers. Both use a *geocentric system* to map the planets, where the planets appear to be moving around us.) One of the many aspects of Shakespeare's genius was his intuitive ability to be an archetypal thinker way ahead of the field. The world did not catch up with his insights in this area until Carl Jung published his work on Archetypes in the 1930s.[1]

Making the 10 Archetypes accessible

Richard was researching and activating several other archetypal systems in the late 1990s and early 2000s, including the pantheon of Greek gods and numerous Jungian concepts, with a different number of Archetypes embraced by each. But as we continued to do experimental workshops together every year, it gradually became clear that the 10 is the most complete set. Between them they really do encompass the whole gamut of primary forms and impulses that we humans respond to. And, in combinations of different Archetypes, they offer hugely rich, varied and nuanced mixes of characteristics that everyone we have introduced them to can easily relate to and identify themselves with.

The practical problem for a while was that 10 Archetypes is a big "cast" for people to hold in mind at one time, so it took us a number of different experiments until we were able to describe them through the Five Realms. We then reduced the number of Archetypes that we asked individuals to focus on from all 10 to three Leading Actors and two More Offstage Actors. At this point the richness of the full palette became easily accessible and these now operate as a key thread in all the workshops run by Richard's organization, Olivier Mythodrama, using great stories from Shakespeare as mythic case studies and exemplars for leaders.

That is the simple answer to why these 10 Archetypes. The more complex concepts that underlie the correlation between the 10 in the sky and the 10 inside of us all is explored in more detail below.

Archetypal astrology

Calendars continue to be set by the sun and the moon's cycles. Sea captains still know how to navigate their ships by the stars, and well-studied astrologers learn how to make meaning of patterns in the sky. To the ancients, more so than today, the heavens were alive and filled with stories. Modern archetypal astrology carries on that tradition but adds a depth psychological perspective and bypasses fatalistic predictions. As human consciousness has evolved, so has astrology.

In Western thought there is a long tradition of defining universal constants that underlie all phenomena. Plato called them *Ideas*, Pythagoras *Mathematical Forms*, Kant *a priori categories of the human psyche*, and Schopenhauer *prototypes that are the original forms of all phenomena*.[2] Jung called them *Archetypes*. Archetypal astrology says that the planets are representations of such universal constants.

In general, astrology makes meaning of the sky. There are several subcategories in astrology, including financial, medical and vocational astrology. When a chaotic world no longer makes sense, certain underlying patterns remain intact. A certain order is never lost. We can look skywards in times of breakdown because the only visibly reliable constants that remain, no matter what surrounds us, are the consistent wanderings of the planets across the sky. We do not know what will appear on our screens six months from now, yet we do know exactly where the planets will be on any given day. Such surety allows us to find patterns in the sky, reading how the planets are situated, particularly in relationship to each other. Over millennia, planetary constellations have been observed and recorded as celestial patterns. Then worldly affairs have been correlated to such patterns and, over time, and mostly empirically, meaning has been gradually gained from these patterns. This is explored in detail in *Cosmos and Psyche* by Richard Tarnas.[3]

Ever since the Babylonians began tracking the movements in the sky 5,000 years ago, every major culture has created its own version of astrology, its own way of making meaning of what they observed. Babylonian, Chinese, Aztek, Hindu, Arabic and Hellenistic astrologers, to name just a few, all learned to read the night sky. Remarkably, when compared, each system, on an archetypal level, agrees with the others. The movements of the planets against the fixed stars has been widely regarded as a reliable way to make sense of the world. Once limited to a select few of learned astrologers, this cross-cultural language is available in our era to all with the time and interest.

To paraphrase Nietzsche, "We can take any what if we know why".[4] Astrology can answer "why" questions. Time and again archetypal astrologers witness that even the most rational people, when shown their astrological chart, are able to make sense of otherwise apparently senseless events. Meaning-making occurs by correlating the "story above" (represented by a symbolic chart of the sky) with the "story below" (their internal experience). When this connection is made, the ancient axiom of "as above and so below" is recognized, a principle that Jung referred to as *synchronicity.*

Synchronicity

Jung defined synchronicity as "a coincidence in time of two or more causally unrelated events which have the same or a similar meaning."[5] The concept of synchronicity is one of the most difficult to understand for the rational mind, as most of us are deeply trained to think causally. We therefore assume that "this over here affects that over there". One key reason that depth psychology and astrology can often be marginalized is that, for most of us, correlating events synchronistically goes against the grain of our training. Seasoned astrologers are often asked: "Do you really believe that the planets affect me?" This is a causal question. The Moon affects ocean tides and the Sun can change Earth's magnetic fields. But from the astrologer's perspective, the planets don't cause things to happen on Earth. To be clear, the planets *do not* make us do anything. Rather, as planetary constellations form in the sky, they also synchronistically manifest on Earth, and we can use this information if we have access to it. The connection is through synchronicity.

So, the planets do not determine anything but their positions on the stage of the heavens can offer insights as to the "mood below". For example, if Saturn and Mars (the Strategist and the Warrior) are prominent above, the two express themselves together and this is reflected on the world stage below. If Saturn is leading, the mood may be one of "focused aggression", whereas if Mars is more dominant, we may recognize "a passion to challenge authority". These are two simple ways to show the subtleties of "as above, so below". On the world stage, this could be the difference between an invasion and a rebellion. On a personal stage, this could be the difference between a martial arts class (focused aggression) and starting a demonstration in the street (challenging authority).

The quality of time

Besides synchronicity, a second key idea to understanding archetypal astrology is *the quality of time*. When discussing time, it is typical to use quantitative terms, e.g., "little time", "lots of time", "losing time" and "wasting time". The implication is that time should be measured in quantities. In other historical eras people also understood that time has different *qualities*. We still say, "This is not a good time for me", which shows our innate capacity to understand how there are different *kinds* of time. In his previous book, *Planets in Play,* Laurence wrote that, "The core idea behind astrology is that the movements of the planets show the quality of time similar to the way a clock on the wall shows the quantity of time."[6]

If we accept the notion that every moment has a different quality, then the quality of the moment in which we begin a project becomes important. In Ancient Greece this was understood. Those seeking counsel from the Oracle of Delphi would ask, "Is this the right time to begin... (a particular undertaking)?" It was understood that the choice of the right time was crucial to the success of the undertaking. Such thinking is practically non-existent today. But by embracing an archetypal perspective, it can add a meaningful perspective to decision-making.

Archetypes at Work™

Astrological imagination continues to infuse our Archetypes at Work™ assessment method and tools as the system itself expands and grows in response to its practice in the field. It gives us access to universal principles, usually ignored by predominantly rational approaches, that can unlock new perspectives for individuals, teams and organizations. For example, a classic Warrior organization in search of a new territory may struggle to find anything out of the usual, until they embrace the Dreamer and the Storyteller to help them.

Archetypes at Work™ offers a method to explore what characters might be useful to listen to – for individuals, communities and whole systems – so as to respond in more diverse ways to the complexities of our time.

Notes

1   C.G. Jung, (1933), *The Collected Works of C.G. Jung Volume 9i, The Archetypes and the Collective Unconscious,* translated by R.F.C. Hull (London: Routledge & Kegan Paul, 1959)
2   Keiron Le Grice, *The Archetypal Cosmos: Rediscovering the gods in myth, science and astrology* (Cornwall, UK: TJ International, 2012)
3   Richard Tarnas, *Cosmos and Psyche: Intimations of a new world view* (New York: Penguin, 2006)
4   Friedrich Nietzsche, *Twilight of the Idols and The Anti-Christ,* "Maxims and Arrows", translated by R.J. Hollingdale (London: Penguin Books, 1990)
5   C.G. Jung, *Collected Works of C.G. Jung,* Volume 8, "Synchronicity: An Acausal connecting Principle", translated by R.F.C. Hull (London: Routledge & Kegan Paul, 1960)
6   Laurence Hillman, *Planets in Play: How to reimagine your life through the language of astrology* (New York: Jeremy P. Tarcher/Penguin, 2007)

If you, your team or organization would like expert assistance from our Archetypes at Work™ coaching and consulting practice to apply the learnings from this book, please visit

www.archetypesatwork.com

For more information on the authors' other practices, see

www.oliviermythodrama.com and
www.laurencehillman.com.

APPENDIX 2
KEY WORDS

Sovereign
Royal, Ruler, Visible, Heroic, Luminary, Generative, Playful, Heartful, Magnanimous, Loyal, Present, Spacious, at the Centre of Things
Radiates: Purpose, Generosity, Courage, Will, Self-Confidence, Vigour, Strength, Vision, Vitality, Charisma, Ambition

Strategist
Structured, Rational, Principled, Ethical, Pragmatic, Organized, Controlled, Mature, Contained, Precise, Deliberate, Measured
Respects: Time, Focus, Rules, Mastery, Limits, Discipline, Duty, Hierarchy, Boundaries, Tradition, Wisdom, Objectivity, Goals, Capital, The Establishment, Law and Order, The Truth in Numbers

Nurturer
Supportive, Caring, Reassuring, Protective, Responsive, Instinctive, Parental, Trusting, Nourishing, Sensitive, Empathetic, Receptive, Cosy
Values: Relationships, Potential, Growth, Feedback, Togetherness, Time to Reflect, 'Keeping the Hearth', Legacy, Conservation, Emotional Intelligence, Natural Cycles, Tending Gardens, Feeling at Home, Full-Body Listening

Lover

Alluring, Sensual, Sociable, Desirable, Charming, Passionate, Seductive, Creates Longing, Acts as a Muse, Accumulates Self-Worth and Net-Worth

Adores: Design, Style, Luxury, Money, Pleasure, Relationships, Beauty, Fine Art, Fashion, Decorations, Harmony, Song, Fantasy, Enchantment

Dreamer

Imaginative, Poetic, Sensitive, Idealistic, Compassionate, Spiritual, Visual, Boundless, Imaginal, Believing

Inspired By: Fantasy, Symbols, Infinity, Mythology, Non-Dualism, Dreams, Intangibles, Metaphors, Mysticism, Visions, Ecstasy, The Transcendent, The Invisible, Art, Music, Archetypes, Lateral Thinking, Negative Capability, Emergence, Holding Paradox, Possibilities, Altered States

Storyteller

Communicator, Translator, Mediator, Synthesizer, Advertiser, Conceptual, Critical, Versatile, Adaptable, Agile, Trickster, Mercurial, Quick-Thinking

Connects With: Ideas, Metaphors, Information, Multiple Perspectives, Puzzles, Juggling, Multi-Tasking, Wit, Details, Logic, Intelligence, Making Connections, Creating Narratives, Clever Articulation

Renegade

Intuitive Disruptor, Eccentric Inventor, Liberator, Rebel, Provocateur, Maverick, Unique, Has Epiphanies, "Eureka!"

Thrives On: The Zeitgeist, Freedom, The Future, Disruptive Technologies, Revolution, Uniqueness, Structural Collapse, Surprise, Revelation, Flashes of Insight, Emerging Ideas, Brilliance

Transformer

Magician, Healer, Regenerator, Change Agent, Deep, Powerful, Psychological, Magnetic, Intense, Inexorable

Honours: Renovation, Roots, Research, Transitions, Upheaval, Total Change, Power, Deconstruction, Transformation, Secrets, Death and Rebirth, Break Down to Break Through, The Underworld, Mystery, Hidden Gold

Warrior

Champion, Spearhead, Amazon, Defender, Trouble-Shooter, Brave, Fierce, Passionate, Forceful, Decisive, Fearless, Surgical, Leads from the Front

Drives: Competition, Challenge, Action, Direction, Tactics, Risk-Taking, Seed-Planting, Making Things Happen, Adrenaline, Competitive Advantage

Explorer

Enthusiast, Adventurer, Teacher, Optimist, Wide-Ranging, Striding, Honest, Philosophical, Expansive, Jovial, Multicultural, 'Can-Do' Attitude

Seeks: Progress, Knowledge, Truth, Nature, Justice, Joy, Hope, Abundance, Ascendance, Oneness, Success, Big Ideas

Leadership Shadows

Sovereign

Too Much: Egotistic, Self-Centred, Narcissistic, Grandiose, Overpowering, Childish, Selfish, Ridiculing, Proud, Arrogant, Ostentatious, Haughty, Putting Others Down, Compulsively Centre Stage, "They can't do it without me"

Too Little: Apathetic, Weak, Uncentred, Dull, Dispirited, Unassuming, Lethargic, Lifeless, Low Energy, Abdicating, No Vision, Repressed Ambition, Low Self-Esteem, "Who am I to make a difference?"

Strategist
Too Much: Narrow-Minded, Closed, Unyielding, Inflexible, Inert, Depressive, Pessimistic, Over-Controlling, Stagnant, Leaden, Rule-Bound, Risk-Averse, Rank-Focused, "Don't reinvent the wheel", "Don't rock the boat"
Too Little: Unrealistic, Impractical, Unstructured, Disorganized, Undisciplined, Scattered, Procrastinating, Always Late, Never Completes, Misses Deadlines, "I'll get to it eventually"

 Nurturer
Too Much: Compulsive Care-Taker, Overshares, Oversensitive, Smothering, Overprotective, Food Addict, Unnecessarily Repetitive, Excessively Emotive or Emotional, 'Over-Feeds', "They will always need my help", "They can't do it for themselves"
Too Little: Unfeeling, Insensitive, Lonely, Isolated, Numb, Undernourished, Unable to Slow Down, Lack of Self-Care, Emotionally Absent, Missing Instincts, "Feelings are overrated", "I don't ask for help"

 Lover
Too Much: Materialistic, Superficial, Backstabbing, Greedy, Gossipy, Ostentatious, Jealous, Flaunting, Sleazy, Gaudy, Fake, Money-Obsessed, Overly Flirtatious, "I can sell anything to anyone", "Nobody can resist me"
Too Little: Styleless, Money-Phobic, Unaffectionate, Charmless, Unfriendly, Dispassionate, Frosty, Few Social Graces, No Eye for Beauty, Unresponsive, "I can't sell", "I'm not desirable"

 Dreamer
Too Much: Unrealistic, Vague, Confused, Escapist, 'Lost', Gullible, Indecisive, Ungrounded, Naïve, Uncertain, Unbounded, Fantastical, 'Head in the clouds', 'Pie in the sky', 'Castles in the air', "So many dreams, so little time"
Too Little: Unimaginative, Dry, Disillusioned, Dense, Dispassionate, Non-believer, Limited Mindset, Unable to

Visualize, No 'Inner Music', Can't Imagine Competing Views of the Future, "If I can't measure it, it's not real"

Storyteller
Too Much: Scattered, Unpredictable, Hyperactive, Heady, Fickle, Sly, Speedy, Busybody, Tells Tall Tales, Deceitful, Peddling Misinformation, TMI (Too Much Information), Creates 'Fake News', Never Grows Up, Addicted to Communication and/or Social Media, "You can't have too many ideas"
Too Little: Uncritical, Confused, Uninformed, Ignorant, Inflexible, Outwitted, Single-Minded, Lacks Mental Confidence, Feels Less Intelligent, Literal, Slow to Catch On, 'Out of the Loop', "Wait, I don't get it!"

Renegade
Too Much: Detached, Intellectual Arrogance, The Eternal Revolutionary, Misfit Genius, Overly Opinionated, Emotionally Absent, Uncaring, Robotic, Overly Eccentric, Contrary, Technology-Obsessed, "I just don't fit in!"
Too Little: No Ideas, Conformist, Boring, Repressive, Change-Resistant, Afraid of The Unexpected, Lacking Creativity, Technophobic, Not Curious, Living in The Past, "There's nothing wrong with the old way!"

Transformer
Too Much: Manipulative, Relentless, Obsessive, Totalitarian, Change Addict, Power-Hungry, Pop Psychologist, Fascinated by Death, Compulsive Navel-Gazing, Conspiracy Theorist, Paranoid, Self-Destructive, Vindictive, Sadistic, "To be alive is to suffer"
Too Little: Shallow, Change-Resistant, Uninitiated, Naïve, Simplistic, Gullible, Avoidant, Pain-Averse, Afraid of Death, Takes Things at Face Value, Unable to 'See Through', "Don't open a can of worms"

Warrior

Too Much: Bully, Impatient, Aggressive, Intimidating, Furious, Raging, Destructive, Vicious, Explosive, Reactive, Winning at All Costs, Sore Loser, Looking for a Fight, Too Quick to Act, Pre-Emptive Strike, "Fire, Ready, Aim!"

Too Little: Victim, Pushover, Weakling, Indirect, Quiet, Hesitant, Submissive, Undefended, Cowardly, 'Limp', Fearful, Too Nice, Risk-Averse, Low Energy, Playing It Safe, "I'm keeping my head down"

Explorer

Too Much: Restless, Tactless, Greedy, Overbearing, Zealous, Preaching, Inflated, Obnoxious, Boasting, Too Big, Too Loud, Overlooking Details, Oblivious to Other's Pace, "Grow or die!", "My truth is right!", "Bigger is better"

Too Little: Pessimistic, Inhibited, Hopeless, Constricted, Joyless, Cynical, Naïve, Narrow-Minded, Unfulfilled Potential, Missing The Big Picture, Stay-At-Home 'Local Yokel', "I'm only safe with what I know"

APPENDIX 3
EASY REFERENCE

For those wanting an easy reference to each section connected to an Archetype, please find relevant page numbers and chapters below.

Sovereign

Strategist

Nurturer